BLACK
SPORTSMEN

BLACK
SPORTSMEN

ERNEST
CASHMORE

Routledge & Kegan Paul
London, Boston, Melbourne and Henley

First published in 1982
by Routledge & Kegan Paul Ltd
39 Store Street, London WC1E 7DD,
9 Park Street, Boston, Mass. 02108, USA,
296 Beaconsfield Parade, Middle Park,
Melbourne 3206, Australia and
Broadway House, Newtown Road,
Henley-on-Thames, Oxon RG9 1EN
Set in 10/12 Plantin by
Rowland Phototypesetting Ltd, Bury St Edmunds, Suffolk
and printed in Great Britain by
St Edmundsbury Press, Bury St Edmunds, Suffolk

Library of Congress Cataloging in Publication Data

Cashmore, Ernest.
Black sportsmen
Bibliography: p.
Includes index.
1. Athletes, Black – Biography.
2. Athletes, Black – Great Britain – Biography.
3. Sports – Social aspects.   4. Blacks – Social
conditions.   I. Title.
GV697.A1C27   796'.092'2   [B]   82-554

ISBN 0-7100-9054-4   AACR2

He had decided by this time that his future, if any, lay in getting into the professional fight game. All the men he worked with on the section gang knew about this ambition of his, and many talked to him about it. Some of them were fighters or former fighters themselves. They were friendly and glad to swap stories about the fight game, but they were not very optimistic about his chances to make a go of it. A Negro fighter has to be mighty good, they reminded him again and again, so good that he simply can't be overlooked – and even then the going is hard.

> (From the biography of Henry Armstrong, former featherweight, lightweight and welterweight champion of the world, 1936–40.)

I don't think this is such a bad thing. Sometimes, it's hard to get to the top and it may be better for a good few than a lot of mediocre ones. I think the black sportsmen who develop are going to be so good; you see, there's a lot of mediocre white sportsmen in a lot of different sports, but there aren't too many black sportsmen and most of them are good. And I don't think it's a bad thing because black kids can relate to someone who's good. . . . It helps, but, at the end of the day, the change that black sportsmen are going to make to the lives of everyday black kids is only marginal. All you can do is give them hope; just show them that you can do it.

> (Justin Fashanu, England international footballer in the 1980s, in response to the above quotation.)

CONTENTS

FOREWORD

The questions this book sets out to answer are: Why are so many black kids currently entering sport and why are so many succeeding? In trying to give answers, Ernest Cashmore brings out many of the important issues which affect the lives of all black youths in modern day society and, in the process, squashes many of the fallacies about blacks that have been handed down through the centuries. What becomes obvious is that there is no clear-cut reason why blacks turn to sport due to something like perhaps natural 'feel' or 'ability'; but there are lots of factors and Cashmore's study tries to spell out as many of them as possible.

Top black sportsmen are relatively new in Great Britain. Until quite recently, there was only a handful. I remember, as a boy, watching Clyde Best of West Ham and before him there was hardly a mention of blacks in football. This book shows how boxing and athletics had more black competitors in history, but even here the real impact has come over the last few years. Part of the reason for this is that black kids are latching on to people like Cyrille Regis and Laurie Cunningham. They feel that, if they can be a success, then they can too.

In my early days, white kids used to follow Denis Law and George Best, but now black kids as well have their models who they're trying to copy. The principle behind this is simple: everybody wants to be good at something. Black kids feel they have a much better chance of achieving something in sport than they have in other areas of society.

Why? Well, one of Cashmore's suggestions is that black kids in Britain tend to lose a little bit of ground in school. They lose interest and then fall behind and this disadvantages them. But in sport, they

Garth Crooks. Photograph courtesy of *Match Weekly*

see the chance of being the 'number one' and, as a result, they give it their complete and total interest. This is a very strong point and my own experiences may throw some light on this. All five of the children in my family were into athletics and sport generally, my sisters Valerie and Sandra being really good at netball. Now, Jackie is still at school; she's 5 feet 3 inches and not particularly good at athletics. She's coming up to leaving school, she's going well and is taking GCE 'O' levels. But, when she was 13 or 14, she started off slowly and began to lose a little interest. The teachers probably thought she wasn't too bright and began to push her into sport. But she wasn't that interested. My mother always believed she was quite capable academically and, eventually, she began to get to grips. Now, at 15, she's top of her class in English and history and in the top three for several other subjects.

School teachers, if they're not careful, can get this terribly blinkered attitude about black children not being capable academically but being good in sport and my sister had to contend with this. In my family, we've all done quite well athletically and, out of the four children who've left school so far, two 'O' levels has been the minimum. So when Cashmore refers to the 'push' of teachers at school, he makes a good comment: it definitely does happen.

This links up with the point about sport becoming a central life interest of many black kids, possibly replacing school and, later, work. This definitely happened with me; I knew at an early age that I was going to be a footballer, I was going to be damned good and I wanted to be the best. I remember once when I was 18 and I'd been dropped from the Stoke City first team. I'd had a run in the first team. I'd had a taste of what it was all about and I liked it. As far as I was concerned, my progress was working exactly as I wanted. But I'd been dropped by Tony Waddington (then the team manager) purely because it was an important match and I hadn't played particularly well for a couple of games before and he wanted his most experienced side – which was typical 'Wad'. Geoff Salmons was my team mate and he said to me: 'You're only 18, you've got 15 years in the game. Why are you so disappointed? Do you want to be special or something?'

I'll never forget that remark till the day I die because I couldn't understand why anybody would want to do something and not want to do it the best they could. I could never understand why he said that. I don't know whether it was because I was black, because I was young or because I was a bit bouncy and cocky at the time. Blacks do want to be exceptional whereas the average white sportsman will be complacent. A white sportsman will be content to be moderately successful; the fact that he's been there is good enough for him.

When I was at school, I gave everything to football. I neglected my academic subjects. At that age, about 13 or 14, I didn't know how to even the two out and give the two areas an equal amount of time and energy. And this is where you need teachers and, most important, parents. I know a white kid, Richard McKenzie, who is 13, and he's into every sport going. And he's in the top five in his class, because his parents are there to help him. He's able to give both his best shot. I think West Indian parents are not aware of what black kids want to do and they don't help them in this way. It's not very often you get a West Indian parent-child relationship where they can both sit down and the parents make it perfectly clear why it's important to work at school and, at the same time, the kid can explain to them what he gets out of athletics or football or whatever. There is definitely a gap between the parents and the child.

For West Indian parents, children are to be seen but not heard. They don't want to listen to what the kid has to say about the classroom. You read books and study and work hard, but don't hold any arguments with your parents. The parents bring their principles with them from the West Indies along with their ideas about discipline. But the kids go to school in England and they learn a different way. The two things are like oil and water: they don't mix.

The gap I refer to is responsible for many of the problems connected with black kids and Cashmore gives his interpretation of this in chapter five. One of the possible results of this is that black kids get frustrated with their home and school lives and 'drift' away, as Cyrille Regis puts it, and take all the wrong ideas with them. As Regis says in the book, he went through the same phases as most black kids, but he had a strong mind and a little more determination and managed to pull away.

I believe most of us in sport have gone through similar experiences, but none of us has allowed ourselves to let our colour become an excuse for failure. Black kids have the popular image of being hoodlums in Brixton or pickpockets or rebels. But this is not so typical and you can look at sportsmen as examples. When I first came to Tottenham I knew I could give a good account of myself on the football field, but I wanted to prove to people in London that I could go anywhere, eat anywhere, talk intelligently and hold my own everywhere. I could see the element of surprise in people because I was black and I didn't conform with what they expected. The fact that I'm still getting that reaction keeps me on my toes because, if I'm not, I'm not so much letting myself down or my family, but thousands of black kids. I haven't become paranoid about it; just very conscious of the fact that people need to be given new views on black youth. We're not all into a reggae scene trying to find a new identity, but we're still black and proud of it.

With this in mind, I was surprised to read in the book about Daley Thompson, who asked Cashmore on their first meeting, 'Why do you want to talk to me?' He didn't feel himself to be black in the same way as many of us others. But I understand how he feels because in no way in his life has 'black' been the dominant factor. As far as he's concerned his attitude and commitment isn't because he's black. He hasn't been interested in *why* he might not get a job or something. What he's been interested in is what it takes to get it and going away and getting it and not making colour an excuse.

I find this both amazing and tremendous and the book brings out the various ways in which black sportsmen – whether successful or unsuccessful – have reacted to their blackness. Like Thompson, they didn't use it as an excuse; but, if they felt it would harm their chances of success they tried harder – and this is really the theme of the study. I honestly believe that, when I became a professional footballer at Stoke, I had to do that little bit better than the equivalent white kid. Make no mistake about it, I had to do it and I was aware of that. I just sensed it was the case. And I was happy doing that. It didn't bother me because, in trying harder, it wasn't going to do me any harm. 'Banksy' (Gordon Banks) drove me terribly and 'The Wad' was always keeping a watchful eye over me. They all kept a watchful eye over me because I was the only black kid at the club at the time.

I have experienced racialism in football from a few other players and from crowds and in society generally. But I was prepared for it and, like other black sportsmen, I've had to prove myself. So Cashmore is right in saying that the whole experience has a sense of challenge in it. This is the theme of the work and this is one part of the answer about the rise of black sportsmen. I don't think we black sportsmen are naturally gifted. It doesn't matter whether you are black or white in terms of your body and your mental attitude.

There's no reason, physical or psychological, why a black man can't do what a white man can and vice versa. In this book, Ernie Cashmore goes some way to explaining exactly why the emergence of black sportsmen is nothing to do with such factors, but is all about the way we are conditioned in history and society.

Garth Crooks
Tottenham Hotspur Football Club

ACKNOWLEDGMENTS

A piece of work such as this is always a collective enterprise, involving many, often hidden, collaborators. Here I can mention just a few. Obviously, my biggest debt is to all those black sportsmen and sportswomen, who had enough interest and sometimes patience to talk to me about themselves and their colleagues. I hope that, when they get to read the book, they'll find the results interesting and valuable.

I found tremendous support and co-operation from the six clubs I used as research bases and would like to thank the officials of the Birmingham Birchfield Harriers Club, the Haringey Athletic Club, the Birmingham City Amateur Boxing Club, the Repton Boys' Club, the Newtown Warriors Football Club and the Continental Youth Club. In particular, I would extend my appreciation to, in the order I met them, Sandy Gray, Frank O'Sullivan, Kevin Reeves, Dave Hoare, Peter Lawrence, Tony Burns and Barry Dennis. Mel Watman and Barry Trowbridge of *Athletics Weekly* were extremely helpful in supplying information on black athletes in the UK.

The research on which most of the book is based was sponsored by the Social Science Research Council and I would like to thank the members of the various committees who supported me and had enough faith in the value of the project.

Friends and colleagues who read and commented on early drafts included Bob Mullan, Dave Podmore, Barry Troyna and my department's head, Colin Bell. I greatly appreciate their efforts. Immense secretarial assistance came in the form of Julia Cox whom I thank for typing every word of two scripts plus numerous other things. The jacket cover design came from the skilful hands of my friend Mick Davis and the foreword from the hands of my friend Garth Crooks, who's pretty useful with his feet too! Thanks to both of them.

EC
1982

Chapter One
INTRODUCTION to sources

If I hadn't made it, I wouldn't have put it down to my colour. I would just have said: 'Well, I wasn't good enough.' But I did make it and the colour did make a difference in a way I didn't expect.

Maurice Hope, boxer

Trying twice as hard

There was rain in the air outside; inside, the air was suffused with a mixture of cigar fumes and evaporating sweat – the fumes from the audience, the sweat from the boxers whose endeavours were the principal attraction of the evening. In the lobby, Maurice Hope and I talked casually, neither of us knowing that the idea behind this book was evolving from our conversation.

He had, some months before, wrested the World Boxing Council title from the Italian Rocky Mattioli and was reaping some of the ancillary benefits for his achievements: he was guest of honour at the boxing show. Yet, despite being Britain's only world championship claimant at that time, he was relatively unknown outside boxing circles and had boxed most of his important contests outside the UK, winning the European title in 1976 in Rome, then drawing in his first world title attempt in Berlin in 1977, before finally taking the title in San Remo.

He did not crave recognition, but was understandably regretful about his lack of it. In his words, he had 'sacrificed a lot' to get to the top and, now that he was there, it was an anticlimax. Yet he was unmoved and found the situation in keeping with his whole career which was strewn with obstacles. In his analysis, such obstacles were vital to his development in boxing. My interest was aroused when he reasoned that it was his blackness which constituted the major drawback in his life at one level, but at another, proved an indispensable asset to his eventual success. 'It does something to you when you get in the ring,' he explained. 'Knowing you're black makes you try even harder.'

Slightly perplexed, but fascinated, I invited him to elaborate and he outlined how, since arriving in London in 1961 at the age of 9, he had been rocked by the awareness that his colour could place him in a position of possible – or probable – disadvantage. Before leaving his native Antigua, he had no recognition of this. But his experiences of street life in Hackney and his boxing ventures in Bethnal Green taught him that blackness presented him with a unique set of problems. By the time he was approaching school-leaving age, he had formed, from his angle of vision, two alternatives: 'To buckle under, or be determined and ambitious.' He opted for the latter route and took up the gauntlet he saw set before him by steeling himself for a career as a boxer, a career in which he distinguished himself as a man of immense resolve and purposefulness.

Hope and I continued our conversation a few weeks later, this time at his terraced house in Stoke Newington. He fleshed out the bones of the skeleton he had constructed, making it clear that, in a very massive and consequential way, his perception of blackness had affected his whole career. But not necessarily in a negative way: he had used his blackness to become a better boxer. How he used it opened up a new realm for investigation.

It could have been Hope's unknowing repudiation of the popular notion of black people which fired my imagination. Conventional wisdom dictates that the experiences at school, in the transition to work, at work itself and in society generally, tend to imbue the black youth with a jaundiced view of the world; recoiling from the 'pressures', he retreats to a street-corner gang existence, detaching himself from society and cultivating a posture of indifference or even hostility towards the rest of society. The pressure is seen as too burdensome for the black kid, who 'buckles under' it and withdraws into his enclave complaining about 'Babylon' and its inequalities but without doing anything about them.

What Hope had to bear was exactly the same kind of pressure as other blacks of his generation. Sons and daughters of Caribbean and, to a lesser extent, African migrants of the post-war period, did have to face racialism and there is evidence to support this (for instance, Daniel, 1968; Patterson, 1969). Hope perceived this as acutely as anyone else; he had experienced being called a black bastard, being physically abused, being spat at, being excluded. He was black and it was conveyed to him in a most unambiguous way that this would mean pressure for him, but it was the way in which he responded that challenged conventional images of black kids. Being black was a potential impediment he transformed into a stimulus. It hardened him and hardness proved an extremely valuable asset in the ring.

Was Hope unique? Well, with my interest intensifying, I went to see a number of other black sportsmen who had achieved a measure of success to compare their perceptions and experiences. A vague but discernible pattern emerged. Boxers, footballers and athletes who eventually broke through at the highest level, in championships in football league, in international meetings, made it not so much in spite of their blackness but because of it. People like Garth Crooks, Mike MacFarlane and Garry Thompson traced back how they could have made their blackness the basis for defeatism, admitting that 'there's no way a black guy can make it in this society.' But they did not: in their eyes, blackness was a resource to be used; and use it they did – to strengthen their resolve, redouble their efforts and forge a will to succeed.

Black sportsmen presented me with vivid examples running counter to the stereotypical black youth and, as such, they lent themselves perfectly to my general purposes, for I am hopefully in the process of shattering some of the popular images of blacks. How I long to see the black kid depicted as something other than the tam-donning, dope-smoking, unemployed gang member, structuring his life around reggae music, blues parties, and thieving, and phrasing his life's ambitions in terms of one day to the next with little or no positive orientation to the world and an outlook flavoured by prejudice and ignorance. In the past, I have been guilty of reinforcing this icon; now I am committed either to destroying it or affecting major reconstructions. Black sportsmen I saw as contributors to my task and they were ready allies.

With my impressions stored up from the initial set of interviews, I came to see an intriguing challenge. Visits to sports grounds in London and Birmingham had made me realize just how many second generation black kids were following the likes of Hope and Cunningham and channelling their efforts into sport. The kids at places like Haringey and Repton were not, in the sporting vernacular, 'messers': these were young but serious sportsmen seeking to emulate the 'stars' and acquiring the requisite mental and physical equipment to do so. Taxing work, determination, application, steadfastness, resilience: these were some of the qualities needed to make the grade as a sportsmen even at the more modest levels. If they believed they had 'natural ability', they well knew that it had to be refined and fastened by a bridle of discipline.

These kids were obviously pursuing success and they were sinking inordinate amounts of energy, week in, week out, into their efforts. They were highly motivated, prepared to learn, willing to comply with demands, eager to listen; perhaps they didn't want to follow rules, but they did. Yet could these be the same kids who were, with law-like consistency, achieving little of significance at school, who were showing no aptitude or promise of improvement, who seemed undermotivated, feckless, lacking in both ambition and determination? The abundance of energy, commitment and enthusiasm many black kids manifested in sport contrasted strikingly with the languor they took to their formal education. The end-product of their orientation to education was year after year of miserable results. Blacks consistently performed badly compared to whites and Asians: they 'underachieved' (see The Runnymede Trust and the Radical Statistics Race Group, 1980, chapter five).

All sorts of reasons were advanced, including language barriers, teachers' racism, biased curricula, deprived homes, inadequate material conditions and, most pejorative of all, lack of intellectual equipment. None of these struck me as particularly penetrating answers to a thorny problem. But, by exploring the aspirations and motivations of groups of blacks who were highly charged and who brought extraordinary energy to their chosen tasks, I thought I might find some clues as to the kinds of things which move black kids: what makes them tick. It soon became obvious to me that no study of black sportsmen could proceed without a very careful consideration of why blacks fail in other areas, the most important one being school.

There are, of course, those only too ready to malign my whole project and offer instead a much shorter and simpler account. In answer to the problem I set myself (reports of which were carried in the provincial press in 1980), a certain Mr A. Hatton of Birmingham wrote: 'If you visit some of the pubs, clubs and places of enquiry, you will get the solution to your enquiry . . . just speak to the majority of working people, blacks do not have the intellect or inclination for academics' (personal communication, 12 June 1980).

Whilst accepting that 'inclination' was absent I could not agree that blacks lacked the intellect to do well at school and my work was, in a way, intended to lay bare as false such assumptions. So, it came as something of a disappointment when a Ms Mel Chevannes, who ran a black supplementary school in the West Midlands, wrote to the *Wolverhampton Express and Star* to protest at my testing 'hypotheses that black people are "happy-go-lucky or very physical in their outlook"' and that my aims were to 'damage even further the life chances of black children' (25 June 1980). The suggestions, ridiculous as they were, pointed to the sensitivity of the area I had moved into. By looking at black sportsmen I had invited the accusation that I was unwittingly accepting the traditional stereotype of the black man physically endowed with the properties to excel in sports, but incapable of performing well in academic pursuits. If anything, this whole book is intended as a pulverization of the stereotype.

I replied to Ms Chevannes through the same newspaper thus: 'Generally, black kids do not demonstrate interest in school work and do not sink much enthusiasm into their efforts. They do, however, demonstrate a vigorous approach to sporting pursuits.' A reasonably well-supported statement, I thought, though the late Maurice Ludmer found it 'astonishing' and wrote in *Searchlight*:

> The reason why sport is such an attraction is not hard to understand. It is an area of activity where it is possible to compete on an equal basis, with less of the difficulties of overcoming the discrimination found in commerce and industry in terms of employment (July 1980).

Whilst agreeing in part but disagreeing substantially with the assumptions of Ludmer, I felt – and still feel – that the attraction of sport for black kids is a little more complex and that any full understanding cannot assume that sport constitutes an area freed of racialism, or that black youths are attracted to it simply because they see it as such. Contrary to such a view, black kids believe that, for them, being successful is more difficult than it would be for the white person of comparable proficiency. Many believe it is tough for a black person to make it and that leaves them two choices. The most available is to drop out, resign. The other is to take stock of the overall situation; if it's doubly difficult for a black person, then a

redoubling of effort and determination and perseverance is necessary. If it's twice as hard, you try twice as hard.

Although Hope was the first sportsman to convey this view, it was
replicated time and time again by black footballers, athletes and
boxers. Hope's manager, Terry Lawless, himself white, told me of
how he first became aware of this. During the 1950s, he talked to the
handlers of a black American opponent of Randolph Turpin. He
asked one of them: 'How come there are so many great black boxers
in the States now?' The answer was: 'Well, it's so tough for black
guys to make breakthroughs that they try like mad to be better. And
when they do eventually make it, they're really, really good.'

In a way, black sportsmen in Britain are responding to what they
perceive as a challenge. The reasons for their getting involved in the
first place are multiplex, involving many related processes, which I
will endeavour to uncover. But a sense of challenge permeates the
whole experience. This book is about that experience.

Wrong reasons, right results

Discussing successful black sportsmen, Horace Lashley of the Commission for Racial Equality wrote: 'it is unlikely that their success
can be divorced from the British schooling they have received.' He
goes on: 'PE is regarded as a subject of low priority and status within
the curriculum. It is not surprising, therefore, that the black community resents this focus on the "success" that black youngsters
enjoy at PE' (1980, p.5).

Most components of education are highly valued and thought of as
necessary to the overall development of the child. Physical education
is an exception in this regard. As Lashley points out, we have not
recognized 'prowess on the sports field as genuine *educational* success.' This derives from the dualistic conception of mind and body
and the associated belief in the mind as superior and the body
inferior. Howard Danford and Max Shirley call education 'a vitally
important process involving the mind and emphasizing intellectual
development, while recreation is a relatively insignificant operation
centering around the body, amusement, fun and frivolity' (1970,
p.26).

This split which ensures that the main emphasis in educational
achievement rests on cognitive or intellectual pursuits contrasts with

the situation in the Soviet Union where the central unity of the human being pervades all levels of education. Physical education is highly valued and forms part of a fully integrated educational programme based on a unitary conception of man.

The work of Norman Shneidman has been of some value in highlighting the way in which sport in Soviet society is 'directed towards the *all-round development* of the human individual' (1979, p.7). It is regarded as a matter of national importance and, as such, it is emphasized in much the same way as other elements of education. As Shneidman makes it clear: 'While different components of the educational process aim at the development of different qualities and values, it is impossible to draw a clear distinction between them and to separate physical education from other segments of communist upbringing' (1979, p.6). Without wishing to champion the Soviet system and the way in which it 'manufactures' its sportsmen, I believe the general philosophy underlying the integration of sports with other components of education is much more realistic than the irritating duality with which we labour in the Western world where educators are prone to see justification for particular studies in terms of their practical value.

I agree with Eldon Snyder and Elmer Spreitzer that: 'Like all of education, physical education should provide opportunities for students to try their hand at a variety of activities as sources of possible self-realization. To be able to recognize opportunities for self-actualization is a basic skill that can be carried through life' (1978, p.170). Such characteristics as initiative, purposefulness, persistence and self-control are developed through sport and, while I am not sold on the idea of sport as a builder of 'character', I do believe that these capacities serve important functions in self-actualization, that tendency of all human beings to develop their full potentialities.

I will argue later that kids involved in sport are able to broaden their intellectual scope, partly because they can bring the characteristics chiselled out of sport to bear in other aspects of life, and partly because, through improving health, the kids increase their capability for intellectual work and reinforce their resistance to mental stress.

I think there are many benefits to be gleaned from sustained involvement with sport and would emphasize strongly its creative dimensions. The reasons behind thousands upon thousands of black kids immersing themselves in sport may stem from basic inequalities which I find unacceptable, and, indeed, immoral, but I cannot affirm that sport is some device for the perpetuation of these inequalities any more than I can agree with some critics, such as Paul Hoch, that sport is a mere instrument of capitalist domination designed to slough off energies or divert them into meaningless channels (1972). Black kids may be in sport for all the wrong reasons, but that does not render the results wrong.

My biases are already clear: I see sport as a supremely creative enterprise in which the competitor exerts a mastery and control over himself and his environment. Blending discipline with spontaneity, rigidity with flexibility, the sportsman develops and refines skills, forming objectives, sometimes meeting them, often falling short, but always extracting meaning and gratification. My conception of sport elevates it to the realms of art, where the producer finds room to express himself and the consumer studies and appreciates; both seek satisfaction. This view might be too romantic for some who prefer to see sport as a destructive force, leaving black kids, their hopes shattered, with no qualifications, few prospects and little career orientation. What follows will be an attempt to examine sport in both of these differing lights.

The attempt is structured in terms of an historical overview of blacks' attachments to sport, starting the analysis in the eighteenth century and seeking to document the social sources behind the enduring link. The chapter sets the tenor for the whole work in so far as it tries to examine the social conditions under which blacks became involved in sport, first in the USA and then in Great Britain. My contention is that no account of the emergence of black sportsmen in contemporary Britain can ignore the social and historical circumstances in which that emergence occurred.

The popular view of black sportsmen's rise is more simple: they have a 'natural ability' that equips them to do well in physical enterprises. For many reasons, I reject this, not only because it is vile in its implications but because it is theoretically suspect and unsubstantiated by research. Its main proponent has been Martin Kane and I give some attention to his work in chapter three.

Over a period of three hundred years, black people have achieved a growing presence in sport in Britain yet it seems pathetic that we have no account for it apart from reference to the mysterious attribute called natural ability. To begin with there is no single ability, rather there are several like speed, accuracy, strength, endurance and resilience which combine in manifold ways to determine the 'raw material' to be shaped. This 'raw material' is formed through an interaction between what we are born with and what we live through, or as James Michener puts it: 'Heredity establishes the perimeters of what we can accomplish; environment determines whether we acquire the character to reach those perimeters' (1976, p.130). There are certain properties we inherit but it is the conditions we live under which dictate how we will develop them and to what purpose we will put them.

Brian Wells notes: 'Of course, *all* behaviour is ultimately controlled by the influence which our genes exert upon the development and function of our biological system' (1980, p.29). I am more concerned with the ways in which social mechanisms work to permit the growth and refinement of abilities necessary for sporting involvement. By examining social processes, I am not throwing out the baby with the bath water: I do concede that inherited properties play a part. But ability conceived in a singular way is not sufficient; one cannot assume a situation of perfect competition in which those possessing the necessary physical attributes will emerge as the best sportsmen: the notion of natural ability is not sufficient. My alternative theory does not deny the influence of genetic characteristics, but, when history throws up a patterned sequence of black people entering sports in large numbers, excelling at them and continuing to demonstrate extraordinary zeal for particular disciplines, a more penetrating analysis of the social conditions beneath the sequence is necessary.

This is exactly what I have attempted in this book, beginning in chapter four with my version of why so many black kids commit themselves to sport, then moving, in chapters five and six, to the experiences in family life and at school and how these affect the ties to sport. In chapter seven, I explore the important relationship between education and sport, which is so vital to any understanding of the rise of black sportsmen. American research has been instructive and I survey this before moving to my own views. Perhaps one of the most disturbing elements of black youth's attraction to sport is that they tend to eschew more 'earthly' pursuits and go in search of sporting success. Given that the chances of establishing oneself in sport are extremely small regardless of colour, this is a rather dangerous channelling of objectives. Sport is a slender thread on which to hang one's hopes for the future. How and why sport assumes the status of a central life interest for black kids are the questions I set out to answer in chapter eight.

What is it in sport that black kids find so compellingly attractive? It cannot be the cheap medals and worthless trophies they hope to accumulate and the chances of making big money are so tiny as to make it untenable as a career. In chapter nine, I offer an alternative: through sport, the black youth generates a fresh, exhilarating and positive image of himself, in short, a new identity. The organizing theme of the book is distilled in chapter ten, where I delineate exactly why black sportsmen regard themselves as at a possible disadvantage in sport, how they perceive blackness as an impediment and, most crucially, how they react to it.

Finally, I round off with some of the social implications of the continued involvement of black youth in sport. Much of my attention is devoted to both the positive and negative aspects of sport within education systems and society generally.

In April 1980, the National Association of Head Teachers reporting to the Rampton Committee on the education of ethnic minorities stated: 'If there is a difficulty of cultural identity among second generation West Indians, there is also much to counter-balance that deficiency including their natural sense of rhythm, colour and athletic prowess.' The reader, after completing this book, must decide how much sense this makes.

Chapter Two

ENTER THE BLACK SPORTSMAN in history

Desire and dedication. Without both, a dream is a fragile thing. And desire and dedication are easier to come by when the alternative is a one-way ticket back to the ghetto.

Bob Waters, American sports writer

Bad men and Uncle Toms

During the American War of Independence, beginning in 1775, a certain General Percy of the British forces captured the town of Richmond, after which he named a slave whom he met there. Impressed by the slave's apparent physical prowess, Percy took 'Bill Richmond' under his tutelage and groomed him for prize fighting. Richmond travelled through Europe gaining a rudimentary education on his tours before basing himself in England where he continued to box with a measure of success while working as Lord Camelford's valet. Although not an outstanding boxer himself, he assisted a number of other young boxers including the more famous ex-slave champion Tom Molyneux in whose corner he worked during the Virginian's classic fight with the English heavyweight champion Tom Cribb in December 1810, Cribb finishing victorious (Egan, 1812).

Molyneux, like Richmond, won his freedom as a result of his boxing and it was he, more than any other early black sportsman, who 'showed how prize fighting could be the means by which a man of his colour might gain prominence and a certain undeniable importance akin to a theatrical star' (Farr, 1964, p.3). Together, the cases of Richmond and Molyneux present many of the themes which characterize the entire history of blacks' collective involvement with sport. Richmond was the first black man to find in sport a route out of the despair and misery which were integral parts of his enslavement. Through his competence in sport, he was able to leave Richmond and establish himself as something of a sporting celebrity in Europe and England where, according to Edwin Henderson, he came to know, among others, Lord Byron (1949, p.16).

Molyneux was both sponsored and trained by his forerunner, who came to be his mentor (Knebworth, no date, p.31). There was a close relationship between the two. Both men improved their education whilst engaging in sporting exploits and, indeed, Molyneux was fêted in the London circles of the early nineteenth century. Molyneux built on Richmond's earlier successes and became a figure of public renown. For both men, sport was a 'way out'.

But, although these two set precedents, there was no conspicuous increase in the number of slaves gaining their freedom. Indeed, for the most part, slaves demonstrating boxing proficiency were pitted against each other locally at the behest of slave masters; few trod the same paths as Richmond and Molyneux (McPherson, 1976a, p.123). The years on either side of emancipation in 1865 saw blacks filtering into other sports, most successfully in horse riding and baseball (see Quarles, 1964). In the latter, social circumstances permitted them to compete only against other blacks (from 1898 to 1964), thus prompting what Robert Peterson called 'a uniquely American spectacle called Negro baseball' (1970, p.3).

Ninety-eight years after the first Molyneux–Cribb duel, a black man ascended to the apogee of sporting achievement. John Arthur Johnson was born in 1878 and worked on a milk wagon, in livery stables, in bakers' shops, at Galveston docks and in various other occupations while establishing himself as a boxer of some distinction. When, in 1908 he challenged a white man, Tommy Burns, for the heavyweight championship of the world, he carried into the ring far more than his gloves and gear: he carried the hopes of a considerable portion of black America. His status by that time had taken on an additional dimension: 'When Johnson battered a white man to his knees, he was a symbolic black man taking out his revenge on all whites for a lifetime of indignities' (Gillmore, 1975, p.5). Fighting as 'Jack Johnson' he overcame the barrier known as the 'colour line' which effectively forbade blacks from boxing whites and wrested the supreme prize under the most dramatic circumstances. Police had to enter the ring in the fourteenth round of the prize fight to rescue the pre-fight favourite Burns from further, unnecessary punishment (Farr, 1964, p.60). Such was Johnson's dominance that Jack London wrote: 'Plucky, but absolutely helpless, the white man seemed to be a victim of a playful Ethiopian who did just as he would' (quoted by Gillmore, 1975, p.29).

That Johnson had so much social significance as a black man challenging white oppression, albeit in a symbolic way, was attested to by the scenes following his dismissal of Burns and after his defence against the revered bastion of white pride, Jim Jeffries. 'Gentleman Jim' had previously retired from the ring rather than do combat with a black man, but was tempted in an effort to curb the mounting confidence of blacks and re-establish white dominance in the sport. In less than fifteen rounds, Johnson had delivered the goods for his people. 'It was my honour, and in a degree the honour of my race,' he later reflected. The aftermath of the fight was tumultuous with blacks, enraptured by the triumph, celebrating in the streets. Whites responded, provoking conflict in virtually every state (Levine, 1977, p.432). Al Gillmore calls them the 'Jack Johnson Riots' and reckons the fight itself 'had the effect of a second emancipation' (1975, p.60).

Responses from whites were swift for, within days, calls for the abolition of boxing were heard and films of Johnson's fights were soon suppressed for fear of further riots. Many blacks were also concerned, particularly after Johnson showed a predilection for escorting white women. Their apprehensions were summed up by the *New York Age*: 'As a black champion, he has given the Negro more trouble by his scandals than he did in twenty years as a black tramp' (quoted by Gillmore, 1975, p.99).

No one was more strident in his condemnation than the black leader Booker T. Washington who charged Johnson with being: 'A man with muscle minus brains.' Though Washington's rival Marcus Garvey lauded Johnson and held him up as man to be revered by blacks (1967, volume I, p.13). Despite the controversy, Johnson captured the hearts and imaginations of most black Americans in a way which only folk heroes had done previously. The myth developing around Johnson took on an existence of its own and he became known as a hero of black folklore, fitting into that tradition of 'bad niggers', moral hard men who were, according to Lawrence Levine, 'admired because they had the strength, courage and ability to flout the limitations imposed by white society' (1977, p.420).

One folk tale about Johnson suggested he was protected by an extraordinary power. In 1912, he was believed to have attempted to board the ill-fated *Titanic* only to be refused, thus saving his life. In fact, blacks used the *Titanic* disaster as a symbolic setting for the confrontation between the privileged whites and the poverty-stricken blacks who were excluded from the vessel (Levine, 1977, p.427). Johnson was elevated into the panoply of black culture heroes and martyred after he was forced into exile in Europe for seven years from 1913 after his arrest under the Mann Act.

Not surprisingly, Johnson's ascendancy led to the search for the 'Great White Hope', someone who was capable of wrenching the title from Johnson's grasp and restoring supremacy to the whites. The crusade eventually produced Jess Willard, who, in April 1916, challenged Johnson in Havana, Cuba. Sixteen thousand people watched an astonishing scene as Johnson was knocked to the canvas in the twenty-sixth round and made no attempt to regain his feet, merely shielding his eyes from the sun. Allegations of a 'fix' were unsubstantiated but rumours were rife. So ended the reign of the first black sporting symbol of significant proportions. Willard re-drew the colour line and the heavyweight crown was insulated from black threats. Over the next eight years, the unemployment rate grew to 5 per cent and the Ku Klux Klan's membership to 4½ million (Roberts and Kloss, 1979, p.133). Not until 1937 was the colour line erased, when Joe Louis beat James J. Braddock to start a succession of black champions interrupted only by Rocky Marciano (1952–5) and Ingemar Johannson (1959–60).

In 1946, when Louis was nearing the end of his far less controversial occupation of the champion's berth, Johnson was killed in a road accident in North Carolina. His career had gone into an ignominious period following his deposition and he had spent time in prison in Kansas, fought bulls in Barcelona, performed stunts in circuses, played 'Othello' across the country and even boxed all-comers in exhibitions at the age of 68 years.

Joseph Louis Barrow was, like Johnson, a formidable boxer who exerted total domination for a long period. Johnson reigned for six years, Louis for eleven. There the similarity ended. Louis, in the black American vernacular, 'tommed out'. He did not use his position as a potential leader to mobilize black sentiment or cull support for black people; he simply conformed to the mould of a black sportsman without showing much inclination for socially significant causes. The image Johnson had smashed was restored by Louis: he was controllable.

Not so Muhammad Ali, who was without doubt the most socially important sporting figure after Johnson, and his career parallels that of his predecessor in many ways. An Olympic gold medallist in 1960, Ali came to prominence shortly before his assumption of the world heavyweight title in 1964. As Cassius Clay, he proclaimed himself 'The Greatest' and split the heavyweight division asunder. Once champion, he relinquished his name believing it to be a relic of slavery and announced his allegiance to the Nation of Islam, the segregationist sect popularly known as the 'Black Muslims' (see Lincoln, 1961; Essien-Udom, 1962).

For three years, Ali made inflammatory statements about what the Black Muslims called 'white devils' and proved somewhat embarrassing with his views on black–white separatism. He lost no opportunity to use his status as an ideological lever for black causes, eventually refusing to serve in the army on the grounds that blacks had no interest in the Vietnam War. For this he was relieved of his world title and, like Johnson, was involuntarily immobilized. While Johnson was prevented from defending his title in the United States, Ali had his taken from him.

His return to the ring reached a climax in 1974 when he once more became the world's supreme heavyweight with an eighth-round win over George Foreman in Kinshasha and, apart from a temporary spell in 1978, held the championship until his first 'retirement' in 1979. As with the latter-day Johnson, his exploits in the autumn of his career were inglorious: pathetic exhibitions, a shameless contest against a martial arts exponent, Anonio Inoki, and a misguided come-back fight against Larry Holmes in 1980, when aged 38. Having done so much to point up the plight of blacks in the 1960s and 1970s, Ali reduced himself to little more than a comic figure in much the same way as Johnson had. Very wealthy comic figures, it should be noted.

Quite obviously, the black population which attached so much importance to Johnson in the early years of the century was very different to the one which looked to Ali for leads in the 1960s and 1970s. Indeed, according to Louis Lomax, there had occurred 'The Negro Revolt', meaning that there had been a gradual but discernible rejection of the notion of blacks as inferior and a series of social movements orchestrated to sound this (1963). Martin Luther King's civil rights campaign had resulted in legislation against the segregationism which existed in parts of the USA well into the 1960s. King denounced not only whites for their paternalism and racialism, but blacks also for their enduring 'slave mentality'. His aim was to restore pride in being black and inspire black Americans to campaign for equal rights.

Improvements in the general conditions of blacks had taken place between Johnson's era, when white supremacist groups like the Ku Klux Klan articulated deeply-held sentiments, when at least three hundred and fifty blacks were illegally lynched and mixed marriages were forbidden, and that of Ali, when conflict manifested itself in the Watts riots and radicalism came in the form of the black power movements. From the time when Ali was stripped of his title until 1975, the material conditions of blacks deteriorated; unemployment tripled so that figures of 35–50 per cent were commonplace in urban ghettos (Roberts and Kloss, 1979, p.72). Ali proved a personal focus for his movements and the Nation of Islam became a forceful agent of cultural change amongst blacks, offering, through the leader Elijah Muhammad, a reassertion of the lost culture of black people with the creation of separate hospitals, schools, farms and industries. Social isolation was encouraged to preserve racial purity and 'freedom from contempt'.

By 1977, the movement's name had changed to the World Community of Islam in the West. 'Bilalian' replaced 'Muslim' (Bilal was an Ethiopian thought to be the first black follower of the prophet Muhammad). Several prominent black sportsmen followed Ali's example and underwent conversion to the faith (two world light-heavyweight titles in the 1980s were held by converts, Matthew Saad Muhammad and Eddie Mustapha Muhammad).

Sport has been called by many, including such opposing writers as Robert Boyle (1963) and Paul Hoch (1972), a 'mirror' reflecting, in often exaggerated ways, aspects of social life. The period between Johnson's demise in 1916 and the rise of Ali, provides a good example of how reflective sport can be. Caution must be shown when reviewing the progressive eradication of the colour line and the subsequent successes of blacks in many fields of sport. It would be unwise to assume that because sport became an arena where colour lost its significance – if, indeed, it did entirely – the rest of society

followed suit. It seems feasible to agree with the sports historian
Edwin Henderson that, with the exception of show business, sport
was the only area 'in which blacks were able to assert themselves'
and so 'on a large scale, Negroes identify with people in sports and
entertainment' (1970, p.4).

Certainly, as I will argue later, sport and show business constitute
the two spheres in which blacks have made immense contributions
and which seem to throw up figures with whom black kids tend to
identify and on whom they model themselves. There are reasons for
this, reasons rooted in social circumstances rather than natural abilities and these can be highlighted by examining the period between
Johnson and Ali.

Willard's restoration of white dominance in heavyweight boxing
in 1916 coincided with the re-establishment of the colour line. He
and subsequent champions refused to defend their titles against
blacks. Their policies drew little disapproval from sports authorities
or the rest of the white population. Harry Wills, a black boxer, was a
contemporary of Jack Dempsey who reigned from 1919 (when he
beat Willard) to 1926. It is perhaps surprising that Dempsey is
ranked among the greatest champions of all time when he was
artificially protected from the challenge of black opponents. Wills,
from Louisiana, campaigned for a shot at the title, but Dempsey had
acquired a status somewhat akin to Johnson's. But, whereas Johnson
had been 'bad', Dempsey was a symbol of everything wholesome in
white America.

Racial disturbances and the 'Red Scare' were parts of the changing
social climate in which Dempsey fought in the aftermath of World
War I, yet 'Dempsey seemed something stable, something people
could depend on', according to Randy Roberts (1974, p.66). Dempsey defended his title only six times in as many years and constantly
snubbed black challenges, one interesting one appearing in the pages
of the *New York Times* from a certain Prince Mohammed Ali Ibra-
him of Egypt whose special weapon was a 'pyramid punch' (4 March
1924, p.14). But it was Wills who posed the most potent threat from
the number one contender's corner. Dempsey's manager Tex
Rickard was, as another outstanding black heavyweight of the time
recalled, 'determined to keep the title white' (Gains, no date, p.54).

Gene Tunney disposed of Dempsey in 1926 and, after that, Larry
Gains observed, blacks' frustrations about the colour line spiralled:

Harry Wills' campaign had caused a lot of soul searching.
Dempsey with his image of the ex-hobo riding the roads to fame
had been big enough and glamorous enough to blur the
controversy from the minds of the crowd. But now that Dempsey
had gone, the question had to be asked (no date, p.82).

Answers came in the form of an alternative world championship for
the excluded black boxers. Gains himself was one of the holders, as
was George Godfrey, whom Gains rated as at least the equal of
Dempsey. As Gains (from Toronto, but now living in Croydon) told
me in an interview in 1980: 'The only time Godfrey had the hand-
cuffs off was when he was fighting another black man.' The black
title lost its meaning after Joe Louis began the black occupation of
the heavyweight scene in 19⅝7 and, after that, the colour line was
erased, in boxing at least.

Athletics, too, had moved away from the days when black sportsmen in the USA were forbidden to compete against whites. 1936 was
the year in which a performance of theatrical proportions signalled
the arrival of black athletes on an international scale. Black athletes
had already represented the United States: George Poage at the
Olympic Games in 1904; de Hart Hubbard won the long jump in
1924; Eddie Tolan won the 100 yards and Ralph Metcalfe competed
in 1932. But, after this, the scene was set for the 1936 Berlin
Olympics where, as Richard Mandell points out: 'Racial policy
permeated all aspects of German life in the Nazi era. German sport
was not excepted' (1971, p.58). Jews bore the brunt of such policies,
but blacks were similarly despised as Hitler's refusal to recognize
Jesse Owens signified. James Cleveland Owens, as he was christ-
ened, eclipsed the achievements of every previous Olympian when
he swept through to win the sprint and long jump events, only to be
rebuffed at the presentation ceremonies. The Games were to be used
as what Mandell calls 'The Nazi Olympics', a spectacle to under-
score the supposed physical and intellectual superiority of the Aryan
race. Owens, together with Archie Williams (400 metres), John
Woodruff (800 metres) and Cornelius Johnson (high jump), punc-
tured that myth decisively, winning gold medals for the USA.

Owens, along with Louis, became an establishment figure. Mandell depicts him thus: 'a self-effacing gentleman, Jesse Owens was
both a paragon and a refutation and therefore was considered "a
credit to his race" ' (1971, p.225). A 'credit' he may have been, but

Owens was expelled from the American Athletics Union for refusing to compete in a Swedish tour and was eventually reduced to freak show racing against horses and motorcycles. He also made it clear that he was against black boycotts organized around the 1968 Olympic Games in Mexico, at which Thommie Smith and John Carlos demonstrated on the victory rostrum with a gloved black power salute. The two were banned from international athletics for their parts in 'The Olympic Project for Human Rights' (details of which can be found in Edwards, 1970).

Owens was submissive in the extreme and, though at first adulated, he was later despised by more vociferous blacks. He may have established the credibility of blacks as sportsmen, but, as Harry Edwards notes in allusion to Owens: 'From their [whites'] perspective, the only difference between the black man shining shoes in the ghetto and the champion black sprinter is that the shoe shine man is a nigger, while the sprinter is a fast nigger' (1970, p.20). It is a sobering statistic that in the twelve months either side of Owens' triumph there were twenty-six lynchings of blacks in the USA. Also, it was not until 1947, eleven years after the Berlin Olympics, that black and white athletes were allowed to compete openly in a full track meeting in the USA (Henderson, 1949, p.96).

The year before that, 1946, baseball allowed a black man into its major league for the first time. Strict segregation had held firm for years and, as in boxing, a world series for blacks was organized in the 1920s. But Peterson contends: 'By the early thirties, gentle waves were washing against the hull of organized baseball' (1970, p.175). And, at the start of the 1940s, a baseball administrator named Branch Rickey began his search for the man destined to become the first black player in a white team. Like Louis and Owens, Jackie Robinson was an uncomplicated, uncontroversial, non-drinking, non-smoking and, importantly, non-political sportsman. In 1946, he played in Montreal and in the following year, he transferred to the Brooklyn Dodgers, where he had to weather a strong protest by the rest of the team before making his debut. Lomax describes Robinson as a 'moderate' and his sympathies with the National Association for the Advancement of Coloured People (NAACP) underlined his initial reluctance to be involved in mass direct action (1963, p.103). The organization favoured social change through legal processes. Robinson became much more confident and outspoken in the 1950s and eventually criticized the NAACP for its gradualist policies.

Presumably, his testing years as the first black in major league baseball affected his perceptions; he was abused verbally and physically, was sent threatening notes, was boycotted by many teams and at one stage, came to the brink of a nervous breakdown (Henderson, 1970, p.71).

Henderson believes that Robinson was 'wrapped in all the dreams and aspirations not only of negro people but of all Americans of whatever colour who knew that segregation was wrong' (1970, p.69). The hostility of his reception may have daunted other administrators from recruiting black players, but there was a gradual incursion of blacks into baseball in the 1950s and 1960s.

The basketball equivalent of Robinson was perhaps Chuck Cooper, who, in 1951, signed for Boston Celtics and precipitated a rush of black players to the major league clubs. Within sixteen years, over half the registered players of the National Basketball Association were black. The impetus behind this increase was probably provided by a decision given by the United States Supreme Court in 1954 which declared forced segregation unconstitutional in all public educational institutions. Previously all-white colleges with heavy emphases on sporting achievements were then able to recruit blacks for their institutions. Two pieces of apparent racialism surfaced in basketball. First, in the 1967–8 season, 'dunking', a shooting strategy employed almost exclusively by blacks, was outlawed. Second, in the 1972–3 season, the management of the American Basketball Association's Dallas franchise removed four of its ten black players (of an eleven-man squad) because, according to the coach: 'Whites in Dallas are simply not interested in paying to see an all Black team' (quoted by Edwards, 1973, p.214).

One all-black team whites seemed very interested in paying to see was the Harlem Globetrotters, which began life as 'The Savoy Big Five' and changed its name in 1927. It is difficult to categorize the team alongside the previously mentioned sportsmen simply because it was more a comedy outfit than a competitive unit. Its historical and current popularity with whites is accountable in terms of its members' conformity to the image of the black man as physically adept but lacking in the intellectual equipment to harness his skill to firm objectives. The goals were more in making audiences laugh than scoring baskets and so they were clowns, even if skilful ones. The team was regarded by many, including James Michener, as having a negative impact: 'I strongly suspect that the Harlem

Globetrotters did more damage racially than they did good, because they deepened the stereotype of "the loveable, irresponsible Negro" ' (1976, p.145).

It was not a historical accident that the sports in which blacks were overrepresented compared to their proportion in the general population were those demanding little in the way of equipment or facilities. Such events as rowing, swimming, shooting, fencing, skiing and yachting were, as Edwards puts it, 'outside our cultural reach' (1970, p.79). The desegregation of education helped bring sports such as American football inside their reach during the 1960s and, by 1972, black players comprised 40 per cent of the total of professional footballers, most, however, occupying 'positions with the fewest intellectual and leadership demands' (Eitzen and Sanford, 1975, p.959).

The general pattern established by blacks' involvement in sport in the last two hundred years is that they have excelled in all those areas within their cultural reach and such excellence is repeated generation after generation. Blacks in the USA achieve success in sport in numbers that belie their minority status in the population at large. In the mid-1940s, explanations for this were offered in the form of theories which presented anatomical features as the cause of the blacks' advantages. 'A long thin shank, a long heel, a peculiar patella, a stronger tendon of Achilles or larger adrenalin glands' were some of the attributes thought to enable blacks to dominate certain disciplines (Henderson, 1949, p.362). However, there are social sources for the high value placed on sport by blacks and, in this short and somewhat cursory account of blacks' involvement in American sport, I have hoped to bring out some of them.

Obviously, when sport offers itself as one of the few accessible routes away from deprivation, as it was to the early slaves, it takes on an attractive quality. Those slaves distinguishing themselves through their sporting efforts in the ring were able to win their freedom and, in some cases, elevate themselves to social prominence. As a consequence, those figures became inspirational to other slaves who attempted to emulate them: the Richmond-Molyneux effect. Even today, sport is seen as a 'way out' and black sportsmen provide important reference points for young blacks. As I will indicate, black sportsmen of distinction wield considerable influence, often unknown to them, and unwittingly act as lures for black kids, as Bill Richmond probably did in the late eighteenth century, not only in the United States, but in England too. Yet, given their potential influence, few outstanding sportsmen have used their position to challenge the notion of the legitimacy of sport as a way out and a method of social mobility, and few have pointed out that blacks' continued domination of sport is more a reflection of limitations in other areas of a society permeated with racism than of blacks' talent. Thommie Smith and the other members of the 1968 Olympic protest against black–white inequality were vivid exceptions. His expulsion by American authorities contrasted strikingly with the reception he received from Rap Brown, Stokely Carmichael, Elijah Muhammad and other black leaders (Edwards, 1970, p.107). George Foreman, who also won a gold medal (for boxing) in Mexico, held the stars and stripes as he received his medal and was celebrated throughout the United States by whites. But, then again, he was more in the Louis mould, 'a good nigger', rather than the bad Mr Smith.

Foreman's opponent in 1974, Muhammad Ali, is the other important articulator of protest, and his dominance over other heavyweights for a period of fourteen years was so complete that he was impossible to suppress, even though his enforced incapacitation for four years did seem to dull his sharpness in criticizing white racism. He saw that it was this very racism that was responsible for forcing blacks into positions of marginality. He emerged from a culture in which positive values were attached to sport and, in a black perspective, for good reasons – that was where other blacks were making it. Ali himself has acknowledged this: 'I started boxing because I thought this was the fastest way for a black person to make it in this country' (quoted by Torres, 1971, p.83). From this viewpoint, racism contributed in significant measure to Ali's achievements as it did to every other black sportsman's. The effects of racism were not restricted to the USA, but were apparent in England too, where my focus now shifts.

Escape: the British experience

The existence of successful black sportsmen in Britain is not the recent phenomenon it is often considered to be, though the upsurge in the post-war years makes it appear that way. Unlike the USA, where emancipation released slaves from plantations to develop into a large indigenous population, Britain acquired its black contingent initially through immigration. In the twenty years after 1951, Britain's settlers from New Commonwealth countries increased from 0.2 million to 1.2 million, the majority being black workers attracted to England in the 1950s and 1960s by expanding job opportunities (for more details, see The Runnymede Trust and the Radical Statistics Group, 1980). Recruitment schemes such as those of London Transport were operated in the West Indies to encourage immigration. Most West Indians settled in areas where the chances of employment were highest, London and the Midlands attracting the majority.

The sportsmen came mainly from the children of this first wave of immigrants in the 1950s and 1960s. But not all: for black sportsmen have staked a presence in Britain, albeit a small presence, since 1777 when Bill Richmond was uprooted and given his freedom in recognition of his sporting achievements (at this time, Walvin, 1971, p.12, estimates there were 15,000 blacks in London). He handled and advised Tom Molyneux, the next black figure on the sporting scene, and actually fought until 1815, five years after the famous Molyneux–Cribb encounter, which Henderson describes as 'the first great fistic battle of the century' (1949, p.17).

Henderson's early work, *The Negro in Sports* (1949), contains references to a number of other slaves who followed Richmond and Molyneux to England where they campaigned as boxers, thus effecting an escape. Jim Wharton for example, born in Virginia in 1813 (five years before Molyneux's death in Scotland at the age of 34), campaigned in England in the 1830s. In the second half of the century, Britain received, amongst others, Bob Smith from Washington DC and Bob Travers, who was noted for his contests against Jem Mace and Patsy Reardon.

Slightly later came heavyweight Peter Jackson, born in St Croix, West Indies, in 1861, four years before emancipation. He travelled as a seaman to Sydney where he won the Australian heavyweight title before transferring to San Francisco where he was persuaded by the Earl of Lonsdale to operate in England, a move which enhanced his status greatly, as a contemporary noted: 'I knew him in the days of his greatness when sitting on top of the pugilistic world, fêted and lionized, he might well have been excused some slight vanity' (quoted by Henderson, 1949, pp.20–1). Viscount Knebworth notes an early colour line drawn by the world heavyweight champion John

L. Sullivan who took on white challengers but refused to fight Jackson (no date, p.56).

By 1896, however, Peter Corris reports: 'Jackson became a publican and a drinker and his decline was rapid' (1980, p.53). He was reduced to playing Uncle Tom in a touring version of Stowe's *Uncle Tom's Cabin* and, in this sense, became something of a prototype.

Travelling with Jackson when he left the USA was perhaps the most awesome of all black boxers to come to England. Born in Halifax, Nova Scotia, George Dixon moved to Boston where he acquired a knowledge of boxing. Fighting as 'Little Chocolate', his campaign in England culminated in his winning the world bantamweight title by stopping Englishman Nunc Wallace in eighteen rounds of a contest at the Pelican Club, London, in 1890 (though he had informally been recognized as the premier bantamweight for some years before). Like Jackson, he enjoyed a comfortable life style, staying in quality hotels and dressing rather ostentatiously. His inability to make the weight limit forced him to relinquish his title, but two years later, at the age of 22, he moved back to the USA and won the featherweight crown (subsequently losing it, regaining it, losing it again and winning it back finally in 1898).

While Jackson and Dixon were performing regularly in the English rings, a black man distinguished himself on the track. He was Arthur Wharton, a Jamaican about whom little recorded evidence exists apart from his sprinting achievements. Running for Darlington, he became the first man to run 100 yards in even time (10 seconds dead) under championship conditions when he took the Amateur Athletics Association (AAA) title in 1886 at Stamford Bridge. Interestingly, he remained in sport, becoming the first black professional footballer when he signed on as goalkeeper for Preston North End. He kept in touch with athletics, running in the professional Powder Hall competition in 1889. (For further details on the historical aspects of athletics, see Watman, 1968.)

In 1902, Andrew Jeptha migrated from Cape Town to Liverpool, working his passage on a freighter. He had been boxing in South Africa for three years and, according to boxing historian Gilbert Odd, had remained unbeaten for the first two years (1978, pp.18–19). After moving to Willesden in north-west London he became the scourge of local boxers and eventually became the first black man to hold a British title when, in 1907, he beat Curly Watson in the fourth of a scheduled twenty rounds to take the welterweight championship at the 'Wonderland' venue in the East End of London. He continued to box until 1910 when a deteriorating eye condition signalled the end of his active career.

Jeptha is not popularly credited with being the first black British champion. This is because the British Boxing Board of Control (BBBC), the governing body of the sport, was not formed until 1929 and quite openly barred non-whites from challenging for British titles until 1948. Charles Donmall, in this period the secretary of the BBBC, justified the discrimination by pointing out that: 'It is only right that a small country such as ours should have championships restricted to boxers of white parents – otherwise we might be faced with a situation where all our British titles are held by coloured Empire boxers' (quoted by Henderson, 1949, p.340).

If anyone was a source of embarrassment to the BBBC because of this rule, it was Larry Gains who was born in Toronto in 1900 and moved to England rather late in his boxing career when 30 years old. Gains' involvement in the sport was a perfect example of role modelling for, in 1913, he fleetingly met Jack Johnson. From that time, he made it his ambition to become 'another Jack Johnson', as he told me: 'It was a kind of inspiration to me as I was the only black kid in the area. Every time we used to fight from then on, I used to pretend I was Johnson and the other kid used to say he was Sullivan or somebody.'

The ambition was what Gains, in his autobiography, calls the 'impossible dream'; the colour line effectively prohibited him from challenging for the world title, though he did beat George Godfrey for the black version of the championship in 1928. After moving to England, he fought for over two years without being defeated and reckoned: 'Ninety per cent of the public wanted to see me win the British title. There wasn't prejudice amongst the public then 'cause there was only a handful of coloured here, anyway.'

His ring record alone demanded the attention of the BBBC and he believed that: 'It was through public opinion that I eventually got a title. The board thought, "we've got to give Larry Gains a title; give him an Empire title and he'll be satisfied with that." I reckon I was the People's Champ.' Accordingly, he was granted an Empire title challenge in 1931 at Leicester where he duly disposed of England's Phil Scott in under two rounds. He continued to campaign successfully without ever managing to secure the British title he wanted to win and retired in 1939 with the racist rule still intact. This rule was eventually changed after the war so as to permit the Leamington-born middleweight Dick Turpin to contest the British championship. He did so successfully in 1948, outpointing Vince Hawkins at Birmingham and thus becoming the first black champion to be recognized by the BBBC.

Black involvement in athletics had continued in the inter-war period, first through a Guyanan, Harry Edward, a prodigious sprinter who was interned in Germany during the war, but returned to England taking seven AAA sprint titles in the 1920–2 period. He still remains the only man to win the 100, 220 and 440 yards in one AAA championship (in 1922). Also from Guyana was Jack London, though he was brought to London when just 3 months old. He went to the 1928 Olympics, equalling the 100 yards record in the semi-final. In the following year he won the 100 yards AAA title; he had for a while reigned as the British number one high jumper. He was also the first sprinter in Britain to use starting blocks. After retiring, he went into show business. Between the wars, the credibility of black sportsmen generally was enhanced by the tours of the West Indian cricket team in England. Later, the 1950 series against England, won by the tourists, gained black cricketers recognition as world forces.

World War II was an important factor in the emergence of the two black athletes who, according to Mel Watman, ranked alongside Roger Bannister in terms of national popularity. Collectively, Bannister, McDonald Bailey and Arthur Wint formed what Watman calls 'the Holy Trinity' (personal communication, 1981).

Bailey competed as an unheralded schoolboy in a AAA meeting in the late 1930s, then returned to his Trinidadian birthplace. He joined the Royal Air Force during the war, after which he settled in London. Between 1946 and 1953, he was virtually invincible over 100 and 200 yards, achieving an all-time AAA record of sixteen titles (including two relays). He won a bronze medal for Britain in the 1952 Olympics. One of his 'trade marks' was an all-white kit to contrast with his dark skin. 'Unusual, but totally accepted', is how Watman described him. 'A big hero'.

As 'heroic' was Arthur Wint, also in the RAF during the war. He joined Polytechnic Harriers (also Bailey's club) and took the AAA 440 yards and 880 yards titles in 1946 and added three more titles before 1952. Representing Jamaica, he won the 1948 440 yards Olympic title in London and added two silvers to his haul. He studied at the University of London whilst competing and qualified as a doctor of medicine. After retiring from sport, he became the Jamaican High Commissioner in London. This was in contrast to Bailey who attempted to capitalize on his athletics success by venturing into rugby league. Business interests in the music industry occupied his later years.

It is wise to remember that these men were competing at a time when the black presence was of only tiny significance. Curiosity may have been aroused by their performances but, according to Watman, 'they enjoyed incredible popularity at the time and there was never any suggestion of race as a factor' (personal communication, 1981).

During the decade after the war, immigration, most particularly from the West Indies, rose sharply in response to the employment opportunities I mentioned earlier. Active in that period was Lloyd Lindbergh Delaphena, born in Kingston, Jamaica, in 1927. He played soccer for Middlesbrough in the immediate post-war years and, in 1950, moved to Portsmouth where he played professionally until 1958, after which he drifted away from the club never to contact Portsmouth again (W. J. B. Davis, Portsmouth FC Secretary, personal communication, 1979).

More black boxers were becoming active during the same decade. Indeed, on one night in June 1946, five black successes prompted the ambiguous headline from a London newspaper: 'Black Night For British Boxing' (Henderson, 1949, p.340). As well as the home-grown Turpin, boxers like Yolande Pompey from Trinidad and Cliff Anderson from Guyana were making regular appearances. They were, however, not allowed to take part in British title contests. Regulation 31, paragraph 4 of the BBBC's constitution specified that a title contestant 'must be a British subject who was born and is normally resident and domiciled in the United Kingdom . . . and has been resident in the United Kingdom for a period of not less than ten years.' This effectively ruled out the overwhelming majority of black boxers based in Britain. The ten-year qualification still stands.

The life of Dick Turpin's brother Randolph fits almost perfectly into that pattern created by Jack Johnson, Peter Jackson and Jesse Owens: an emergence from abjection and poverty to world recognition and wealth amounting to £300,000 from boxing earnings alone, followed by a slide into debt and obscurity and a reduction to the kind of fairground exhibitions engaged in by the others (Birtley, 1976).

Turpin was born in the Midlands town of Leamington Spa in 1928. His father was an immigrant from British Guyana, his mother a local woman who, according to Turpin's biographer Jack Birtley, had to withstand the stigma attributed to those making 'mixed marriages' (1976, p.13). Inspired by the example of his eldest brother Dick, he began boxing in 1937, the year in which Dick made his professional debut. His career climaxed in 1951 when he upset Sugar Ray Robinson by taking his world middleweight title after fifteen rounds at Earls Court. His reign as champion, however, lasted only two months and he was stopped in the tenth round of a return contest in New York City.

For two years, he persevered in an attempt to regain the title but was outpointed by Carl 'Bobo' Olsen in October 1953. Thereafter, his form fluctuated as irregularly as his training and his domestic affairs. Lacking any financial acumen, he ran into difficulties with the Inland Revenue which filed a bankruptcy petition against him for the unpaid tax on his ring earnings: the order was for over £17,000. His career plunged to humiliating depths when he engaged in 'boxer v. wrestler' bouts and even consented to making a fully fledged comeback in a boxing promotion at Peterborough (which was not licensed by the BBBC) at the age of 35 (Birtley, 1976, p.133). On 16 May 1966, he committed suicide by shooting himself, though rumours of a 'gangland murder' remained, according to Birtley (1976, pp.140–53).

Boxing continued to attract black participants after the initial post-war period. Among the more conspicuous were Yolande Pompey, who challenged unsuccessfully for Archie Moore's world light-heavyweight title in London in 1956, and Hogan 'Kid' Bassey, a Nigerian who moved to Liverpool in 1952, three years later won the Commonwealth featherweight title and, in 1957, won the world featherweight title, before eventually returning to Nigeria as national boxing coach.

Neither athletics nor soccer prospered from black participation in the same way as boxing, but there were exceptions. Roy Hollingworth, a discus thrower from Trinidad, and Clive Long from Guyana gained international athletics honours in the 1960s, though it was a Jamaican, Marilyn Fay Neufville, who, over the period, rose to prominence in athletics, eventually gaining the Commonwealth

Games gold medal and, simultaneously, the world's 400 metre record (51 seconds) in Edinburgh in 1970 when she was 18 years old. Neufville ran for Cambridge Harriers in South East London though she opted for competing for Jamaica in the prestigious games.

Leeds United's winger Albert Johanneson became the first black player to appear at Wembley in the 1965 Cup Final against Liverpool, who won 2–1 after extra time. In the early 1970s, Clyde Best, a Bermudan, played for a spell with West Ham and, I am told by one of his former team mates, was made to feel isolated by fellow players. John Miller, the son of a Jamaican father and English mother, aroused interest by being mooted as the first black player to represent England. 'Miller for Munich' (the site of 1974 World Cup Finals) anticipated Maurice Smith in the *People* (19 December 1971).

Blacks continued to involve themselves in boxing after the war though it was not until 1970 that a black boxer emulated the Turpins in winning a British title: Jamaican-born Bunny Sterling became the first immigrant boxer ever to win a British title when he beat Mark Rowe at Wembley. He had been domiciled in England since 1954 and so fulfilled the BBBC residential qualifications. The racially inspired threats which Sterling told me he received after taking the title illustrated the resentment felt at a black man being a British champion.

It was only because of fortuitous circumstances that Bunny Johnson was allowed to carry through his successful challenge in 1975. The BBBC ordered an eliminating series of contests to decide who should gain official contender status. Johnson was highly ranked but had been based in England for a few months under ten years. He was excluded on these grounds when the eliminators were announced even though, by the time the fights would have taken place, his ten years would have been up. In the event, John Conteh dropped down a division and Johnson took his place, proving the legitimacy of his claim by beating two contenders and then the champion to become the first black heavyweight champion of Great Britain.

Conteh's decision brought benefits in the form of a world light-heavyweight title in 1975 though his desire to sever links with the main promotional power bloc led to his eventual demise. Born in Liverpool to a West African father in 1951, Conteh won ABA, British and Commonwealth titles but was stripped of his world title by the World Boxing Council for failing to go through with a contracted defence in 1977 and failed three times to regain the championship before retiring in 1981.

By the time of Johnson's accession, the second generation West Indians' enthusiasm for sport was beginning to germinate and, by the end of the decade, decisive steps had been made in both athletics and soccer. International representations in athletics came in abundance with Ainsley Bennett, Mike MacFarlane and Daley Thompson and football went through a veritable upsurge in the 1978–9 season with the likes of Viv Anderson, Laurie Cunningham, Cyrille Regis, Garry Thompson providing the vanguard of a train of black first-division players. Anderson became the first black player to play in a full international game for England in 1979.

Cunningham detached himself from the British game negotiating a £1 million transfer to Real Madrid in 1979, the same year in which Maurice Hope of Antigua emulated Dixon, Turpin, Bassey and Conteh by winning a world boxing title. London-born Mike Mac-Farlane established himself as the top black British athlete by winning the 200 metres European title, though his form thereafter lapsed and, although he made the 1980 Olympic sprint team, he failed to make the finals.

A surfeit of black footballers appeared in the early 1980s, some, like Garth Crooks and Justin Fashanu, of exceptional competence. In boxing too, blacks continued to participate: out of 448 professional boxers registered with the BBBC in 1981, approximately one-third were black and four out of the ten British titles were held by boxers of West Indian origin or descent and Cornelius Boza-Edwards, a Ugandan who moved to London in 1974, won the world superfeatherweight title in 1981. Athletics continued to prosper by the increasing infusion of blacks into sprint and jumping events, though it was a decathlete, Daley Thompson, who, in 1980, became the most successful black British-based athlete since Arthur Wint, by winning an Olympic gold medal and, for a spell, holding the world's decathlon record.

The early 1980s was a time of immense fertility for blacks in sport: as well as their presence in athletics, boxing and soccer, Desmond Douglas established himself as the top table tennis player in the UK; Eugene Codrington consolidated his captaincy of the British karate team (composed mainly of other blacks) and Roland Butcher became the second black player to play for an MCC touring side (the first being Basil D'Oliveira of South Africa). Though less of a working-class sport than the others, cricket has played a part in gaining blacks' acceptance as legitimate sportsmen through exposing black West Indians as players of enormous proficiency.

Clearly, the intense involvement of blacks in sport is no recent phenomenon and any study of black sportsmen must pay careful attention to history. To gain an understanding of the persistence and excellence of black sportsmen, the analysis has to begin in the eighteenth century. I outlined earlier how several of the themes developed in early slave days continue throughout the course of black involvement in sport. Sport constituted an avenue of social mobility for any slave willing and capable enough to pit his sporting skills against another. It is no surprise that the gladiatorial sport of boxing was the most accessible route. Slave masters matched their gladiators and rewarded the successful with relief from plantation duties, the possibility of travel and, ultimately, freedom. Few or no other routes were available and so it was a most logical decision to opt for the sporting escape. But only the very superior pugilists made the ultimate escapes and so it was in every boxing slave's interest to wring out his best efforts on every occasion. If training and competing were exacting, they were not nearly so exacting as plantation work.

Boxing was also the sport in which blacks first grew to prominence in Britain, though, of course, their presence was the result of the predilection of the wealthy to engage their interests in the noble art and therefore encourage the cross-fertilization between Britain and America. The first black sportsmen to appear in Britain were either slaves or ex-slaves. As in America, boxing overwhelmingly dominated the attentions of blacks simply because it was the sport in which other blacks had been allowed to compete and they had done so with extremely conspicuous success. I have emphasized the part played by people like Jack Johnson in uplifting the morale of other blacks and providing reference points for the ambitions of many, and I will argue for the importance of successful black sportsmen in galvanizing blacks' interests.

Athletics, to a more limited extent, commanded some attention, beginning in the late nineteenth century with Arthur Wharton who later became the first black footballer to play league soccer. At that time, athletics was more genuinely an amateur sport, less the 'invisible' crock of gold it is today with its often overt forms of 'shamateurism'. So, although a rich source of status and prestige, athletics could not compare with professional sport in terms of material gain. Because of this, boxing remained the major sporting area for blacks right up to and beyond the World War II period, though it was not until 1948 that they were allowed to contest a British title. The blacks, like Bailey and Wint who were in athletics, tended to be from established occupational and social backgrounds and, to them, sport may not have yielded a direct material benefit. But, indirectly, the prestige accorded them because of their achievements no doubt aided their later successful careers. And, even in itself, prestige through sport is a valuable commodity for those unlikely to receive it from any other direction.

The elliptical path paved by Peter Jackson in the 1890s was followed by another black comet, Randolph Turpin, in the 1950s. Leaving poverty and strife behind them, both went into orbit via sport only to return dispirited to their take-off points. Stories such as these are more regular in the USA where, according to Nathan Hare, black boxers begin with visions of wealth and glamour but complete their careers 'dissatisfied now with their present lot'. He gives the example of Johnny Saxon who, three years after winning the world welterweight title, was charged with burglary and eventually institutionalized at New Jersey State Mental Hospital: 'Boxing does not leave all its scars on a fighter's face' (1973, p.325). Such scars were left on Jackson and Turpin, but it would be facile to accept these as rules rather than exceptions. And, in any case, it is ridiculous to condemn boxing itself for attracting black aspirants when the reasons for their involvements are rooted in historical and social processes.

It is not so curious then that blacks have manifested a predilection for sport and have achieved high orders of success in their chosen disciplines. Maurice Hope, no less than Jack London or Lindy Delaphena or Tom Molyneux, was involved in sport because of the social circumstances common to black people. Not particularly these circumstances in an objective sense, but the way in which they are perceived and oriented to by black people. And the source of those circumstances lies in the imperial expansion of the seventeenth century, the settlement of the West Indies and the expansion of the trade in slaves, gold and sugar between Africa, the Americas and Britain. Slavery meant that whites maintained their domination over blacks and so kept a rigidly structured inequality. Such an inequality has been modified and refined in the decades since emancipation, but blacks have never quite shed the remnants of their shackles and have stayed socially unequal.

Men of sport must be understood in relation to their historical and social conditions. Where opportunities exist in realms offering longer term and, therefore, more secure futures, sport does not figure prominently for it is always precarious, invariably venturous and frequently treacherous. Where such opportunities are absent and material conditions suffer, resulting in apprehensions about employment, housing and diet, more accessible areas are approached. Sport and entertainment are two such areas. They are both gladiatorial in the sense that the participants train or practise and exhibit their skills and enthusiasm for one end, the amusement of others. Training and preparation may be the most isolatory activities, but sport itself is performed to be appreciated. When all is said and done, the modern day season ticket holder or the viewer of closed circuit television, no less than old time slave masters, have decisive effects on the destinies of sportsmen.

Historically, where there has been a demand for sport, the particulars of participants seem to lose significance. Thus the severe animosity against Jews culminating in the Aliens Act of 1905, a product of what Bernard Gainer calls 'The Anti-Alien Mentality' (1972, chapter 5) did not prevent sport's patrons delighting at the scores of immigrants seeking material rewards through boxing. As with the blacks, sport for Jews became a possible way out of the dreadful circumstances which beset their lives.

That sport and, for that matter, entertainment may not be viable avenues from despair is less important than the fact that they were seen as such by groups who saw no alternatives. 'Shout down any coal pit in Yorkshire and half a dozen fast bowlers will come up' was an adage born out of the 30s depression when cricket was one of an extremely limited range of alternatives to a miserable, lowly paid struggle in coal mining.

The potency of sport in magnetizing certain minority and underprivileged groups is obvious. But there are no inflexible rules concerning its power to draw on such groups: first generation Caribbeans in the UK showed little interest in sport, nor did Asians of either generation on any scale. But the first generation did not see their opportunities as restricted: migration itself was an optimistic move. The prospect of improved material conditions in a new social environment was a strong one, as many studies indicate (for example, Patterson, 1963; Davison, 1966; Peach, 1968; Lawrence, 1974). Although their reception by whites was more hostile than they anticipated, their conditions were still improvements on what they had left behind and their thoughts for the future would have turned about accumulating money through regular, if uncomfortable, comparatively rewarding employment. Asians were products of a culture emphasizing the value of education as a means of social advancement and, because of the tight control they were able to exert over their children, could imbue the second generation with similar values. Various factors militated against this happening with Caribbean children and I will spell them out in the chapters to come.

The tenor of the work so far indicates my view that any account of the rise to prominence of black sportsmen in Britain is hollow unless constant reference is made to the social conditions amidst which black people lived and live. I hope it is already apparent that the intense enthusiasm for sport generated by blacks in both the United States and Britain is no historical accident. Nor is it due to black people's possession of special gifts or talents which equip them more satisfactorily for certain sporting events.

The latter point has been a cause of some concern because, in the 1980s, black kids continue to involve themselves in sport with a fervour which alarms many, fearful that blacks' achievements can only reinforce traditional stereotyped images about blacks being adept at physical pursuits, but inept at intellectual ones. One does not logically follow the other, of course, but trying to establish theories purporting to explain blacks' achievements as resulting from alleged natural gifts unique to blacks, by implication, reinforces the stereotype. In the next chapter, I will consider one such theory.

A chronology of blacks' involvement in British sport

The forerunners

1777	Bill Richmond moves to England from Virginia
c.1805	Tom Molyneux follows Richmond to England
1810	First Molyneux–Cribb contest
1811	Second Molyneux–Cribb contest
1815	Bill Richmond's last fight
1818	Tom Molyneux dies in Scotland
1850s	Jim Wharton campaigns in England
1860	Bob Travers loses to Jem Mace
1860s	Bob Smith of Washington DC active
1886	Arthur Wharton of Jamaica wins AAA 100 yards title in even time
c.1886	George Dixon and Peter Jackson move to England
1889	Wharton relinquishes amateur status
1890	George Dixon beats Nunc Wallace for world bantamweight title
c.1890	Wharton plays for Preston North End FC
1891	Peter Jackson v James J. Corbett declared no contest
1892	Jackson wins Empire heavyweight title from Frank Slavin

The turn of the century

1902	Andrew Jeptha moves from Cape Town to England
1902	Jeptha beats Curly Watson for British welterweight title
1922	Harry Edward wins 3 AAA titles in one meeting
1928	Jack London of British Guyana competes in Olympics
1929	London wins AAA 100 yards title
1930	Larry Gains moves to England from Toronto
1931	Gains beats Phil Scott for Empire heavyweight title
c.1939	McDonald Bailey of Trinidad and Arthur Wint of Jamaica appear in England
1940s	Lindy Delaphena of Jamaica plays for Middlesborough FC
1946	Bailey wins first of 16 AAA titles
1946	Wint takes first of 5 AAA titles

The Turpin period

1948	Dick Turpin wins British middleweight title from Vince Hawkins
1948	Wint wins Olympic 440 yards gold medal for Jamaica
1950	Delaphena transferred to Portsmouth FC
1950	Randolph Turpin beats Albert Finch for British middleweight title
1951	Turpin adds European title by beating Luc Van Dam
1951	Turpin takes world middleweight title from Ray Robinson
1952	Hogan Bassey moves from Nigeria to Liverpool
1954	Bunny Sterling moves to London from Jamaica
1955	Bassey beats Billy Kelly for Empire featherweight title
1956	Yolande Pompey challenges unsuccessfully for world light-heavyweight title against Archie Moore
1957	Bassey wins world featherweight title beating Cherif Hamia
1960s	Athletes Roy Hollingsworth and Clive Long represent Britain
1961	Maurice Hope leaves Antigua for London
1965	Albert Johanneson plays for Leeds in Wembley FA Cup Final

The modern phase

1970	Sterling wins the British middleweight title
1970	Marilyn Neufville wins Commonwealth Games 400 metres and breaks world record
1975	Johnson becomes first black British heavyweight champion
1975	Conteh wins world light-heavyweight title
1979	Viv Anderson becomes first black England soccer international
1979	Hope wins world light-middleweight title
1980	Daley Thompson becomes Olympic decathlon champion in Moscow
1981	Garth Crooks becomes the first black player to score in a Wembley Cup Final
1981	Cornelius Boza-Edwards wins the world superfeatherweight title

MAURICE HOPE
fighting for others

Born: Antigua, 1951; father: Antigua (railway porter); mother: Antigua; occupation: professional boxer – formerly a leather tanner.

'If he wasn't a successful boxer, Mo would probably have been doing ten years for something or other now,' reckoned Tony Burns, Hope's former coach from the Repton club. 'Around here, there are two things for a working-class kid to do: steal or box.' Hope opted for boxing and became a world champion.

> I came to England when I was 9, that would have been in 1961, and that's when I saw the world for what it's all about. I was still a child but I saw it, the black and white thing, it was a reality. Not that it came to me just thinking: I realized it at school. Most of my school mates were black, though I had a few white ones. From the age of, say, 11, I began to see that I'm black and others were white and there was no use putting it behind me.

At this age, he started boxing, principally at the instigation of his brother Lex. There were only three other black kids at Repton at the time and Hope had to withstand some daunting reactions to his presence at the club in the East End of London.

> I had to mix and tolerate. There were a few of them who put it straight at me and I was forced into getting into rows. I remember one fellow spat in my face. I'd be in the shower and they'd push me out, actually push me out saying, 'you black so-and-so'. This shocked me 'cause I'd left Antigua with no idea what colour prejudice was, no idea.
>   You can imagine how frustrated I felt. I'm only human. Outside the ring, you feel frustrated, but you try to argue and get some facts. But that's the most you can do outside the ring. You argue with one another and put it down to the fact that people who are

Maurice Hope. Photograph courtesy of C. Y. Moyse

prejudiced are ignorant. It makes no sense arguing with them, so I had to walk away or get involved in fights. Most of the time, I'd walk away. Now, in the ring it's different: it's all legal there.

In a way, he was able to vent his frustrations in his boxing and his sport became like a cathartic experience; it provided a perfect outlet for his aggression.

It doesn't sort of get to me nowadays. I've learned to deal with prejudice, but in a funny kind of way, it's helped me get from the bottom to the top. I still get the comments. The only difference is that, now I'm somebody, they don't say it to my face. But because they don't say it to my face, it doesn't mean to say I don't still get them: now they say things behind my back.

Hope's emergence as 'somebody' was almost glacial. He turned professional in 1973 under the management of Terry Lawless. After winning his first four contests, he was outpointed, but strengthened his resolve winning his next nine, eight inside the distance, including an eight-rounds victory for the British light-middleweight title. After that win, Hope's family and supporters celebrated with champagne in the dressing room and Lawless recalled: 'We only had a few glasses and Mo and I were drinking out of the same one. I can still see the looks of astonishment on his friends' faces when they saw me, a white man, drinking out of the same glass.'

After having a challenge for the domestic middleweight title demolished by Bunny Sterling who stopped him in eight rounds, Hope once more returned with a vigorous sequence of wins culminating in a challenge for the world light-middleweight title held by Eckhard Dagge in Berlin. The result was a highly controversial draw, most ringside commentators agreeing that Hope deserved victory. That was in 1977 and Hope had to wait two years before making his second attempt. Rocky Mattioli, an Italian, had displaced Dagge, but Hope overwhelmed him in San Remo to take the World Boxing Council light-middleweight title. Three defences made him one of Britain's most successful world champions ever before being dethroned by Wilfred Benitez in 1981 (in a fight for which his purse was 400,000 dollars) yet, curiously, he stayed at his terraced house in Stoke Newington, London. This was partly because of his sense of responsibility to black people.

I haven't led a life of freedom: I've sacrificed a hell of a lot. But they all know me as one of them. They see that I do things different. That's why I feel kind of different, like a leader, like an example to them. Things are getting harder and harder and we're going backwards. I also think that a lot of black kids think that this is a white man's country and, when any little thing goes wrong, a set-back, the first thing they jump on is colour. I've been through everything: set-backs and fear. Where publicity is concerned I've had a raw deal. Naturally, I put it down to colour. I've looked at it on both sides, from different angles and colour is something to do with it.

Even in the later stages of his boxing career, he held a most acute perception of the problems besetting black people and he continued to carry such a perception to the ring.

I've really had to work hard to get where I got to and when I fight a black guy, I know that he's had to do the same thing. I think: 'Well, he's had it as hard as me' and little zest goes out of your punching, I just want to beat him on points. I'm professional, of course, and it all changes as soon as he hits me. All of a sudden, I want to get it over with no matter if he's black, white, pink or yellow. But, I know black people who are watching me in the audience or on the TV are thinking it's a black versus white thing.

Before his defence in 1980, against Carlos Herrera, he announced: 'This is a white man's country and the black man is being held back.' Accordingly he dedicated the fight to 'black people of the world', and was criticized for his sentiments. However, Hope, by that time, clearly regarded himself as the embodiment of blacks' ambitions.

People like myself and the footballers and athletes, we're black and have been pressed down. OK? But they can't keep us down forever 'cause we're going to show whites that we're better than them at their own game. We've made it, so we're showing other blacks that they can make it as well.

Asked if he thought an over-emphasis on sport could disadvantage black kids in academic subjects, he answered:

No. I think if you've got it inside you, I don't think you have to turn your back on any one subject and concentrate on another. If you're sensible enough, you know you've got to learn your lessons and not be ignorant to the fact. I know that a lot of blacks are just expecting things to come to them; they're sort of free living, it's our nature to sit down and enjoy life. But you've got to compete. There are a lot of black boxers because blacks are natural fighters. But there are very few that have made it really big in this country. They haven't got perseverance, haven't got the dedication; they want to enjoy themselves, not sacrifice things. Really, I've surprised myself being a black man and being by my nature free living. But it's amazing how I'm affecting black kids. They come up knocking at my door asking me to teach them boxing and even stopping me on the street. My winning has done something for them as well as me. Fighting inside the ring, I'm not just thinking about myself. I'm thinking about black people as well as Antigua and Great Britain and, lastly, myself.

Chapter Three

THAT BLACK MAGIC
of nature

Environmental factors have a great deal to do with excellence in sport. But so do physical differences, and there is an increasing body of scientific opinion which suggests that physical differences in the races might well have enhanced the athletic potential of the Negro in certain events.

Martin Kane, American sports writer

The belief in the existence of an invariable racial 'character' was supposedly disposed of by scholars decades ago. Its persistence only indicates the difficulty with which racial stereotypes and caricatures are destroyed or altered to comply with prevailing scientific knowledge . . . by asserting that blacks are physically superior, even well-meaning people at best may be reinforcing some old stereotypes long held about Afro-Americans.

Harry Edwards, American sociologist

Ability

One of the most apparent features of blacks' involvement in sport is the continued standard of excellence they achieve. It seems that, whenever blacks turn their attention to a particular sport, they rise to a high order of competence in it. In history and in modern times, any sporting pursuit which seriously engages blacks is sure to see them become the leaders in the field.

As I argued in the previous chapter, boxing was the first sport in which institutional arrangements permitted a black presence: almost every weight division produced black boxers of such brilliance that they were virtually without equals (see Henderson, 1949, 1970;

Maher, 1968). The examples of Sugar Ray Robinson, Henry Armstrong and Ike Williams attest to this and heavyweight boxing was dominated by black boxers almost totally from 1937.

Jesse Owens' mastery of multiple athletic disciplines is well known and since then the sprint events have become virtually the property of American blacks with figures like Jim Hines in the 1960s, and hurdler Ed Moses in the 1980s, exerting unparalleled supremacy in their respective events. Basketball was all but taken over by black players; grid-iron football became a platform for such star performers as Jim Brown and O. J. Simpson and baseball, to a lesser extent, absorbed many black players of distinction, including Hank Aaron and Willie Mays, the number one and number three leading home-run hitters, after Jackie Robinson broke the colour bar in 1947.

The pattern was similar in the UK with second generation blacks rising to prominence in the late 1970s and early 1980s, getting a foot-hold first in boxing and later in athletics and football, not to mention karate and table tennis. Blacks' recent involvement in sport began in the 1950s and continued spasmodically through the next two decades, intensifying as the 1980s approached; in the spheres in which they opted to compete, many achieved excellence.

Their visibility in sports and success in certain events led many to speculate on the reasons behind the supremacy of blacks in some sports and non-involvement in others. Generally, blacks in the UK concentrated on boxing, the traditional 'open sport', which was historically the most accessible to them, the sprint and jumping events of athletics and, more recently, soccer. Amongst the sports in which blacks showed no interest were swimming and golf and there was little obvious interest in racket sports while middle distances of the track were disregarded.

Explaining this seemed of no particular concern to those involved with sport: blacks were patently good at some events and not good at others. When pressed for reasons, they would draw on such 'obvious' facts as blacks are physically equipped or conditioned better for some sports, or reference was made to the explain-all theory of 'natural ability'. Even today, these types of explanation are prevalent amongst sporting communities. They would seem to be of integral importance to any manager or coach handling black sportsmen, yet few theorize at any level other than the physiological or, more occasionally, the psychological. It is my purpose to expose such ideas as erroneous and offer in their place an account based on *social* processes.

The theories held, often implicitly, by managers, trainers and coaches are of interest because of the effect they have on all involved in sport. If a coach believes that the black sportsman he is helping to prepare is naturally endowed with the physical equipment to produce fast sprints or hard jabs, or mazy runs through defences, it will affect his judgment as to the areas of speciality into which he should channel the efforts of that sportsman. It will also affect the manner in which the coach attempts to motivate the sportsman, the light in which he analyses his performances and tries to improve them and more basically, the very nature of his personal relationship with his protégé.

Some folk theories of sport have achieved a myth-like status, and they are often seriously entertained and elaborated upon by those in sport. The old chestnuts about blacks having weak ankles and heavy bones which militate against their achieving success in swimming still retain credibility in sporting circles, and there are other similar theories in abundance. Birchfield jump coach Kevin Reeves insisted that blacks possessed 'a muscular structure' which gave them advantages in power events, where short, explosive bursts of uncontrolled energy were needed. Fellow coach Robert Millington reckoned: 'Physiologically, they [blacks] are much better equipped than whites; not so much with what they've got to start with, but what they can achieve in a short space of time. They develop their bodies in no time. Whites can't do that.'

Athletics coaches were unanimous in their opinion on the physical suitability of blacks for specific events and Haringey's black coach John Isaacs made the extreme assertion that: 'A black kid can do a 100 [metres] without any training at all; they can just come along with their kit and knock out 11 seconds. They just have that natural ability.'

The 'natural ability' angle is appealing in its simplicity and comprehensiveness. Athletics coaches allude to it constantly, believing it to be the basis of blacks' successes. 'It's a question of physical make-up: black kids are built for the explosive events. White kids are always at a disadvantage,' speculated Charles Taylor. As a foil for this argument, white sprinter Mark Garmeston offered his view:

There isn't a chance of competing on level terms with black guys.
It's depressing really. I trained hard all last winter and in one race
I came up against a black who I knew hadn't prepared properly.
He just blazed out and killed the rest of the field. It's got to be
something natural.

The argument gains force when applied to boxing where the
emphasis shifts to the muscular flexibility and, as manager Terry
Lawless put it, the 'natural fluidity' of black fighters which gives
them a distinct edge over their more rigid white counterparts:

You see a black guy in the ring and he moves around in this
relaxed way, totally lacking inhibition in his movement. It's the
same when you see black guys at a dance or a disco; they have this
natural fluidity in their bodies. Whereas a white guy will be
starchy and throw punches only when he's sure he'll land, a black
guy will stay loose and throw six or seven jabs in the hope that one
or two will land.

Continental Football Club manager, Mitch Daley, himself a West
Indian, expanded a similar notion into a full-blown philosophy on
black footballers:

Take the white player: he's very rigid, upright, stiff. Now, the
black man he's different: he likes to step on the ball, control it,
express himself with it. He has natural flair which gives him the
ability to do anything with the ball he wants to.

And he believes that it is precisely because black footballers know of
each other's natural ability, that they are able to construct the most
intricate and seemingly planned movements without any preparation
at all: 'They've got the receivers built into their heads and can pick
each other up on the same wavelength.' So, the natural ability goes
beyond the physical and manifests itself mentally when players are in
the process of play.

On the other hand, Jim Smith, ex-manager of Birmingham City
Football Club, believes that black players make only limited use of
intellectual abilities when playing soccer: 'They seem to use very
little intelligence; they get by on sheer natural talent most of the
time.' Daley countered this with his idea that black players can use
the mental facility only with other blacks, believing that even the

black players who had commanded football league places had not been allowed to play to their utmost because they were engulfed by whites who were on 'different wavelengths'.

Overall, the view that blacks' success in certain sports is not chiselled out of hard work, determination and perseverance, but out of a somewhat intangible capacity called 'natural ability' holds sway amongst coaches, managers and even amongst athletes themselves. Modifications to the general view are only minor and it is obvious that relationships between black sportsmen and their coaches and managers are structured by such a view.

It is stressed repeatedly how some sportsmen had the potential or the promise yet lacked the application to develop it. Blacks are thought to have natural advantages and, if they do not capitalize on them, they are seen as lazy and lacking in conviction. So, tensions occur in relationships where the sportsmen are thought by their coach to be naturally gifted and yet they fail to achieve success. Sportsmen who believe themselves to be blessed with natural advantages, after being told so by others, become depressed by the lack of success of the magnitude they had come to expect after being fed the natural ability line. Leroy Brown, at one stage a prodigious sprinter, reflected on a career which never materialized: 'I just don't know why I couldn't put it together when it mattered. Physically, I was all right. I knew I had all that it takes; the others told me.' He dropped out of athletics after a season without a win.

For the most part, black sportsmen accept that they have advantages, in an unspecified way, over their white counterparts. A natural propensity for physical rather than intellectual pursuits was cited by Coventry City footballer Garry Thompson: 'I think blacks are the most athletically gifted race. We may not be the cleverest but we're athletically gifted.' This view was endorsed by Repton boxer Jimmy Dublin, who confirmed: 'It's natural; we're just good at sport. We don't do very good at reading and writing, but we're made for physical things.'

It will be obvious by now that my account of the emergence of black sportsmen runs contrary to such views and I cannot accept that blacks are 'made for physical things' any more than I can that their continued failure in more formal academic realms is based on inadequate intellectual resources. The point is: virtually everyone in sport, to some extent, accepts that blacks have a natural ability at sport which functions at both physical and intellectual levels. As sprinter Ainsley Bennett put it: 'Most black kids seem to be natural and fluent in what they do and what they think.'

Agility, speed, muscular power, sharpness of reflex, accuracy of judgment, these I presume to be some of the attributes with which blacks are thought to be born. Certainly, they are useful characteristics for sportsmen, as are the more psychological ones, intuitive vision, resistance to pressure and the ability to remain calm under stress being among the more obvious ones. But few sportsmen or coaches could be more explicit on this point than Haringey's sprinter John Skeets: 'It's part of our make-up, physically and mentally.' Hardly a scientific viewpoint, but efforts have been made to review the available evidence and assess the plausibility of such an idea. Although not specifically related to sport, Robert Malina's work begins with the observation: 'populations differ in a variety of biological and cultural characteristics and motor performance and strength are no exception' (1973, p.333).

Malina looks at the ways in which black youths in elementary schools seem to possess different basic motor skills to whites: they can, amongst other things, run quicker, jump longer and grip stronger. There are a number of reasons for this and Malina is aware of how such phenomena as poverty, crowded home conditions and poor diet can affect physical performances. However, the upshot of his research is that differences in motor skills do exist between black and white kids.

Now, although he ignores many of Malina's suggested causes for these differences, Martin Kane uses his evidence to support what is, without doubt, the most exhaustive attempt to find some biological foundation for theories purporting to explain blacks' natural ability. It is instructive to preface an exposition of the theory with Kane's somewhat ingenuous comment on the ancestors of modern blacks:

> the West African was no savage. He created an architecture of respectably high standards. He was a skilled and artistic weaver . . . a highly competent woodworker . . . a good herdsman . . . a fine farmer. . . . He had not, though, for the most part, reached that fine state of civilization in which he was able to make gunpowder . . . he never invented the wheel and the plow (1971, p.81).

Through the medium of *Sports Illustrated*, Kane analysed three strands of thought, all originating in the belief that blacks possess unique, natural talents. For his article, 'An assessment of black is best', Kane assembled copious data and marshalled the support of medical scientists, coaches and sportsmen (1971). The result is an argument organized in three categories, all of which connect in the idea that sporting superiority is racially linked. This in itself is, of course, highly problematic since the concept of race is regarded by contemporary social scientists as, at best, misleading and, at worst, viciously destructive to understanding. The argument, therefore, proceeds from a precariously weak premise: that human populations are divided biologically into discrete, bounded units, designated 'races'. (For a further discussion, see Baxter and Sansom, 1972, part one.)

Kane's first category of race-linked physical and physiological characteristics, then, is in doubt from the start but he delineates them as follows: proportionately longer leg lengths, narrower hips, wider calf bones and greater arm circumference among black athletes than among whites; a greater ratio of tendon to muscle among blacks, giving rise to the condition typically termed double-jointedness, a relatively dense bone structure; a basically elongated body structure among black athletes, enabling them to function as more efficient heat dissipators relative to whites (1971, pp.74–5).

Quite apart from the conceptual fragility of the enterprise, Kane's work suffers from a problem of method: his evidence for the above assertions was collected from a sample of sportsmen who had already achieved a level of success, in other words the sportsmen he studied had 'made it'. The attempt was not to take a sample of the total black population, but of the minority of sportsmen of proven excellence. The absence of black swimmers is explained by Kane as the result of such factors as bone and muscle density, distribution of fat and small lung capacity. Cold climates are said to affect blacks adversely because of their body fat deficiencies, weak ankles would account for the lack of black hockey players, etc. In short, genetic factors are regarded as crucial in determining the eventual performance in sport. The inference is quite clear: blacks are innately different from whites, these differences are genetic and so can be passed from one generation to the next, and they have a critical effect on sporting performance. And whether they like it or not, the vast number of coaches and sportsmen who harbour similar ideas on the natural ability of blacks also implicitly, and occasionally explicitly, hold what amounts to a racist explanation of black sporting success.

The first category of Kane's analysis has to be called into question because it is patently obvious that black people do not share physical and physiological characteristics. Stand former British heavyweight and light-heavyweight champion boxer Bunny Johnson alongside the diminutive British international sprinter Ainsley Bennett and one begins to get the idea. Some black athletes do look alike and have similar builds, but there is also much physical diversity amongst them and between them and whites. What are the salient physical diversities amongst them and between them and whites? What are the salient physical characteristics shared by 20-stone Repton boxer Ray Tabi and Danny Thomas at 5 feet 8 inches, relatively short for a top football defender? These extreme examples highlight the ludicrousness of trying to draw together the physical traits of black people when it is clear that there exist as many differences between individual blacks as between blacks and non-blacks.

To foul up the analysis further, Kane's alleged physical characteristics are meant to predispose blacks to the sports demanding speed and strength while whites, because of their body make-ups, are rendered liable to go for endurance events. One supposes that Kane would find the performances of Henry Rono of Kenya, Miruts Yifter of Ethiopia, and Suleiman Nyambui of Tanzania difficult to explain. In fact, he claims that the Kenyans, in particular, have black skin but have a number of white features! A not dissimilar offering came from a Birchfield sprint coach who suggested that the Africans were 'built differently to West Indians . . . and this makes them better suited to the longer distances.'

Wherever they are now, black people are descended from Africans, but over the centuries their genetic heritage has become diversified and complicated by various permutations of mating. Why Kane ignored this and chose instead to propose a one-dimensional view of black people sharing physical characteristics is perplexing, but his next step is utterly stupefying: he suggests that blacks have psychological characteristics which are also determined by race.

In this category, blacks have a greater capacity than whites for remaining relaxed under pressure. This conforms neatly with what a great many coaches, especially in boxing, believe. Lawless, as well as remarking on the lack of inhibition in throwing jabs, connected this with a more general 'relaxed approach', and others concur with this, agreeing that the black sportsman shows a remarkable tendency to bring to his work a resistance to tension. Often the ability not to become tense infuriates coaches and managers who think that a sense of urgency and resolve are missing in the performance of a sportsman who seems too relaxed.

Frank O'Sullivan, head coach of Birmingham City ABC, regarded 'the majority of black kids' as 'too casual in their approach' and as a consequence 'they can't react to pressure.' As well as being an aid then, being cool is also seen as an obstacle to digging deep into the ultimate reserves under stringent conditions to produce a better performance.

Kirkland Laing, former British welterweight champion and an ex-member of the Lawless camp, provided a nice example of this. He, more than anybody in sport, personified cool: he boxed with the most consummate self-assurance, drifting around the ring almost somnambulistically, often dispensing with his guard and rapidly discharging clusters of punches. In his 1980 title defence against Colin Jones, a white Welshman, he performed with his usual calmness, accumulating points with ridiculous ease for the first eight rounds. Then, quite unexpectedly, he took a clubbing right hand to the head and lost complete co-ordination. He did not react but lay back grasping the top rope. Jones mounted a quick two-fisted assault and the title changed hands in those brief, dramatic seconds. Laing was at pains to stress that at no time did he feel under pressure: 'It was that I'd never been caught before and I didn't know what to do. It was the shock of it more than anything. I suppose I could've been too cool!'

This story is tangential, but it illustrates the downfall of a sportsman who epitomizes Kane's 'couldn't-care-less' black sportsmen. Lloyd C. Winter, an established American coach, lends Kane's theory some credence: 'As a class, the Black athletes who have trained under me are far ahead of whites in that one factor – relaxation under pressure' (Kane, 1971, p.76). But let me balance this with an inside view from triple jumper Aston Moore:

> Everyone used to say to me, 'how do you manage to stay so cool and relaxed for a big event, Aston?' If only they could know how I feel everytime I compete! If they could have only known what's going on in my head. I suffer from so much tension it's not true. The thing is I disguise it. But my head is totally taut.

It should also be understood that black sportsmen work sedulously at perpetuating their popular image of being relaxed at all times. Examples of blacks consciously and deliberately projecting this image, radiating cool and total relaxation, abound, but two in particular stand out. One is a track side scene: five white runners and two black limbering up, shrugging shoulders, stretching legs and trying desperately to loosen up in an intensifying ambience; sitting on the grass some way away from the main group is a black guy awaiting his call to marks; while the others shuffle about nervously, he remains casually sitting, seemingly unoccupied with the imminent race as he nonchalantly sharpens the spikes of his running shoes with a nail file. The other concerns a light-middleweight boxer of Repton and Young England, Leon Young, who, when asked which aspect of his boxing he was trying to improve, answered: 'My laziness, really. I'm trying to be relaxed like Frank Edwards [also of Repton] and get a lazy jab like his.'

What these examples illustrate is an attempt by black sportsmen to convey an impression of themselves as cool: they like people to believe they are always relaxed and unflustered. In other words, they work at it – which is a quite different thing from saying they are psychologically predisposed to remain relaxed under pressure. Ainsley Bennett revealed: 'I give this careful impression in training and competition that I'm lazy and never provoked into action, always relaxed, even if I'm not.'

What limited evidence there is on the relative propensity of blacks and whites to be relaxed suggests that, in contrast to Kane's view, black sportsmen were more 'concerned' and 'serious' – uptight – than their white counterparts (Ogilvie and Tutko, 1966). They also exhibited a more controlled orientation to their sport, a finding which goes against Mitch Daley's theory on the spontaneous, free-flowing approach of black footballers compared to whites.

While it is most certainly the case that black sportsmen try to present the image of being cool, calm and unaffected by tension, I doubt if there is any foundation for pointing to psychological states. If anything, the psychological condition of the black sportsman should be tension-packed given the social circumstances surrounding his involvement. As I will suggest in chapter eight, the black sportsman sees sport not as a hobby, but as a central life interest, a sphere in which he might find scope for self-expression and a possible avenue out of his mundane, everyday existence. Consequently sport is of paramount importance to him and every event has to be approached as if it is the most demanding in his life; failure is not easily assimilated, as a result. Also, many blacks perceive themselves as severely disadvantaged in both society generally and sport in particular. In every competition, they believe the odds are against them and one consequence of this is that they always know that they have 'to be twice as good' and, as indicated in this book's theme, 'try twice as hard'. Hardly the type of perception designed to elicit a relaxed orientation.

There is a curious way in which psychological factors might come into play, and Harry Edwards has reasoned this through:

> many white athletes, some of whom may themselves be of exceptional athletic potential, *believe* blacks to be innately superior as athletes. These white athletes under such circumstances may start off at a psychological disadvantage. The 'white race' thus becomes the chief victim of its own myth (1973, p.197).

Whites allow themselves to be psyched out. The afore-mentioned view of Garmeston that 'There isn't a chance of competing on an equal level with blacks' would support this. One is left to wonder how many whites have fallen foul of 'their own myths' and begun at a 'psychological disadvantage' to blacks because of the misguided belief in 'natural ability'.

Another angle on psychological differences between blacks and whites is given by Worthy and Markle who argue that white sportsmen do better at self-paced activities, 'ones in which the individual responds, when he chooses, to a relatively static or unchanging stimulus', whereas blacks have an edge in reactive activities, 'in which the individual must respond appropriately and at the right time to changes in the stimulus situation' (1970). So, for example, in football, whites should be more suited to take penalty and free kicks (self-paced) and blacks to more spontaneous out-field range shooting (reactive). Worthy and Markle cite basketball, finding that whites excelled in free throws from a static position and blacks at field goals on the move. Their findings were repudiated by Jones and Hochner (1973) but supported by another study by Dunn and Lupfer (1974) who assessed the performance of 55 white and 122 blacks in a modified game of soccer, calling the forwards' functions self-paced and the defenders' reactive. Blacks were superior at the reactive activities.

Interesting as such studies are, they leave too many questions unanswered. Even if one accepts that the thesis accounts for why blacks are overrepresented in reactive activities such as boxing and soccer, and underrepresented in self-paced sports such as golf and swimming, it does not explain why blacks do not excel in such reactive sports as motor racing, tennis, fencing, squash or even skiing!

Second nature

Slavery is the key to unlocking the third chamber of Kane's theorem about why blacks excel in sport: 'Of all the physical and psychological theories about the American black's excellence in sport, none has proved more controversial than one of the least discussed: that slavery weeded out the weak' (Kane, 1971, p.80).

The historical experiences undergone by blacks during slavery are invoked to explain why blacks are so demonstrably well equipped physically and psychologically for the demands of sport. In essence, the argument advanced runs that the slaves, originally wrenched from their African homelands, had to withstand the 'most inhuman conditions' during the passage to the Americas and the seasoning period which followed (when they were 'broken in' in much the same way as wild horses – with force). About half the captured Africans survived the rigours of capture, passage, seasoning and eventually worked on plantations and, Kane concludes: 'only the strongest survived.' Calvin Hill, a former footballer with Dallas Cowboys, extends the theory: 'Well, Black athletes are their descendants. They are the offspring of those who were physically tough enough to survive' (quoted in Kane, 1971, p.76). Maurice Hope held a similar view, though he favoured social rather than genetic factors: 'Black people are natural fighters; they've been fighting for survival and they've been in that condition all their lives. So fighting comes natural.'

Coach Kevin Reeves concurred: 'The weakest didn't survive and, over the years, the strongest features of their physical make-up have become refined.' Lee Evans, the controversial black Olympic sprinter, contributed a further element to Kane's model when he added:

'Then, on the plantations, a strong Blackman was mated with a strong Blackwoman. We were simply bred for physical qualities' (quoted in Kane, 1971, p.79).

Whilst not doubting that the slaves were treated by their conquerors and masters as akin to live-stock rather than like human beings, it strains credulity to say that, in the decades after emancipation in 1865, the stock somehow remained 'pure'. The sexual behaviour of blacks has hardly been controlled in such a way as to create a gene pool in which specific physical traits related to power, speed and agility became dominant. (In fact, even in slavery, it was quite common for slaves to have white fathers or grandfathers; certainly nowadays, most blacks have some sort of white ancestry.)

Also, physical characteristics such as power, speed and agility were perhaps of lesser importance to survival than ingenuity, tact and intelligence. Of course, some were able to pull through on sheer physical strength, quickness and resilience, but there is evidence to suggest that shrewdness or guile were useful properties to have when it came to self-preservation. Extending this theme, David Targett, medical officer of Aston Villa FC, reasoned that:

> Intelligence is essential to the modern sportsmen; there are so many losses and benefits to be weighed up that a sportsman needs a rational, calculating mind. I think nearly all the top sportsmen are reasonably intelligent people. They have to be.

No sphere in which physical prowess is necessary, whether survival in slavery or excellence in sport, is devoid of the need for intellectual properties. No one who seriously appreciates sport believes that even the most overtly physical sports are founded solely on physiological characteristics. In the physically gruelling sport of boxing where 'brawn' is said to rule, the most stringent demands are made upon mental agility, speed of thought, anticipation and sense of strategy – at all times, it is necessary to 'box clever'.

Despite the two serious drawbacks to this strand of Kane's theory, the non-existence of a pure gene pool and the uselessness of purely physical attributes without intellectual characteristics, I must stress that many modern black sportsmen hold theories which seem to harken back to their slave heritage. Boxer Brian Johnson, for example, suggested that: 'Blacks are conditioned to sport by their slave ancestry . . . toughness is part of our make-up, it's been drummed into us.'

This type of view is very prevalent amongst black sportsmen, though some even trace the causes back to Africa, an environment which was thought to foster physical abilities useful for running fast, jumping far and being strong. Like Justin Fashanu: 'Back in Africa, there were the conditions for running about and fighting – speed and strength were essential.'

I find this final strand of Kane's theory as unacceptable as the first two in its pretensions to scientific validity and equally as objection-able in its racist undertones. All three categories gel into a coherent formulation which states that blacks' achievements in sport are related to factors determined by their race. Sport is seen as the black man's second nature. He takes to it as a duck takes to water. I will argue that the affiliation is not nearly as simple as the formulation implies. I have contended that the success, and for that matter failure, of blacks in sport has nothing to do with so-called physical characteristics which they are all meant to share, nor with psycholo-gical predispositions which they clearly do not have, and certainly not with physical inheritances which are said to have been somehow transmitted genetically from their slave forefathers. All three of Kane's categories suffer from implausible assumptions which belong in the realms of racist folklore rather than scientific inquiry. The whole model of race-linked characteristics ensuring success in sport has the solidity of a house of cards.

One of the serious problems with Kane's work is that, despite its theoretical fragility, it is simple, comprehensive and, unfortunately, appealing; it explains everything to do with blacks' sporting success as rooted in race. Less obvious is the misguided logic it offers, for, if it is accepted that blacks have the natural ability and talent to do well in sports, then it can do no harm to encourage their participation in sport. The outstanding results they continue to produce would seem to confirm the validity of the first assumption that they are naturally gifted.

The counterpart to this is that they are naturally limited intellec-tually and so not actively encouraged to excel in academic and the more cerebral pursuits and, of course, they do not. So, the prophecy of blacks' doing well in sport but poorly in intellectual realms is self-fulfilling. And by accepting it, the believer tacitly ignores the complex social mechanisms which uphold the mistaken logic.

One beautiful example of such logic came from Tony Zaidman, a white field athlete from Haringey, who said: 'Black people are good at sports just like Jews are good at making money!' This is not so far away from saying: Blacks are naturally superior in sports and physical endeavours; whites are naturally superior at intellectual pursuits. Without impugning the motives of any believer in this, I point out that it reeks of a vile and dangerous racism. Fresh substance is given to old stereotypes. That blacks do reach standards of excellence in sport, while failing in academic spheres, is beyond doubt. But by accepting an explanation of this which is manifestly racked by conceptual, methodological and theoretical shortcomings, one gives purchase to the type of idea which is likely to prove injurious to the general interests of ethnic relations and the particular interests of black people.

In the chapters which follow, I will attempt to offer a more satisfying and, hopefully, iconoclastic alternative; satisfying because it will place the explanatory emphasis on definite social processes which perpetuate the invidious position of blacks both in and out of sport; and iconoclastic because it will at least go some way towards smashing the outdated image of the black man as possessing natural physical abilities that are determined, in the last instance, by his race.

For every black sportsman that becomes a Maurice Hope, a Daley Thompson or a Laurie Cunningham, there are thousands upon thousands who either slide into ignominy and failure or, in the sporting idiom, 'go nowhere'. Considering the disproportionate number of black kids who feed their ambitions into sport and zealously cultivate goals around sport achievements, the high number reaching standards of excellence is not so surprising. Underlying the visibly successful black sportsmen are countless other black youths enthusiastically chasing sporting objectives and, perhaps later, organizing their life's ambitions around their sporting discipline.

The reasons why so many seek futures in sports, and in rather specific areas of sport, do not lie in the rather obscure realms of anatomy, physiology or psychology. I argue that race may be a factor in the puzzle but only in so far as blacks feel their belonging to a specific race may affect their futures. The idea of race is in people's heads only, but they act on that idea.

I reject natural ability arguments as vehemently as I reject the notion of 'born sportsmen'. Sportsmen are not born: they are made and they are made through social processes. How? This will be the question to be answered in the coming chapters.

JUSTIN FASHANU
law of the jungle

Born: London, 1961; father: Nigeria (lawyer); mother: Guyana (nurse); foster-father: England (engineer); foster-mother: England (music teacher); occupation: professional footballer.

When he was 3 years old, Fashanu was taken from his mother and placed in a Dr Barnardo's home in London. His mother had been deserted by the father and, with five children to support, could not cope. After a year in the home, Fashanu and his younger brother John were taken by foster parents to East Anglia. He went to school in Attleborough and it was here he developed what he considered a 'natural advantage' in sport.

The reason I became a footballer was simple: I could run faster than anybody else, that's about it. I didn't have any skill whatsoever, but I could run with the ball and hold it. I think blacks were designed to use our speed and agility. I'd never do anything that didn't come easily to me. I wouldn't do anything that took a long, long time before it showed a reward.

Blacks start off with an added advantage of being able to move. So you've got a good start over whites. Then it's up to you. If you've got 10 yards and you don't want to run, that's the end; whites will soon overtake you. I thought I'd got the initial start and I wanted to keep ahead all the time.

Unlike many black kids who consider themselves singled out as possible sportsmen because of stereotyping, he found only his PE teacher took an interest in his sport.

I was the one black kid in all the school and school teachers around here have got their set ways. Everybody was there to be academically acknowledged at the highest level they could and sport was just something that came as well. So everybody bar the PE teacher hated me playing football and everything they could do

Justin Fashanu. Photograph courtesy of *Match Weekly*

to stop me playing football they did. If they needed a punishment to hurt me, they'd stop me playing. They put as many blocks in my path as they could. But the PE teacher was strong-willed and I associated myself with him more than anybody else.

Even my mum and dad (foster-parents) used to hate me playing. Their natural children are very well qualified academically – they only played tennis – but my brother and I were into sport. And I think that's good for me 'cause I'm so independent now. At the time I used to think: 'I wish my mum and dad were like other people and come and watch me play and be involved with the football.' Because nobody could tell me about sport, nobody could guide me, which is what I needed. Even at the age of about 13 I'd be guided only by people who I thought knew something about the game, and who were not trying to stitch me up – I was always thinking people were trying to stitch me up for some reason.

In his words, he 'sold' himself to the Norwich City Football Club, persistently going to the training ground when aged 14 and 15, until the club offered him an apprentice's contract. He was convinced that a career lay in sport and reckoned the media influenced his perception of himself.

Before I left school, the local papers were full of me. They were always saying things like 'This boy will go all the way to the top' and that, and I suppose you could say I took notice of the media. But I was into boxing pretty heavily as well. I'd met Gordon Holmes, who knew the London managers and he was guiding me. Gordon was like another father to me. He was sport-minded. I took notice of him 'cause he knew everything about football as well as boxing. I was split between boxing and football when I was 16 and, at one stage, I wanted to turn professional boxer and thought that, as I was on Norwich's books and I couldn't get a pro boxer's licence till I was 17, anyway, I'd play football for twelve months and then steam into boxing [he was a double ABA junior finalist].

Then, lo and behold, at 17 I'm in the first team. So I couldn't jack it in when things were going well. I was still boxing by going down the London gym of Danny Peacock – Gordon was a friend of his. I still love boxing but things have happened so quickly in football.

The thing with me and with 'Crooksy' [Garth Crooks, his friend] as well is that, if you're black in a small community where there aren't too many blacks and you've got a little bit of style, then you cannot go wrong. If you can be just a little bit clued-up and not be Rastafarian with dreadlocks, you cannot fail. The jet setters like novelty and things like that! As long as you hold yourself well and don't embarrass people by letting them think, 'Oh he's so thick' or 'his ways are so silly', you're all right. You have to have a little bit of presence about you; and that's what made me here. I'm not the kind of fellow that's going to creep to anybody, but I didn't cause aggravation unless I had to. I didn't give anybody a chance to hate me.

Not that he was so popular with crowds outside Norwich or other players. 'I got slaughtered,' he reckons. 'I'd rear up on players if they said anything and footballers aren't the bravest people in the world, so they used to think twice before they said anything to me and that helped me.' He did not regard such experiences as without worth:

They're good for you. If you've been through it, it's in the bank. If you've had it easy all the time, as soon as trouble comes, you don't know how to handle it. If I was to break my leg tomorrow I'd be as sick as a parrot, but it wouldn't be the end of the world. I'd live off my wits even though I've geared myself to be a footballer. Football isn't the be all and end all to me. I know I can always do something to earn a living. You have to have confidence in your own ability and being black is a good thing as far as I'm concerned 'cause I've had to sample bits and pieces of how life can be nasty and it's done me good. It's made me independent; I don't like to be beholden to anybody, I like to be my own boss.

Maybe his life in Attleborough afforded him insulation from the rigours of inner city life, but he never understood his colour to be an obstacle.

In fact, it never occurred to me that it made a difference until I was in a trial and a scout said 'We're quite interested in the coloured lad' and that was the first time I realized they thought of me as anything other than my name.

In his early days with Norwich he took 'stick' from fellow players and the opposition, but reflected on this favourably in a way which says much of himself and of other successful black sportsmen.

At the end of the day, it doesn't matter what colour you are, black, blue, pink, white or green. If you've got a strong enough personality and you want to do it badly enough, you'll get there. It's going to be hard and you're going to have set-backs, but you'll get there. I don't want to sound as if I haven't got sympathy with people 'cause I know it's bloody hard, but I know a lot of blacks who use it [blackness] as an excuse and we've got to be careful that we don't use it like that. You can use it for a lot of things, but when you get down to analyse it, I think it may be the law of the jungle where the strongest survive; and I don't know necessarily whether that's a bad thing.

I've had it all said to me: I've got no bottle and stamina; and I don't think it's a bad thing that people think black players have got no bottle. It may strengthen them. Anyway, it might have been true before. But now we've got a new breed of black sportsmen. The heartache and suffering over the centuries has made them tough and strong and it's been a slow evolution. I think if you've got it too easy in life you don't know how to react. There's something to be said for experiencing bad things and coming back and doing the business.

Chapter Four

THE PROSPECT OF BLACKNESS for kids

When you get to about 13 or 14, you begin to realize that your colour, even if you hadn't thought about it much, means that other people are going to be different to you. And you get the idea that a few qualifications aren't going to make that much of a difference to your life. I mean, they can't change your skin can they?

Curt Nisbett, boxer

I think black kids look towards sport as a means of achievement or a means of getting out of society. There's going to be a great emergence of blacks in sport soon. I mean there's only a few stars, but they only need one or two heroes and the rest will come through. The thing that really motivated me was seeing the 1968 Olympics; I saw Thommie Smith and thought, 'God, that's it!'

Ainsley Bennett, sprinter

That's when I felt different

Status and privilege accrue to successful sportsmen in contemporary society. To be an international athlete, a top flight boxer or a first division footballer is to have access to a range of resources not available to the majority of the population. Modern sportsmen are lionized and fêted, their achievements are models for evaluation, their ambitions are the ambitions of others. They are depicted by the media as glamorous, exciting and interesting. Once near the top of their particular sport, money becomes available: percentages of transfer fees, fight purses, appearance monies make sport a financially healthy occupation – provided success is attained.

The money coupled with the status granted makes sport a lucrative and desirable way of earning a living. But, it is not the only way and it is a most precarious way. A sports career, in the Western world certainly, is reckoned to span about twelve years, terminating sometime after the thirtieth birthday. It can be finished sooner by incapacitating injury incurred during play, training or away from sport entirely. More likely in statistical terms is that it will close down even earlier due to judicious coaches' or managers' recommendations on the inadequacy of the majority of aspirants 'to make the grade'.

Sport is just one avenue, and a narrow one at that, through which a young person can achieve access to resources, prestige, wealth, feelings of self-adequacy. The professions, the civil service, the academic world and commerce are amongst the other routes, but travel along these requires two qualifications: an educational achievement motivation and a career orientation. Black kids seem to fail on both counts. They consistently underachieve at school and demonstrate little desire to make headway along a career avenue to success.

Their collective attitude stands in stark contrast to that of the other major second generation immigrant group in modern Britain. Asian youths persevered assiduously in academic work. By the end of the 1970s, they compared most favourably with white youths in terms of examination results (see Bagley, 1979, for evidence). Indeed, I would project that Asian youths in the early 1980s are poised to outstrip both whites and blacks educationally.

Interestingly, education is a highly valued commodity in Asian culture: it is seen as the starting line to a career. Asian families, for the most part, are organized in such a way as to keep a firm control over their children, integrating them into a tightly knit web of relationships within the community where religious traditions remain strong and create in the members a respect for norms, seniority and morality. The internal control lends the Asian community a stability somewhat lacking amongst Caribbeans and their offspring.

The values placed upon formal education are transmitted to the second generation Asians and consequently many achieve educational success. Dedication and steadfastness go into school and college work. There are few top Asian sportsmen in the UK and that is no small coincidence. Whites and Asians perceive a range of activities available to them. The avenues to prestige and financial security are multiplex and, to a large extent, unrestricted. Sport is but one and, seductive as it may be, it is precarious and, inevitably, short-term.

There are many instances of white youths being pressured by their parents to give up their sport in preference for more reasonable and secure occupations, lest they invest their time and energies in a pointless pursuit of intangible dreams. Often, apprentice footballers refuse to sign professional forms seeing them, as one Midland youth put it, as 'bad risks'; and young boxers would, in the pugilistic vernacular, 'swallow' before they had given their careers time to bloom – usually on the say-so of parents. One 18-year-old insurance clerk from Birchfield explained how he reached a sort of cross-road after his training began to detract from his studies: 'I came to the conclusion that my career came first and, at 18, I had to look at my prospects. Now, I treat athletics more as a hobby than I used to.' Another strategy employed mostly by white youth is to delay a possible career in sport whilst completing higher education. Alan Gowling, for example, gained a Master's degree before pursuing his professional sports career with a variety of football league clubs. Only those whose prodigious skill gives them leverage for negotiating secure contracts are prepared to forsake higher education for sport.

Whites and Asians entertain a variety of ways in which they can advance, usually locating their careers in some long-term perspective and thus making security an important consideration. Blacks, on the other hand, harbour a much more narrowly defined set of possibilities on how they might advance. Whereas sport occupies a somewhat peripheral place in the spectrum of career possibilities for most members of society, it occupies a central berth for a great many blacks.

The enthusiasm for sport as a career, as a central interest in life, is very prevalent amongst black kids, even those facing the possibility of another three years minimum at school. As Derek Brown of Birchfield, who at 13 years old and speculating on a career in athletics, spending two evenings and a Sunday morning training, said: 'I don't let it bother my school work 'cause I can get it all done in my other time, but this [athletics] is what I'd really like to do; I keep setting myself goals every year to get to the top.' (He was also anticipating to gain at least six 'O' levels before leaving school.)

The vast majority of the black sportsmen have aspirations of detaching themselves from the routines of school, employment – or unemployment – and wringing out a career in sports, even athletics, ostensibly an amateur sport but bountiful enough in 'gifts' and sponsorships to make it a lucrative career.

Sport is seen by many black kids as much, much more than a hobby; in the words of decathlete Fidelius Obukw, it is 'a way of finding yourself'. It is simply the salient feature of their lives and so, quite predictably, occupies a lot of their time, absorbs a lot of their interest and provides a lot of their ambitions. Why? Well, the answer is wrapped in a skein of social processes and, in the course of this book, I plan to unravel as many of them as possible. Having rejected physical, psychological and historically endorsed properties as 'naturally' predisposing factors, I now have to offer alternatives.

Bunny Johnson, who was born in Jamaica, but came to England in 1963 when he was 16 provides a good starting point:

> If there was a black kid and a white kid with equal qualifications who both went for the same job, I would have to put my money on the white kid getting the job, because we're in a white-dominated society. And, if the positions were reversed and we lived in a black-dominated society . . . I think the white kid would still get through!

The point is that black people are not only at a disadvantage in the job market on account of their colour, they also perceive sharply that this is so and, despite Johnson's tongue-in-cheek addendum, the consciousness of belonging to a group which feels itself to be at a disadvantage is clear enough.

Black kids, at a stage during their latter secondary-school years, begin to feel different because of their blackness. It may be a gradual, one might say glacial, movement of perception, piecing together items of experience which collectively form an awareness that colour places a black person at a disadvantage. Or the awareness may arrive in a sudden moment of revelation, one vivid encounter bringing with it the perception of blackness. An example of the first came from international sprinter Mickey Morris, born in London to Jamaican parents:

> At school, to start off you integrate with everybody, it doesn't matter about colour right up to the third year [when aged about 13 or 15]. So that in the third year, friends, who you know as 'friends' might call you a 'black bastard' and it doesn't mean

anything. And then, when you find they say it in the fourth year, they mean it and you begin to look at yourself and realize what colour you are.

Instances of the second more sudden realization are rarer. Garry Thompson, the Coventry City footballer, told how he was made to take stock of his colour slightly earlier, just after beginning secondary school in Birmingham: 'I went up to some guys and asked to play football and they just shut me out. One of the older guys called me a nigger, and he influenced the others so that they all started calling me it. That's when I felt different.'

For London-born pro footballer Vince Hilaire, the realization was more gradual: 'I didn't really think about the black and white thing until I was about 14 or 15. I think it's when black kids and whites start thinking about what they're going to do when they leave school. But it doesn't happen all of a sudden; you have to think about it.'

I am not making the exorbitant claim that every black youth reaching adolescence in the 1970s and early 1980s underwent such traumas. Nor, indeed am I claiming that all black sportsmen, at some stage in their development, come face to face with their blackness and are made to reflect on the probable disadvantages it carries with it. By way of total contrast, I can point to Birchfield sprinter Phil Brown, who never really felt himself to be any different from other school children and admitted to having 'no identity with other blacks'. Even more extreme was Olympic decathlete Daley Thompson, who straightforwardly stated that he wanted nothing to do with blacks: 'I've never let the fact that my father was Nigerian [his mother was Scottish] interfere with me. I don't feel black and I don't think my friends regard me as such. Most of my friends are white, anyway.'

These two are in a very small minority of black sportsmen who had not at some stage faced the distressing realization that they were black and so they were different and that difference could significantly limit their chances of access to the kind of resources available to others, prestige, affluence, esteem in the eyes of others. It seems that this perception is a common one amongst black kids, whether they are headed for a sports career or not. My own work and that of Barry Troyna (1978) has strongly indicated that, at around school-leaving age or just before, black youths encounter an incident or many which incline them to reconsider their own identities. Troyna has called the perception of 'a shared destiny' the critical feature of black kids' gang formation during late school years. They come to the recognition that being black places themselves and other black kids in a similarly disadvantaged position: 'It would seem, on the basis of the pupils' own perception of this tendency, that this withdrawal into racially exclusive peer groups results from the pupils' realization of a common identity and shared destiny' (1978, p.64).

All their futures will be affected and so they band together in groups. Such banding was called by boxer Brian Johnson 'automatic' and it starts 'when you're at school, because it happens there. I used to have some white friends at school but they fell away. You identify with other black kids 'cause you know and feel what they do by just looking around you. We have to identify with each other.'

Black sportsmen are not exceptional in so far as they too undergo the turbulence of having to refashion their ideas about career and, indeed, life prospects at around this age. Jackie Jackson, a girl shot putter whose parents were Jamaican, put it like this: 'No matter what they say, all black kids go through a phase when they want to be white . . . and when they come to terms with the fact that they aren't, they have to think of the possibilities.' Those possibilities are seen as restricted and, although many would not agree with Jackson's controversial view that all blacks go through stages of white envy, all would appreciate the point that blacks resign themselves to more limited prospects.

Whether or not blacks' career prospects are blighted by covert racialist policies in the occupational sphere is not the question under consideration. Though, parenthetically, I might note that there is plausible evidence enough to convince the most liberal of minds that such policies do operate (see for instance, Lee and Wrench, 1981). What matters is that black kids believe them to operate systematically and continuously.

Such beliefs are born out of first-hand experience and second-hand stories. An example of the former came from Continental FC's captain Barry Dennis, who, having left school, went to college where he gained a Full Technological Certificate enabling him to take a position in the computer industry. When a senior member of his department left, he expected, not unreasonably he felt, to get promotion, but:

> They brought in a white guy to replace him. He had the same
> qualifications as me but he was from a different department and
> had less experience. I resented this and, frankly, was ready to
> leave over it. The only thing I had going against me was: I was
> black.

He made his gripe known to one of his superiors and the decision
was changed, but only after he had, in his own words, 'kicked up a
fuss'.

The Dennis case was by no means unusual: many of those employed had encountered some form of what they perceived as racialism in the transition from school to work. Perceptions such as these
would have affected general conduct and attitude. The 'resentment'
at being denied possible access to positions of respect and maybe
responsibility manifests itself in a number of ways, not least in the
social posture of black youth in the UK. They create the impression
of resenting society, for they feel that society is structured in a way
that is detrimental to their progress (see Cashmore, 1981b).

There are, however, other more important processes working:
beliefs get transmitted downwards from one generation to the next.
The kids who have experienced the problems of occupational discrimination and believe their opportunities are limited make their
beliefs public to those with whom they most identify – in this case,
other blacks. There is a kind of feedback into the black community:
stories about going for a job, getting turned down and explaining the
failure as caused by being black get fed back to other blacks and so
nourish conceptions about the structure of society. Those conceptions hold that it is not so much the white individuals who are the
oppressors, for they are only part of an overall structure which has
been designed to exclude blacks from positions of seniority. The
currency of the concept of Babylon, depicting the system of white
domination as endemically evil, amongst black kids in the 1980s
attests to this (see Cashmore and Troyna, 1982).

In other words, black kids teach each other about the world and
about how it works contrary to their interests. Repton welterweight,
Franklin Edwards, a telephone salesman, who left his north London
school with three CSEs (Grade 1), illustrated this transmission of
ideas:

This guy I used to know, Babs Eadon, he told me of how he went to get a holiday job when he was doing a Masters degree. Anyway, he gave them a few examples of the jobs he was looking for and they told him he was unqualified. That was even before they'd asked him what qualifications he'd got. They just assumed that, being black, he hadn't got any – and he'd got a degree.

Garry Thompson had a friend named Malcolm Percival about whom he recalled:

He went for a job just after leaving school and the guy at the interview asked him if he'd ever encountered prejudice and he said, 'Well, sometimes.' The guy went mad at him saying, 'How dare you say there's such a thing as prejudice!' And, really, it only showed 'Percy' that there was. That's the way we always thought it was: against us.

The abundance of such stories amongst black sportsmen indicates clearly that, at the point of exit from school, they had fairly clear and well-rounded conceptions about what lay ahead of them in the world of employment. Their peers shared such conceptions and served mutually to reinforce each other. Defeatism is not a useful property with which to enter the world of employment: failure is too conveniently assimilated into a horizon of limited expectations. If you go to an interview anticipating you are not going to get the job, chances are you do not get it. Grim prospects do hang over the heads of black school leavers and the research of Gloria Lee and John Wrench does much to nail down the specific ways in which employment opportunities are much narrower for the black kid seeking apprenticeships in industry (1981). So black youths' apprehension about gaining jobs with career possibilities are not without foundation.

A kind of downward spiral results, the kids growing progressively more pessimistic about their chances, their hopes plummeting and their general postures making it more difficult for them to get jobs. 'Black society, as does the dominant white society, teaches its members to strive for that which is defined as the most desirable among potentially *achievable* goals', observes Harry Edwards about the American scene (1973, p.201). And, although progress in conventional careers may not be regarded as achievable, clearly certain things are, as I will now show.

Models

Black kids are not totally without ambition: they have several guides to follow. Having made the point that blacks identify with each other 'automatically', it is no surprise to learn that, when it comes to organizing aspirations for the future, blacks set their sights on blacks who have made it to, or near to, the top of their chosen occupation. Black politicians, lawyers, surgeons, business executives are in pathetically short supply; very, very few have managed to overcome the problem of restricted opportunities, and break what Douglas Glasgow, in his discussion of the chronic unemployment of American blacks, calls 'the cycle of entrapment' – few raise themselves above 'cellar-level jobs' (1980, p.71).

Black incumbents of high prestige positions fall into two main divisions: Stevie Wonder and the late Bob Marley are in the van of the one; Muhammad Ali and Pelé are at the fore of the other. Music and sport are areas in which blacks have made the most celebrated and acclaimed contribution. Even if the odds are stacked dauntingly against blacks in most spheres of society, the numbers of black musicians and sportsmen provide living proof that success can be gained. Here are two domains in which blacks have risen to prominence, seemingly without having to overcome the conventional restrictions strewn around other occupations. The appearance, albeit a misleading one, of an area uncluttered by the constraints characterizing other areas is an attractive one . . . the blacks who follow in the wake of Wonder and Marley make them models for their behaviour. Godfrey Amoo said of Ali: 'I try to copy his style, his footwork and the man generally – everything about him.' Similarly, for Harvey Dennis, there was, 'Pelé . . . just him and no one else.'

In this light, it can be seen that Ali and Pelé were potent symbols. These were the figures who embodied the hopes of black youth in the 1960s and 1970s, not only in England, but in the USA too where

> the athlete has been an important person and model of success for Black youth for a long time. A man like Muhammad Ali not only symbolizes what can be done with talent and ability but shows that the 'man' and his system can be beat (Glasgow, 1980, p.78).

Black kids, suspicious and pessimistic about their chances of gaining success in regular employment in the 'system', look to alternative models upon which to base their own roles in society.

The visible glamour and affluence of the likes of Maurice Hope, Justin Fashanu and Daley Thompson are seductive and in many cases, irresistible. Fashanu himself had thoughts on this: 'If you can relate yourself to somebody, it's a big spur to you, 'cause, if someone else has done it, you can always follow him. It's harder when you do it the first thing. And, like James Brown (the American singer) said on TV the other day, "black kids need black people to associate themselves with."

The energy and enthusiasm black youth have for certain sports and the disproportionately high number wanting to take up sport as a career provides at least the initial indication that they see in successful black sportsmen models for themselves. Hence the preponderance of doleful black amateur boxers in the immediate aftermath of Ken Norton's one-round eclipse by the Great White Hope of the early 1980s, Gerry Cooney. 'You ought to see how the black guys' heads have dropped after Norton got beat,' said boxer Kirk Gibbons of Birmingham.

Not surprisingly, Ali is chosen by most boxers as the most prototypical figure, though Bunny Johnson cites Jack Johnson and many of the newer recruits to boxing look to Sugar Ray Leonard, the quick-fisted American multiple world champion who blazed his way from an Olympic gold medal at Montreal in 1976 to an estimated 30 million dollars by the end of 1981. Nick Pitt's description helps one understand why his appeal was not confined to blacks: 'clean, well spoken [he really was a choirboy], a political eunuch, black but not *really black*, cuddly' (*Sunday Times*, 28 June 1981, p.30). 'You're looking at the next Sugar Ray,' I was assured by one youth before he had even sparred in training! Pelé is the focus of most footballers' attentions. The apparently unbridgeable gulf between him and his contemporaries in terms of sheer footballing skill made him an exceptional and enormously wealthy black man, after a childhood spent amidst the poverty and squalor of Bauru (see Pelé and Fish, 1977).

In athletics, there is a more even spread of influential figures, with political martyr Thommie Smith, who was banned from international competition after his Black Power stand at the Mexico Olympics, influencing the hopes of a great many black kids. His fellow Black Power advocate John Carlos is also frequently cited as a major influence.

Ali, of course, more than any modern figure, crystallized the concerns of black people. He capitalized on his Olympic success by lauding himself, pronouncing himself 'The Greatest', and arrogantly winning the world title under the most outrageous circumstances. Immediately after, as I have previously noted, he became a member of the black segregationist sect, The Nation of Islam, and publically denounced the white world and its domination over blacks. 'Aint no VietCong ever called me a nigger,' was his simple, but penetrating, reason for not accepting the draft for which he was stripped of his world title and forced into inactivity for three years (only to return from adversity and carry on boxing, often successfully, for world titles until aged 38).

He was a black man raised in poverty, but who used his initiative, wit and boxing skill to rise to prominence, command multi-million dollar pay days and criticize the 'man and the system' which ensured him such monies! It is little wonder that this figure cast what almost amounted to a spell over aspiring black sportsmen. No one escaped his all-pervasive influence. It was an influence summarized by Herol Graham, himself a redoubtable boxer who wallowed in his reputation as a 'Flash Harry', as follows: 'There weren't many blacks in my area [in Nottingham] and I'd get called black. . . . There was only him [Ali] for me then 'cause he was black and there was racialism.'

Ali's cutting edge was his intellect: not only was he a renowned sportsman of brilliance, but he also commanded the world's attentions through his insight, sarcasm and satire. In this respect, he deviated from the conventional ideas about blacks possessing physical but no mental prowess. Mickey Morris summed it up: 'He's a great sportsman *and* he's got a brain.'

Generally, black kids' aspirations are coloured by the achievements of other blacks with whom they share an affinity. History shows that sport has been one of the two major areas in which blacks have been allowed or even encouraged to do well. In sport, as in entertainment, black performers have ploughed a tradition and the furrows of that tradition deepen with every successive round of kids entering the fields of athletics, boxing and soccer in direct emulation of their models. The lack of black swimmers, golfers or squash players indicates the extremely limited extent to which black kids are inspired in those areas. It is not that they are not capable of competing; it is simply that there have been no great black performers in these areas in history (due to lack of opportunities and facilities) and no tradition exists.

But questions remain. Virtually all kids, black or white, entertain hopes, often little more than visions, of emulating their role models or 'schoolboy heroes'. Most are brought back into line by their parents and made to organize their lives around achievable objectives, to persevere at the more mundane, sometimes uninteresting but attainable positions in society. Then why are so many black kids allowed to let their wilder notions run rampant and dictate how they structure their ambitions and careers?

Why is it that black kids are so amenable to the influences of their peers? It is through other black kids that some aspirations are fostered and others snuffed out by stories of racialism. Why is it that black kids develop their sporting progress to the point that, by the time they leave school, their educational motivation is rather low, while their sporting motivation is soaring? And, finally, why is it that black kids find support for the idea that they have only limited employment opportunities ahead of them, not only from their peers but also from the school? All these questions must be answered if a satisfactory appreciation of blacks' relationship with sport, and indeed society, is to be attained.

In this chapter, I have argued against the natural ability of black sportsmen theory and offered the bones of an alternative, suggesting that the intensity of blacks' involvement with sport stems from their perception of restricted opportunities in other major occupational areas. Various factors, including actual experience and transmitted beliefs, play their parts in solidifying the conception of society as biased against black achievement in all spheres except music and sport and so, looking to those characters who have achieved the desirable commodities of prestige and affluence, black kids zealously follow their example.

But to understand fully why and how they are allowed to do this, the above questions must be tackled and to do this I need to document the black kids' experiences at two levels: the family and the school. These experiences have extreme consequences and an interpretation of them will occupy the next three chapters.

Bunny Johnson. Photograph courtesy of the *Birmingham Evening Mail*

BUNNY JOHNSON
a point to prove

Born: Jamaica, 1947; father: Jamaica (car worker); mother: Jamaica (part-time machinist); occupation: professional boxer – formerly welder, insurance salesman and nightclub owner.

Just before the Christmas of 1963, two unrelated boxing enthusiasts, both named Johnson, wandered into a Birmingham gymnasium and asked to work out. The one Johnson's enthusiasm faded and he soon drifted away from the sport; the other had his first competitive contest in the following January and so began one of the longest and least celebrated ring careers in British boxing.

Sixteen years and one month later, Bunny Johnson became the fourth black boxer to win a Lonsdale Belt, the most coveted award in British boxing (Randolph Turpin was the first in 1956, Bunny Sterling the second in 1973, Maurice Hope the third in 1976). Johnson presents an intriguing case study. He arrived in England in 1963 when aged 16 and almost immediately immersed himself in sport; as such he was one of the very first sportsmen to emerge from the second generation West Indian immigrants. In 1975, he realized an ambition he had nursed since his arrival: to become the first black heavyweight champion of Great Britain.

My interest in boxing began in Jamaica. I wasn't really good at anything sporting-wise, not to compete rigorously, anyway. I wasn't an outstanding athlete at school; I had more of an interest in reading. That's how I got interested in the sport: I read about the first black champion, Jack Johnson and it created my interest for the first time. From then on, I thought, I'm going to do it and I'm going to do it well.

But in Jamaica at the time, there were no facilities for kids, just for professional fighters, so I just used to look at them through the fence, sparring and punching the bag. I didn't really know how to take up boxing. When I came over here I got to know about Kyrle Hall [a Birmingham amateur club] and went along there with my pumps and shorts and that was my introduction to boxing really.

He had completed his secondary education in Jamaica but his mother implored him to continue in England.

> She always encouraged me academically; she wanted me to become a lawyer. I'd read about the Old Bailey and that sort of thing. So you could say I was prepared for the 'English way of Life' from what I'd read. My mother would always try to influence me. I was still under the influence of my parents compared to my English counterpart and it was a strict influence. After work, I used to come home and watch television and, at weekends, I'd maybe ask to go to the pictures. But I hadn't really made any friends so I was still in a very narrow circle. That was until I met this fellow Johnson and we went to Kyrle Hall. Then I widened my circle to boxing friends.
>   I still kept the idea of being a lawyer through studying at night school, but, after a short while I decided I was really going to follow up a boxing career. Quite early, I made up my mind that all I wanted to be was a top flight boxer, to follow Jack Johnson in my own way and become the first black British heavyweight champion.

The early 1960s were turbulent times for blacks as the reverberations from the spate of immigrant intimidations following the Notting Hill and Nottingham episodes had barely subsided. But Johnson did not sense hostility in his teens.

> Maybe it was because boxing is an enclosed network, you work in teams as amateurs. Or maybe it was just the environment: there was a majority of blacks at the club so the whites were in a minority. So even if they felt hostility, they were going to keep it to themselves. Wouldn't you? I never experienced any direct insults.

A proficient rather than brilliant amateur, Johnson went professional in 1968 and progressed well, winning thirty-two of thirty-eight contests. Throughout 1971 and 1972 he remained in Britain's top three heavyweights, but was overlooked when the BBBC ordered a series of eliminators to decide the next British title challenger.

> The nationality rule was a beautiful get-out for them, but I only had a few months to go before I'd been here for ten years and would have been entitled to fight for the title. For nationality you can read 'racialism'. I couldn't interpret it as anything but racialism. But, at

that stage, the only thing that prevented me from saying, 'oh well, I'll go and find a regular job instead,' was that I was aware that this thing existed – racialism – and that whatever happened, getting away from it, getting out of the firing line, wouldn't help me. I could prove my point much better if I kept on. I'm determined, so I kept on. I had a point to prove.

And prove it, he did. John Conteh's withdrawal from the eliminating series left Johnson as the only credible replacement. As Johnson put it: 'You could say that was a bit of "luck", in inverted commas!' The opportunity was not lost and Johnson eventually captured the title he sought. Never a 'natural' heavyweight, he suffered weight disadvantages against bigger men and lost the title to Richard Dunn. He then switched his efforts to the light-heavyweight division, the British championship of which he won spectacularly (in one round) in 1977. Two defences in 1979 and 1980 (an all-black contest against Hackney-based Guyanan Dennis Andries) brought him a Lonsdale Belt. A year later he was in more conflict with the BBBC which delayed granting him permission to fight in Australia after he had left the country. After four months, he vindicated himself, beating Mike Quarry in seven rounds – again, 'proving the point'.

I know I've never had some of the breaks I deserve but I don't allow myself to dwell on this. That's the way it goes; inequalities exist, but I have to look at it healthily. That is making being black secondary. My initial motive in going to do something is having the desire to do it, thinking I can do it and moving towards it. I'm black and I've got to be better than the next applicant, but I don't let it hold me back.

The way I approach anything is to do it to the best of my ability, whatever. But, then when you've done it to the best of your ability and you can't really see the rewards, then you have to analyse why. Then you go back and you think: 'Well, although I've done my best, maybe I have to find that little bit extra as a black person.' And either you say to yourself 'I can't find it' or you can go on and get to the middle of things and keep trying to find it. A lot of black kids don't do that. Too many of them are saying: 'There's racialism, so what's the good of trying?' But, if they give up, they can't really contribute to the better quality of society.

Being black has always been in my subconscious, but I've tried never to let this come to the fore. I don't feel bitter about being excluded. Bitterness isn't part of my philosophy; I've always said if you let bitterness overwhelm you, you let it distract you from your path. I've got no time for it; it cramps your style. I've never lost my belief in myself. You see, one thing that influenced me was reading about the great American champs and I saw how all the good champs were side-tracked, avoided, yet always seemed to make it late. Jack Johnson, Archie Moore, I could make a list of them. They all seemed to make it, there were lots who didn't – with the exception of Floyd Patterson and Joe Louis. So I always thought: 'If you're good enough, you have to keep on, 'cause if you stop, you haven't got a chance, obviously.'

I've said all along if I'd been a white man with my ability, I feel I'd be a wealthy man. But the boxing power structure is white and it's going to be a slow change.

Chapter Five

ALL OR NOTHING from families

The only sport my old man was interested in was beating up the rest of the family.

Howard Brown, boxer and full-contact karate fighter

If you don't make the goal at school that they've set you, you're considered by your parents as a failure and that's when your head starts to go down.

Danny Thomas, footballer

They've never seen me play

It is tempting to see the source of black kids' sporting involvement and success as the family. A rough-hewn psychological explanation would hold that, because many second generation Caribbeans and Africans in the UK are raised in single-parent families, in almost every case the parent being the mother, the children pass into an emotional void at the ages of 13 or 14 and seek out father figures in the shape of sports coaches with whom they form compensatory attachments.

Positive, meaningful, often intense relationships with coaches yield stable, lasting bonds with sport and so guarantee commitment and perseverance. The surrogate father guides his protégé through his turbulent teens into his twenties when he develops into a mature and secure sportsman with an abundance of technique and a conviction challenging enough to take him to success.

The explanation is appealing and has much merit. It lends itself quite suitably to the UK sporting scene which is populated by many black sportsmen growing up in broken homes, settling on the side of the mother and eventually seeing the father as an anathema, as did Repton heavyweight Ray Tabi:

> As far as I'm concerned, my old man died when I was 12 [his age when his father left home]. The man's a complete cunt. I hate the bastard. We crossed each other on the street some time ago and he went to talk; I just pushed him aside and told him to fuck off. I wouldn't talk to the cunt.

The hatred is vivid but instructive, for Tabi is representative of about half of those sportsmen from single-parent families. The next step of adopting a coach as a father figure is more dubious, however, though a great many sportsmen would describe their trainers or managers as Maurice Hope describes Terry Lawless: 'He's been like a father to me; no, more than a father, actually.'

Without wishing to drown the explanation in cold water, I feel that a few sprinkles are needed to chill it down. For example, the case of Hope, who did not come from a broken home, is atypical: most black sportsmen have much more instrumental relationships with their mentors, seeking to learn techniques, draw inspiration and get motivated for important events. These are the usual limits of the sponsor-protégé relationship in sport.

It is fair to assume also that there is a high proportion of black sportsmen who come from single-parent families, but, in absolute terms, there are huge numbers of black kids who are reared in broken homes who do not enter sport in any serious way. What remains missing, therefore, are the processes compelling some to take up sport and others not to. Presumably, there are psychological needs at work influencing a young person to look for suitable father figures of which there are many in sport. Fine, but we are still unclear about the exact nature of these processes. Perhaps many of those from broken homes search for surrogate fathers, but only those with the physical assets necessary for sporting success, such as strength and speed, are able to foster attachments in the sporting fraternity. The others lack the faculties to stay in sport and so lose the option to form a stable relationship with the coach. It all remains rather vague and some clarity should come from an examination of the actual backgrounds and domestic circumstances of black youth in sport.

An extreme example of parental involvement in children's sports is the phenomenon which Dorcas Susan Butt calls the 'sports parent', the parent 'who pushes the child onward in the sport . . . sometimes encourages the youngster and sometimes criticizes, and will often go to any degree to further the child's interests . . . the parent's main interest is to maximize the performance and benefits of his or her own child' (1976, p.120).

There are many 'sports parents' in the UK who follow their sons and daughters around athletics meetings, football matches and boxing tournaments; they attend training sessions, often consulting with coaches and trainers; they invest many hours and considerable amounts of money in their children's sports. Yet few are black. For the most part, black parents are not interested in their offspring's development in sport and are sometimes oblivious to the fact that they are involved in sport at all. Commenting on the influence of his parents on his footballing career, Carlos Francis, brought up in the East End before moving north to Birmingham City FC, said: 'They've never even seen me play. They gave me no encouragement at all and didn't even realize I was so into football. Even now, they don't take an active interest.'

Danny Thomas' experience was a repetition: 'My parents were never interested in sport. They never came to watch me play.' This theme is a recurring one, with some sportsmen actually being belittled by their parents for their involvement, like sprinter Mickey Morris:

> My parents used to ignore me when I used to go home and tell them I'd won a race. I'd be all proud and they'd just say, 'Oh yeah, so what?' It used to get me down so much. Sometimes, they even used to laugh at me because I got so serious about athletics. So, in the end, I never used to tell them anything about the athletics. I don't much now.

Even more extreme and, frankly, disturbing was the case of Jamaican-born boxer Winston Davis who came alone to England (his parents preceded him) in 1970, when aged 13. He communicated nothing about his sporting ambitions to his mother with whom he lived in Rugby. 'My mother used to treat me like a stranger,' he reflected. 'I wasn't close to her. I had to take care of myself. I never got near enough to her to tell her about the boxing and eventually left home as soon as I could.'

The outstanding feature of black parents' relationship with their children's sport is that it does not exist. Black families offer virtually no encouragement. So the black youth's progress in sport is partially or totally neglected by parents. In the case of Repton light-middleweight Leon Young, there was no encouraging influence at all as he was brought up in a Dr Barnardo's home in Barkingside. Similarly, Daley Thompson, the celebrated Essex Beagles decath-lete, was brought up in a home where he was denied parental encouragement for his sport.

The black parents are often apathetic and perform no positive function in their children's progression in sport and stir from their inertness only when some measure of tangible success has been achieved. 'They don't mind so much now I've got a few trophies in a case that they can show their friends and boast about it,' Carlos Francis recollected his parents' change of posture after it became evident that he could make a career out of soccer. Such retrospective interests are not uncommon but often elicit only disdain from the youths who see clearly that their parents' belated enthusiasm is a product purely of the tangible rewards sport brings along.

The passive role of the black family in the children's sport jars with the discordance of a cracked bell when compared to the part played by the white family, usually a source of encouragement from which affirmative, strengthening and, when necessary, consoling influences come. Invariably, white sportsmen are introduced to their discipline by their parents, actually taken to clubs and made mem-bers under the direction of their fathers and, less frequently, mothers. After that, the parents' involvement often continues and may escalate. That white parents support their children morally and financially is confirmed by the number of families in crowds at athletic, boxing and football competitions. On one occasion, for example, the AAA Under-21s and Youths' championships, I counted eight blacks in the whole non-participating sectors of the Alexander Sports Stadium, yet black participants comprised over half of the competitors. Regularly, at athletic clubs, white parents can be seen to drop off (or maybe stay with) and collect their children. Very few black sportsmen are afforded this facility by their parents.

There is nothing in the black youth's experience to compare with that of javelin thrower Paul Brice, a white boy, whose father careful-ly supervised and monitored his training programmes and competi-tions at considerable financial expense. 'I've spent over £400 in petrol alone over the past few months, taking him to meetings and training', Mr Brice confirmed. Nor to that of Wally Swift Jun. whose father, a former British welterweight and middleweight boxing champion, would meticulously plan and implement training programmes at Birmingham City ABC and insist on taking charge of his corner in competitions.

Obviously, a positive sports evaluation by parents is likely to give rise to sporting interests in children and the above examples are illustrative. So where there is a virtual absence of such evaluations, such as amongst the first generation Caribbeans, there is also no direct influence from the family to children. Not that Caribbean parents are totally without sporting involvements: there are rare exceptions in the form of Ray Tabi's father whom he disowned but still acknowledged as his 'first lead into boxing'; and the father of heavyweight Howard Henlan had also been a boxer and was instrumental in stimulating his son's interest. Other boxers too acknowledge sometimes unknown fathers as their inspiration, for example, Danny Evans, who was raised in an orphanage but was vaguely aware that his father was once a boxer and tried to emulate him. There are, however, precious few parallels amongst athletes and footballers. It seems, then, that, for the most part, black parents are not interested in sport and have no role to play in generating and sustaining their children's involvement which intensifies despite the lack of parental support.

A glance back at the collective situation of first generation Caribbeans in the UK is enough to understand why black parents do not encourage their children's sporting endeavours. Simply expressed, they have insufficient time, inadequate resources, not enough basic interest and, crucially, other priorities. John Isaacs, a Jamaican-born coach with Haringey, believed most black sportsmen to come from what he called 'limited family backgrounds', where their parents are unable to give them positive guidance. Certainly, most black sportsmen are brought up in what are, by conventional criteria, large families (the median size being six). Obviously, they would receive less parental attention than children from smaller families. Often the family is disrupted by a split during the sportsman's upbringing, as in the case of footballer Lennox Smith, who, when aged 16, had to undergo the turbulence of his father's leaving (his case is representative of about a quarter of the black sportsmen I encountered).

Often, the child is brought up from birth by only one parent, usually the mother, or is taken into care at a very early age, as in the cases of Young, Thompson and Justin Fashanu. Sometimes, mothers find it necessary to work (mainly in service industries) and so have little time to spend with the children. Under such circumstances, the influence of the father would, of course, be absent and so, therefore, would what is for most white youths the main stimulus behind sporting involvement. Even in apparently well-integrated families, fathers exert only the smallest of influences on the child's sports participation. It seems that sporting interest in the older black community is very limited. As Derek Brown, the sprinter, said: 'I wouldn't say my dad isn't interested in sport; he's mainly interested in horse racing.'

Cricket is the other major sporting interest of first generation Caribbeans – understandably enough in view of the popularity of that sport in the West Indies – but, of course, in the UK, it is a rather club oriented, many would say middle-class, sport, access to which is narrowly circumscribed. There is a much more limited interest in boxing, which is probably due to the lack of significant boxers from the islands. Joe Bygraves, the heavyweight who beat Henry Cooper and drew with Dick Richardson in 1957 to defend his Commonwealth title, Bunny Grant, who outpointed Dave Charnley to win the Commonwealth lightweight title in 1965, and Percy Hayles, who held the same title from 1968 till 1974 (all from Jamaica) provide notable exceptions.

Caribbean interest in athletics has been enlivened by the Olympic success in 1976 of Don Quarrie of Jamaica in the 200 metres and Hasely Crawford of Trinidad and Tobago who dominated the 100 metres event in the mid-1970s. Turning to football, the West Indies have done nothing on an international scale, though the game is popular and played at a domestic level. Not much enthusiasm was transferred in the migration to the UK and the enthusiasm which appeared to grow in the 1980s seems mainly due to the successes of young black players in the football league. Birmingham pro-footballer Mike Stowridge, whose Jamaican parents split up when he was 16 (in 1979), said his progress in soccer was 'without influences – all down to me' and his view encapsulates the feelings of a great many young black sportsmen who see no support coming from their parents.

The overall picture is of the first generation harbouring little interest in sport, apart from horse racing! Perhaps they have no time available nor money to squander on what they consider to be pointless pursuits. A skim across the occupations of sportsmen's parents reveals that most are employed in skilled or partly skilled or unskilled jobs as such things as carpenters, electricians, fitters, machine tool operators, assemblers, plumbers and porters. Deviating from the normal pattern is the father of decathlete Fidelius Obukw, a Nigerian, whose father was a barrister.

The general occupational picture of black sportsmen's parents is consistent with the rest of the first generation Caribbeans in the UK and as nearly all of them came from the West Indies (mostly from Jamaica, but others from Dominica, Antigua, St Kitts, St Lucia, Montserrat and Guyana and fewer still from Trinidad, Nevis and Barbados and a small number from West Africa) this is not unusual. Most came over during the period 1955 to 1963 and took what work was commonly available (the vast majority were unqualified academically). This would have probably entailed working involuntary overtime, possibly long, awkward hours and, almost certainly, making a physical input, one consequence of which would have been a limit on the amount of time spent with the children and energy contributed to their amusement. Compounding this was the fact that some of the budding sportsmen, who were not from broken homes, remained in the Caribbean with relatives while their parents settled into the new environment, so their contacts would have been severely and massively interrupted.

What I am speculating – and it can be no more than a retrospective speculation based on reports from sportsmen themselves – is that black parents were too preoccupied with maintaining a material existence to attend to sport: they were too busy making ends meet. As sport is popularly thought of as a leisure time distraction rather than a central life interest or a possible career, it would have held only a marginal interest to the first generation. As sprinter Mike MacFarlane said of his parents' total lack of encouragement: 'It was 'cause they hadn't got the time to think about it.'

At home, sport has no salience; yet, outside the home, sport becomes the source of expectations and aspirations, quite often the only one. Considering that the youths have little in the way of positive reinforcements at home for their sports, they develop an impressive voracity for sports. The role models in the form of key sporting figures to imitate or emulate are, as I have pointed out, important as external stimuli, providing the youths with evidence of the successes blacks can achieve in certain spheres and heightening awarenesses of the possible routes to the top. But, then, all kids have heroes; they don't all become rock stars or footballers, though. Most opt for the more mundane pursuits as their peers abandon their grand schemes and resign themselves to working in an office, a factory, a building site, or taking a cushioning three years in tertiary education.

Sport becomes relegated to the peripheries, whereas, for many black kids, it retains centrality – not because the other areas are seen as worse risks, but because they are seen as less accessible, they believe there are only a limited number of entrances to the upper reaches of the employment world. And, as I stressed earlier, the props for such beliefs come from within the black community: black kids tell each other stories about how difficult it is to get a decent job if you are black and, in a self-fulfilling way, it does becomes difficult.

The decisive role in the black youth's continued enthusiasm for, participation in and commitment to sport is played by others of similar inclination. Contemporaries in sport and coaches exert the main influences and the family's role in the sports process is redundant. If family members are not concerned about or appreciative of sporting accomplishments, then the black youth cares not; at least his contemporaries will be impressed. 'I couldn't care less,' was the reply of Philip, a 16-year-old sprinter from Birchfield, when asked whether he was displeased with his parents' lack of zeal. 'It don't bother me whether they know about it [his involvement in sport] or not.'

Mickey Morris' continued involvement in spite of his parents' derision, Carlos Francis' determination to defy his parents' ridicule of football as a career, former British and European middleweight boxing champion Bunny Sterling's refusal 'to let on to' his parents about his boxing: these are typical examples of black kids cutting themselves away from the strings of their parents and locating the vital, influential figures in their lives elsewhere. The family's loss of control over the youth is crucial to his development in sport, for, if there was a more balanced social management within the West Indian community, it is likely that the vibrance and energy expended in sport could be directed into more orthodox areas.

But a combination of factors, including a high proportion of broken or at least deteriorating homes and single-parent families, an absence of parent–child contact due to migration and possibly compounded by the necessity of devoting excessive time to earning a living and, as I will argue shortly, a distorted appreciation of the parent's function *vis-à-vis* education crystallize to release the black youth from the influence of his parents and jettison him into a world in which his peers, with whom he shares the common experience of being black in a white society, are the dominant forces. Such forces carry him away from the mainstream of Caribbean life into the tributaries of a distinct black youth culture. In many cases, the work ethic is denigrated and impulse repression is replaced by an incitement to self-expression. Sport is one vehicle for such self-expression.

Thus we have the permitting conditions: the lack of parental control which might have brought the youth into more conventional alignments rather than setting him free to explore the more extravagant possibilities of a sporting career. Now it remains to focus on the circumstances which promote the youth's interests and involvements in sport. Here the spotlight turns to the school, the crucible in which interests melt into each other to produce the mixture of concerns which characterize black sportsmen. This will come into view next.

The ten foot wall

Having made the somewhat contentious statement on Caribbean parents' distorted appreciation of their function in relation to their children's formal education, I am left to qualify and substantiate, particularly as it has a weighty bearing on the general argument of the entire book. The study of black sportsmen and society brings into relief the way in which the youths' orientations to school and what they expect to achieve from education affect, not segmentally but totally, their attitudes, postures and the way in which they apportion their time and energies. Perceptual lenses ground at home and school provide the youth with the equipment he uses to see the society around him. Something not unlike tunnel vision ensues in the case of black kids.

The overwhelming evidence on black youths' achievements at school suggests they do badly (see Tomlinson, 1980, for a review). They continue to fall away alarmingly when it comes to formal examinations and so decrease their own chances of gaining stimulating and challenging employment. Yet there is undoubtedly a very positive value placed on formal education by black families. Parents may shun sport, but one could not accuse them of doing the same with education and, as Haringey's Clarence Callynder pointed out: 'Some overdo it; they push their kids too much at school. You obviously need some encouragement, but not too much.'

Sportsmen, no less than other black kids, are the recipients of pressure from both parents to do well at school. Birchfield triple jumper Keith Hunter reasoned that it works in a compensatory manner:

> In the West Indies, they had no proper education and so didn't have the qualifications to get good jobs. My old man works at Dunlop and he wants to make sure we [he and his brothers and sisters] do better than that.

It sounds plausible and most black sportsmen agree in broad terms that Caribbean parents anticipate that the greater availability of education in the UK will enable their children to advance more meaningfully in a career than they did. (Nancy Foner's study of Jamaicans in London, 1979, supports this.) Immigrants the world over have such ambitions for their children. Why then, given the emphasis on the value of education amongst first generation Caribbeans, do their children do so abysmally and, further, show little interest or desire to do well at school? There are three strands of answer to this, each of which has much purchase; I can do no better than to let the espousers of the three strands speak for themselves.

First, Winston McLeod, a back four player for Continental FC: 'The school system isn't equipped to deal with the black kids' needs. It simply caters for white kids, but black kids have special problems. They come from totally different circumstances at home and the school doesn't fit in with these.' In 1964, at the age of 8, he moved from Jamaica to Islington, London, where he resumed schooling, but found the demands at home often contradictory:

> The West Indian families have different values – they still put a lot of faith in education, but it's the way they bring this home to the kids that causes the problems.
>
> There's the discipline for one thing: our family wasn't too bad compared to others I know, but, generally, the West Indian family is very, very strict. But it isn't just the discipline, it's the type of things they make you aim for. Virtually, every West Indian family tells their sons and daughters that they have to be a doctor or a

lawyer. Doctor is the favourite, that's the one all black kids are meant to go for.

But, of course, they're not equipped in a lot of senses. It's not as if they say to their kids: 'try to the best of your ability.' With them, it's: 'You've got to pass your exams and carry on in education.' It's not 'try to do well.' It's as if they're saying: 'There's a ten foot wall – jump over it.' It doesn't matter if you're only two foot tall.

McLeod added insightfully: 'It makes failure impossible to take. The West Indian family values education, but the way it goes about it makes it impossible for the kids. They're treating the kids wrongly.'

This trenchant delivery needs no elaboration from me; it captures perfectly the chasm astride which the black kid stands: on the one side, the reasonable, more limited demands of the school which he is capable of fulfilling, and, on the other, the often unrealistic insistences of the family reinforced by discipline.

Another strand is contributed by triple jumper Keith Hunter, born in Marston Green, West Midlands, of Jamaican parents, and schooled at Perry Common, Birmingham. 'They're strange people, West Indians,' he prefaced his comments:

My old man had this thing about all of us [a family of ten] growing up in this society and not getting into a black thing. He never had any real education in Jamaica and he wanted to make sure we all did. But the way he went about it! He used to smash the fuck out of all of us; he used to belt all of us, my sisters as well. We were all bruised and cut all over, if the slightest thing went wrong.

His mother was equally committed to the value of education, but never imposed her will with such harshness. The vast majority of black parents are uninterested and even disapproving of their children's involvements in sport and Hunter's were no exception: 'It [sport] didn't help, but now I'm doing good at it, he [his father] doesn't mind so much. But he had this thing about us [seven brothers – two in Jamaica – and two sisters] concentrating more and more on school work.'

In his initial phase of competition, Hunter remained undefeated for eighteen months. Academically, he did reasonably well, picking up three 'O' levels at the first attempt, then adding three more plus two 'A' levels before leaving school to take up a trainee manager's position at Fine Fare supermarkets, continuing his studies on a day-release business studies course. In the event, the job proved a disappointment and, in his own words, he spent most of the time 'stacking shelves, pushing trolleys and sweeping floors'.

The news filtered back to his father, who was unremitting in his insistence on academic excellence and career worthiness: 'The old man was wild about this and he used to kick the shit out of me. Eventually, all the pressure built up and I had a nervous breakdown. I had to take treatment from a headshrink.' Astonishingly, he added: 'I never even told my parents. I kept it from them.'

Extreme as it may sound, the Hunter experience brings out many disturbing features of West Indian family life: the relentless pressure on children to achieve often unattainable objectives at school; the stern physical measures adopted to back up the pressure; the inflexible refusal to accept anything short of total success; and the youth's eventual collapse under the pressure.

At the other pole, there is the case of boxer Cecil Williams, the eldest of a family of six, who moved from St Kitts to Handsworth in 1960 when aged 5 and was brought up by his grandparents. He introduced a quite different strand:

> I was a slow learner. I couldn't read till I was 14. The only thing I was good at was art [he got a grade 1 CSE in this subject].
> Generally, with education, I didn't recognize it for what it was.

'Starved of stimulation' was how he summed up his childhood with his grandparents.

> I can't remember them reading any books or even having any books around the house to read. So I didn't even read comics. My grandparents didn't push me towards academic life. Being as they weren't too clever themselves, they ended up with a dull kid.

Succinctly, he added: 'If your parents are poorly educated, what chance have you got?' By the time he arrived at school-leaving age, he had realized the value of education for his career and so enrolled on a day-release college course, eventually completing a Full Technological Certificate, whilst training to be a painter and decorator.

Presented here is an experience very divergent from the first two: a total neglect and, indeed, ignorance of educational considerations. The child was never imbued with any conception of what education was all about – 'I didn't recognize it.' The grandparents, whom Williams referred to as 'mum' and 'the old man', were, according to him, uneducated and barely literate; they had little comprehension of the values, demands and functions of education and, as a consequence, were unable to make any contribution to the child's involvement at school.

Education, of course, does not end at the school gates: the home is one of a complex of factors which combine to affect the child's chances at school. An active, verbal home atmosphere is, as many studies have shown, of critical significance in determining how the child will fare at school (see J. W. B. Douglas' 1964 study for one of the main contributions to our understanding of how factors in the home environment affect educational careers; also, Douglas *et al.*, 1968; Bernstein, 1971, 1975). Obviously, a child returning from school to find his own study quarters where he has books at his disposal and sympathetic parents who can offer cogent remarks on his work and broaden his outlook with lively, stimulating conversation, will be able to get more out of education than a child who, when doing his homework, has to share the kitchen table with plates, cutlery and cruet as well as the pet cat and having to contend with 'Crossroads' as the main intellectual challenge of the evening.

For Williams, home life was an intellectual void. There was, he said, 'no interest whatsoever' to the extent that: 'When I left junior school, they [his surrogate parents] never even came to the school to see about it. I had to go and find a new damn school myself.' His case is perhaps not typical; neither are the first two. His family knew nothing of education and so gave him no support or encouragement, still less active aid. Hunter suffered emotionally from the opposite: an almost obsessive urging and prompting from his parents, in particular his father, to do well at school and the promise of a physical beating in the event of failure. McLeod's family placed a similarly strong emphasis on the value of education but failed, not because of the methods the parents chose to ram it home – on his own admission, they were not 'overstrict' – but because they set unachievable objectives for him; nothing short of these objectives would satisfy and so there was no reward for his best efforts.

Presented then are two polar opposites: parents, at the one extreme, neglecting their children's education; at the other, overburdening them, whether by abrasive discipline or by setting impossible targets. Both are ultimately destructive to the child's aspirations at school and the achievements he will gain there and, so, consequently, have a deciding effect on the child's eventual career. Quite obviously, the examples constitute extreme types, but, as Newtown full back Alfonso Clark, part of a family of nine, put it, after describing two similar cases: 'There's nothing in between; it's all or nothing from West Indian families' (he was from Nevis). Three CSEs are what he took to his job at a glaziers.

Lest I be accused of caricaturing the West Indian family's approach to its child's education, let me add some tempering comments from sportsmen who found their parents' blend of discipline and encouragement satisfactory. Both professional boxer Achille Mitchell and Aston Villa footballer Noel Blake travelled to the Midlands when they were 9, Mitchell from Dominica, Blake from Jamaica. One would expect both to have experienced upheavals, having completed about four years primary education before having to take up again in the UK. Yet neither told of any problems and both cited their parents, in Blake's case his mother only, as important 'uplifting' influences (as Mitchell put it). Tellingly, neither gained any qualification; Mitchell supplemented his ring earnings with work as a carpenter and Blake became a pro footballer.

Such cases are irregular: for the most part, black sportsmen's family influences fall into the neglecting or overburdening types. Aston Moore of Birchfield, yet another 9-year-old traveller from the West Indies (from Jamaica in 1968) reflected on his parents' giving him hardly any encouragement at all: 'I got the odd comment now and again – "how are you doing?" or whatever. . . . As regards to homework, I just got on with it myself or didn't do it at all.' (He got five CSEs.)

Decathlete Derek Anderson, born in London's East End, his father Jamaican, his mother Cuban, reasoned perspicaciously that: 'I had no encouragement from my mother and very limited contact with my father. They had to struggle bringing us up so they had no real time to bother about anything else.' He attributed his gaining ten 'O' levels, four 'A' levels, a psychology degree and (in process) a Masters degree to his own 'determination to take up the challenge of the idea of the black kid who's got no brains.'

It seems that if Caribbean parents are not too preoccupied with the 'struggle' to bring their kids up, and there is every reason to believe that, due to the aftermath of migration, familial ruptures and large, possibly unmanageable families, it is a struggle, they are so eager to compensate for their own lack of education that they encumber their children with over-ambitious objectives backed by inflexible, often demoralizing, discipline. Yet, I will go on to argue that black kids seriously involved in sport tend to be rather better placed academically than others who may not be immersed in sport. The overall retardation of black youth is due, in no small measure, to the inadequacy of Caribbean families to cope with the exigencies of education in the modern UK. 'The next generation which has grown up over here and understands what their children have to go through will handle them much, much better,' Cecil Williams speculated.

Overall, the family's role in the education process is, at best, non-productive and, at worst, destructive. And, as I have pointed out, its part in the sports process is non-existent – unless it acts as a deterrent. All this is not meant as a massive, unqualified slight against the Caribbean family, for there are understandable reasons for its failure, amongst them fractured relationships and the prime necessities of having to feed, clothe and shelter their children. In Anderson's terms, they 'struggled' and education may have seemed a little remote to them as it was not freely available in most parts of the West Indies until the 1940s.

But there is a very urgent sense in which the Caribbean family fails to encourage sufficiently or places too much pressure on their offspring at school; and there is every reason to surmise that this is of general relevance – not just to sportsmen. Black sportsmen are drawn from the ranks of black working-class youth and these generally grow up under similar conditions, being subjected to the same kind of pressures or lack of them.

Black kids go to school ill-equipped to do well and, of course, the majority do not do well academically. Indeed, they demonstrate little interest in or carry any vim into their academic work; certainly nothing to compare with the avid desire for technique and expertise many take to the sports field. Family influences help account for the languor of black kids at school and the regularity with which they underachieve. But it is the experience at the school itself which prompts the youths to channel their energies into sport. The relationship between the experience at school and the involvement in sport will occupy the next two chapters.

Mickey Morris. Photograph courtesy of C. Y. Moyse

MICKEY MORRIS
learning to be black

Born: London, 1958; father: Jamaica (fork-lift truck driver);
mother: Jamaica (nurse); occupation: athlete – employed by DHSS.

Two sets of contradictory forces accompanied Mickey Morris's development in sport and, indeed, generally. His Jamaican parents gave him absolutely no encouragement in sport and little more in education yet his school teachers exerted often crude pressures on him to participate in the school athletics and football teams. At '13 or 14' he realized that 'most black kids are not respected for their knowledge or their brains.' His initial promise in sports gained him the tag of 'the runner' which he despised: 'So, I thought: I'll try to be academic and good at sports as well.'

Conflict with teachers came when he refused to play in a school football match which clashed with a geography class. He was castigated by a teacher and told he was letting the school down. His commitments were divided between sport and education, and between blacks and whites, but he was loath to let his sports lapse if only because of the purgative effect they brought, as he explained:

At school, you start off, you integrate with everybody right up to the third year so that, in the third year or the fourth year, your friends or who you know as friends, they might call you a 'black bastard'. At that age, it doesn't mean anything. And then you find that when they say it in the fourth year, they mean it and you begin to realize. You begin to look at yourself and realize what colour you are. And that's where the rift begins: then you have to make a choice, staying with my white friends or going with my black friends. Now, I was more readily accepted by my black friends than my white friends. I remember this time after school there was a fight between blacks and whites; I went and stayed in the toilets for a half-hour thinking what I should do and that's when I really took a look at myself and thought about the white kids calling me names and the black kids saying 'come on' so I said 'all right'. So, I made up my mind from then: 'right, I'll have to stay with the black guys 'cause I am black.' I looked at myself properly and carried on from there.

Then, there's a process of learning to be black. I mean you look at yourself and you've got a black face and a Cockney accent and you realize you don't fit. And there's a learning process of being black: you start going to black clubs you start speaking black, you read history, you learn more about blacks and slavery; it's a process of learning. There's a rift that grows at that stage in your schooling between, not only white people, but the actual teachers as well. You try to be a white person or you go to them and try to be accepted and you go back to blacks and they don't like it. So I went through this process and I started to read my thoughts generally, not to be too much one way or the other. I was learning, trying to be impartial all the time. This is really frustrating. To get off my frustration I used to come down to the track and run it out. I used to play football just to get out the aggression. Ordinary kids might go robbing or beating up old ladies, something like that; I used to come down here 'cause I knew that wasn't the right way to let out the aggression.

After being noticed by Haringey coach Sandy Gray, Morris was invited to train with the club (then called Haringey and Southgate). He agreed, still seeing sport as 'an outlet' but 'in time, it just got serious.' The infamous John Carlos who made the black power gesture on the Olympic rostrum in 1968 became a source of inspiration: 'I said "yeah, I'd like to be there."' (Morris even now wears an all-black track suit and black socks, *à la* Carlos.) Muhammad Ali was also influential: 'He's a great sportsman and he's got a brain, he's not stupid.'

Before leaving school, he was interviewed by a careers officer who asked him: 'Do you want a job in a factory?' His initial reaction was one of elation:

I was happy about it when I went home and told my mum, but she said, 'what are you talking about a factory? What about a clerical job or a nice doctor's job?' And I thought 'she's right.' They didn't even offer me the opportunity to say what I wanted to do.

One CSE Grade 1 is all he could muster from school, so, fired by the grim prospect of a factory job, he went to a college of further education where he gained four 'O' levels after a year and then took a job at a wholesale jewellers, where they weren't too optimistic about his chances of promotion.

> They said I'd never make a manager. I said 'right, I'll show you' and got a job in the Civil Service. And I find with my running it's the same: they said 'you're too short.' I thrive on people telling me that so I can react to it. I put myself down as well to prove myself wrong.

His progressions in employment and athletics were in harness. He long jumped for a while before concentrating solely on sprinting 200 metres: he clocked 22.8 seconds in his first year and reduced this to 21.13 seconds, his personal best, making him the club's number one until the rise in form of Mike MacFarlane. But, his career with the DHSS was never eclipsed by athletics and he consciously made exams and promotion prime targets. There was no changed priority for Morris.

> I've never made athletics my route to the top. I wouldn't train full-time; I thought: 'No, I want a good job.' I run for my own satisfaction really. I don't think I could train full-time like MacFarlane and that's one of the things that's kept me going: to know that, as a junior, I was as fast as MacFarlane. I had the potential. It's just a self-satisfaction. I don't tell my parents about it 'cause they only laugh; it's a big joke to them. I think you find it with most West Indian parents . . . it wasn't so much lack of enthusiasm, they just didn't have the time.

On the track, Morris still feels very much a sense of identity with blacks: he presents a funereal image in all-black, a cowl covering his head. This identity gives him what he calls 'a stability, a feeling of belonging'. But it contrasts strikingly with the pin-stripes he sports for work. He keeps the two spheres as separate as possible, leading an almost Jekyll and Hyde existence. 'I've mellowed a lot,' he told me. 'If you'd have come to me when I was eighteen I wouldn't even have spoken to you.' His blackness he now regards as a personal stabilizer rather than a means for rejecting society.

Chapter Six

EXPECTED TO FAIL by teachers

I was pushed into certain sports at school, like athletics. The teachers naturally thought, because you're black, you must have some sort of athletic ability in you; but I didn't even want to do athletics, at all.

Vince Hilaire, footballer

The push

As I have already suggested successful black sportsmen play a passive but vital role: however unwittingly, they act as role models, figures to be copied and emulated. Black kids look to them as blueprints for their own development. They do so because they are black and black youths tend to identify strongly with other blacks, and because they have achieved visible success and black kids want clues as to how they too might be successful.

But it is still a passive role and, while many major figures in sport express a sense of responsibility for black youth, none actively encourage or discourage them from following their examples. In crude terms, they act as 'pull' factors: the past and current successes of Hope, Thompson, Crooks and others effectively radiate attractive powers. The loss of the grip of the family during the critical adolescent years releases the youth from the 'straightening' influences, thus making him amenable to other fields of force. Whereas a white youth may have visions of becoming a successful sportsman, his parents may have a strong enough hold over him to deflect him and set him on course for a 'straight' job; often this is not the case with blacks. Yet the black family plays very little part in supporting, less still in encouraging, their children in sport. The 'push' often comes from school, in particular, from teachers. It is the influence of teachers in guiding black kids into sport and, often, into sporting careers I now want to consider.

In emphasizing the parts played by school teachers in prompting black youth into sports involvement, I am neglecting many other influential figures, including elder brothers and sisters and occasionally even parents. Other members of the family are often important in at least stimulating an awareness of the possibilities of sport and, at most, actively encouraging the brother or sister to take up the sport. The success of one family member can be inspirational as the examples of ABA champion Garfield McEwan, or giant field eventer Robert Weir show; the successes of the older brother bred involvements amongst younger members of the family. In some cases, the successes of the older brother are far surpassed by the younger: Maurice Hope's entry into boxing was preceded by his little-known brother Lex's involvement.

The eldest must have got interested somehow, however, and, in many instances, the initial influence comes from teachers. They often play a pivotal role in the transitional process of moving from casual, playful flirtation to serious, sometimes intense involvement. With the virtual absence of parental encouragement and the rather remote, even abstract, images of successful sportsmen as guides, black kids lack any personal focus for their ambitions. Not images, but people who can direct them or lead them, channel their energies or expand their scope are what they need. The parameters of sporting involvement are, in the first instance, drawn by teachers.

To choose one of many examples, I can point to the case of Nottingham-born Herol Graham, whose parents came from Jamaica and gave him no support in his sporting endeavours, at first in sprinting and then in boxing where he made his mark as a light-middleweight.

> In boxing, I was encouraged a lot by school teachers. Every time I boxed, they'd say, 'Good fight, very good. Keep it up.' And they presented me with a Winston Churchill half-crown for my boxing. We used to have a showcase at school with just my boxing trophies in it.

His achievements in sport made him something of a celebrity at school and his status was in no small way boosted by the teachers' approval.

One school teacher in particular influenced the course of the life of

Kenny Mower, who participated in a number of sports, including middle distance running (at county level), cricket (for Walsall Boys), basketball (he had trials for England juniors) and table tennis (in his spare time!) before concentrating on a career in professional football (for Walsall FC). 'The only thing that affected my sport was my teachers,' he recalled. 'There was one teacher, Mr Richardson, and he encouraged me in all the sports I did, really. He pushed me along more than anybody. Now, I'm a pro footballer, I'm grateful to him for pushing me so hard.'

A similar tale was told by quarter-miler Winston Martin, born in London of Montserrat parents; he got interested in running when 'about 8', and consistently won running events at primary school (in north London):

> When I moved to secondary school, the PE master used to encourage me in my running and, when he saw I had some potential, he took me down the North London AC and made me a member there so I could train a couple of times a week.

Such stories about school teachers taking an interest, lending assistance, providing support and, generally, giving the black youth a shove in the direction of sport are commonplace and the parts played by teachers in the dynamics of sports involvement shine through the stories. They are willing to contribute to and collaborate with the youths, often spending long hours coaxing and prompting. But for all their interest and benevolence many brilliant sportsmen, black and white, would have been lost, possibly wasted in the barrenness of the mundane world; but also possibly recruited to occupational domains fertile with status and affluence. Possibly.

So immersed are many black kids in their sport or sports, they sometimes neglect their academic work. Sometimes, they are abetted in their negligence; but for the moment, let me abstract from the recollections of Sonia Lannaman, a sprinting prodigy from Aston, Birmingham, whose PE mistress introduced her to Solihull AC (she transferred to Wolverhampton and Bilston in 1975 to train under Charles Taylor: 'I outgrew Solihull'). At only 14, she had made the national junior side (in 1970) and, by 1973, she was the European junior champion, but, she reckoned, at a cost:

> I suppose the fact that I'd made it at the age of 14 was important because it meant I would go a long way in athletics. As a result, I

spent a lot of time in training – sometimes a whole afternoon –
when I could have been at school.

At school-leaving age, she was training seriously at least four times
a week and attributed her total lack of educational qualifications to
her athletic indulgences. To compensate, she took a secretarial
course: 'So that meant I had something to fall back on if the athletics
failed.' But only 'if': athletics was clearly her main source of ambition.

Sport does occupy a great chunk of the time of black schoolkids
and the attention they give it is directly related to the rewards it
brings. Lannaman's exaltedness stood out against the bleak, colour-
less squalor of working-class Aston, cluttered with roads of derelict,
condemned or should-be-condemned houses. Like Graham, she was
hoisted on a platform at her school. The prestige and repute connected to sporting success at school made it a viable, intriguing and
challenging venture for her, as it would be for many otherwise
nondescript black kids already faced with the adversity of being
black in what is perceived to be a a hostile environment.

But, very often, the victories on the track and pitch or in the ring
are Pyrrhic: they are costly in other areas. Sprinter Phil Brown
began athletics at the instigation of two PE teachers. After a school
meeting, he was invited by Tony Hadley, a teacher and coach, to go
to Birchfield Harriers where he was told: 'You must join the club.'
In his Handsworth Comprehensive School, he was fairly consistent:
'I was in the A-stream from the first year all the way through.' He
was 14 when he began at Birchfield and that is when his interest in
athletics spiralled. His relationships with his games teacher, a Mr
Jewitt, and Hadley intensified. He started to distinguish himself as
an athlete of no mean promise and, understandably, invitations to
meetings out of the area were forthcoming. 'There were some meetings that were during the week and I enjoyed going away,' he
remembered. 'Games teachers would say, "There's a meeting at
such and such a place on Wednesday afternoon; would you ask your
teacher if you could miss your lessons?" And I'd get the afternoon
off. It was quite nice.'

In July 1978, his ambitions on the educational front were well
stoked up and he took six CSEs. Disappointment came with only
one grade 1 pass – in PE – and he returned to school to take three
GCE 'O' levels. Another year passed and, though his personal best

times in sprinting improved markedly, he failed all his examinations. He re-sat the 'O' levels at the next available opportunity (November 1979) and crashed once more, thus having to abandon his initial ambition of becoming a police officer. After this, he resigned himself more or less to an athletics-oriented existence, taking up the offer of a job in a sports equipment shop, where he would be granted ample time off to compete in meetings and train regularly.

Brown was not a reluctant athlete flummoxed out of academic success by mercenary PE teachers and coaches eager to capitalize on his obvious potential. He flung himself into athletics and, eventually became a top-flight international sprinter; which is just as well, for, had he not realized his early promise, he would have been stuck in a sports shop with no qualifications – which would not have reflected what he considered his genuine educational aptitude.

There are several illuminating aspects of the Brown experience: the early promise of educational attainment; the not unreasonable anticipation of good qualifications; the gradual intensification of involvement with sport; and, crucially, the persuasive parts played by teachers and, to a slightly lesser extent coaches, in fostering an interest in sport, which he admitted was detrimental to his education. 'It's a case of what I know now. . . . If I had my life over again, I'd see the mistakes coming up and I'd correct them.'

The 'mistakes' of being led and compliantly drifting into sport are not unusual. Brown's fellow Birchfield member Aston Moore, himself an international representative, who left Kingston, Jamaica, for Handsworth when aged 9, conceded: 'Educationally, I wasn't really into it. I wish I had been 'cause I took CSEs at school and I got sort of fairly average grades (1 in music; 2 in English; 3 in history, general science and woodwork). Moore's start in athletics came relatively late when he was 14: 'One of the PE teachers at school had a son at Birchfield and, after he'd seen me jumping well at school, he said, "Why don't you come down?" After that, I joined.'

It was through school generally and school teachers in particular that his interest was aroused and: 'When I was approaching the time to leave school, my interest was in athletics; I either wanted to join the army as a PE instructor or I thought about taking a course in physical education.' The latter choice would have required two 'A' levels and his involvement with the Birchfield club prevented his joining the armed forces. He opted for a job as an arc metalworker for a firm that allowed him plenty of time off for competing in meetings and, as he was an international, he travelled overseas often. (Interestingly, he gave up athletics for one year after leaving school – and the influence of teachers – because 'there was no one to say, "go into this and I'll help you do it." ' He resumed to find his best form: 'I was a late developer, I guess.')

Very few athletes enter sport without the assistance and encouragement of a teacher who might innocently create serious tensions, as with Jackie Jackson, whose PE teacher strengthened her commitment to athletics, a commitment which proved destructive to her educational aims, as she pointed out: 'I was spending so much time in athletics that I couldn't give enough time to my 'A' levels.' She was, in her terms, 'thrown out for wasting my time'.

Footballers and boxers, too, often have their entry into the sports world aided by zealous school teachers, though, overwhelmingly, they choose to see only the formative years up to, say, the age of 13 as affected by teachers. There is almost a tinge of predestination in footballers' reflections on how they came to sport in the first place. Noel Blake summed up the general view: 'I always wanted to be a footballer; there was never anything else.' This perception in itself is, of course, sufficient to predispose youths to the influence of seniors who would seem to be able to help in the realization of the ambition. Boxers are less susceptible because many schools do not include the sport in their curricula and, as a consequence, many kids either start independently of school or get involved shortly after leaving school. The ambivalent attitude of schools towards boxing guarantees that many youths, even those encouraged by teachers in the sport, will have to seek access to boxing facilities elsewhere. Birmingham City's Peter Crawford, who claimed a 'school record' for the number of suspensions from Mirfield Secondary School, was taken, along with other pupils, to the then Aston Manor Club (now Aston Villa ABC) by 'a school teacher called Kane who'd boxed for Ireland at one stage'. (Crawford's ultimate suspension from school came two weeks before he was due to take his leaving exams and he gained two CSEs by taking them in the hostel he was staying at.)

Exams? Nothing!

The effects of the roles of teachers in precipitating an active sports interest can be, as I have pointed out, debilitating academically. This is not always so, but according to a great many sportsmen, their overconcentration on sport, often as a result of the encouragement of teachers, led to a neglect of academic work with the consequence that examination results failed to convey accurately what they felt to be their actual capability.

This sometimes leads to a resentment of the teachers responsible for guiding the youth into sport, particularly if it becomes obvious that the interest in the youth was purely because of his sporting success. Herol Graham's case is a useful one to follow through for, in his fourth year at school, he realized that he had 'left it too late' and pinpointed one of the causes:

> There was one particular teacher; if you done sports for him, that came first. Exams? Nothing! You'd got to do your sport for him and, if you didn't, you'd get a bad report. If ever he used to take us for a spare lesson, all he used to do was draw on the blackboard the scrum lineouts and things. We should have been taking French or English, or something. Eventually, we realized that our school work was suffering and a few of us turned him down flat when it came to the sports and he didn't like it. He didn't speak to us after that. If we wanted to speak to him, we'd have to go through the headmaster. We resented that.

A disquieting parallel is found in the career of Winston Martin who reasoned:

> The teachers didn't seem to care about your academic work as long as you were all right in sport. A friend of mine [also black] used to get taken out of his lessons to compete in football. The teacher used to come in and take him and he got fed up of it 'cause he couldn't get on with his other work. So, eventually, the guy said: 'No, I'm not going' to the teacher and the teacher turned his back on him and didn't ever speak to him again.

He underwent a similar experience after a teacher had taken him to North London AC in his first year of secondary school. When his initial interest waned, the teacher paid no more attention to him: 'Then I realized what he was interested in me for and we ended up just walking past each other, completely ignoring each other.'

Enmity arising out of the often inordinate emphasis laid on sports by some teachers is quite commonplace amongst black kids; much less so amongst whites. Maturity brings new perspectives and the idea that they are often manipulated for their sporting prowess brings with it a clarity of perception, a perception succinctly summarized by Birchfield's sprinter Lincoln Asquith: 'I was used by school teachers 'cause I was good at sport. They used me.'

On the occasions when the realization translates into a rejection of the teacher, if not the sport, perceptions become even clearer and can become a source of new-found motivation. Mickey Morris, having left school with a grade 1 CSE, 'managed to scrape four 'O' levels at college' and then progressed admirably through the internal examination system of the Department of Health and Social Security; but not before he had come to terms with what he called 'a home truth'. Shortly before he was due to take mock exams, he was at a geography lesson which was interrupted by a teacher calling for his services in a football match. He refused to co-operate and was told he was 'letting the school down' and given an indication that this would affect his school report, 'and that's when I realized that I was only acknowledged for my sporting ability.'

Paul Morris, a Birchfield triple jumper, reckoned that, after he and some others at his Handsworth school dropped some sports in order to devote more time to GCE preparations, the PE teacher reacted angrily: 'He thought we were ganging up on him as most of us were black.'

The motivation to achieve at school in the face of what are the deflecting influences of at least some school teachers in some cases takes the form of a challenge. Derek Anderson, for example, showed considerable promise in a number of sports and was encouraged to work at them by his teachers, but, when asked whether he ever thought of making sport his eventual career, he replied:

> No. I knew I could do well academically and I did it as a challenge to the conventional idea of the black kid who's good at sports, yet with no brains. There was one black kid in every year at my school [King Edward's, Aston]; just one in each year. But, on prize-giving for sports day, they were always there. I wanted to prove that I wasn't just good at sports.

The remarkable Anderson, in addition to playing rugby and cricket at area and county junior levels, competing as a decathlete for Birchfield and qualifying to coach nine sporting events, gained an impressive tally of educational qualifications culminating in a Master's degree from the University of Leicester. He is, of course, exceptional, but his sharp perception of the way in which teachers orient their expectations of black kids and his response to that perception was by no means out of the ordinary.

It would be ridiculous to suggest that black kids who are constantly being geared up by teachers to thrust themselves into sports, do not, at some stage, recognize that there exists a manipulative element: they feel they are regarded as naturally gifted sportsmen (see Vince Hilaire's opening quotation), but without an abundance of intellectual equipment, who are used for the purposes of bringing prestige to both the individual teacher and the school. Winston McLeod, who played soccer for his school, district, London, Middlesex and West Ham United before a strangulated hernia sustained in a tackle in 1972 effectively finished his football career, reflected on his and other blacks' experiences with teachers:

> Teachers definitely think of you as a good athlete if you're black. They seem to have this idea about natural talent and any kid who shows the slightest promise is put into sport and made to concentrate on that. It's as if they're expecting you to fail academically; and, if the teacher expects you to fail, then you begin to believe it yourself and you do.

This, he believed, to be one of the important reasons why black kids are continually underqualified:

> You get the impression that teachers do have stereotypes about black kids, about them not being too bright at academic subjects but good at sports. All the black kids at my school were winners at sport, but not in education.

Like some other promising sportsmen who believe their intellectual powers were not sufficiently energized at school, he went to college, abandoned his sports career and became a solicitor's accountant.

Continental footballer, Sydney Grant, who was born in Jamaica, but spent the majority of his school years in Leeds, concurred, but with a political proviso: 'Teachers do have these kinds of stereotyped ideas about blacks being good in sports but not intellectually,' he agreed.

> But, I don't accuse them. They probably don't realize they're doing it. It's because they're caught up in a system which keeps blacks in positions where they have to play only secondary roles to whites.

It would be unfair to suggest that teachers, consciously or unconsciously, use serviceable but pejorative, inflexible impressions, or stereotypes, about black youth. And it would be outrageous to impute motives for such stereotyping. But black kids do both and it is both their perceptions and experiences which have crucial effects on their overall career developments.

Many black kids who are now involved in sport have, in some way, experienced the encouragement of teachers in getting into sport. Maybe it was not direct aid and did not have a serious effect, but it seems difficult to imagine any sportsman, black or white, entering sport entirely unassisted. Even Daley Thompson, who insisted he had very little interference from teachers, said they helped him in a non-involved way: 'They were all right; they left me alone and let me get on with what suited me. I did the minimum of work academically and got on with my sport – at first soccer – and they never bothered me.' The 'minimum' yielded nine 'O' levels and two 'A's.

With only circumstantial variation, the theme about teachers guiding youths into sport and nourishing interests recurs. Black kids enter sport usually from school and so the senior figures in this scene play vital parts. The school is the springboard for sport and, even if commitments are made in later years, early involvement and subsequent progress are important in launching an interest.

One might suppose in reading this chapter that teachers have a lot to answer for; after all, they are the ones who are responsible for accentuating sport by turning a vague, ill-formed image into a seemingly realistic pursuit for sporting excellence. Black kids who, in retrospect, would blame their lack of success at school on their over-indulgence in sport would point fingers of accusation at the people who encouraged them and helped sustain an interest which was later to prove nullifying in its effects. But this would be to simplify things for, as I have argued, black kids generally come from the kind of family backgrounds which are not suited for their own educational needs – for reasons which I spelled out in the last chapter, but will summarize as 'neglect' or 'unattainable goals'. Consequently, black youths in many instances are not keen on formal education in any case. Mike MacFarlane, the international sprinter from Haringey, looked back on his school years in Hackney: 'In those days, living was more important than education.' He got three CSEs before going to college full-time.

Garth Crooks, in a similar way, admitted that he needed no prompting to play competitive soccer four or five times a week when aged 14 and 15. Along with other footballers, as I mentioned earlier, he felt a kind of mild predestination, believing himself to be a footballer even while at school; though one wonders how many others who thought themselves predestined are now in factories or on milk rounds.

It would be misleading to profile school teachers as only seeking to maximize their own prestige by cultivating exaggerated interests in sport among black schoolkids and thus jeopardizing their chances academically. Black kids are psyched up for sport anyway. The other factors account for that: home life, perception of limited opportunities, images of black successes. But the push of teachers is an intervening force which may take the black youth from the realms of inflated ambitions and outlandish dreams of becoming a world champion, winning an Olympic medal or holding aloft the FA Cup to the sometimes arduous and frequently unrewarding world of practical ambition, gritty perseverance and strengthening resolve. The teacher supplying the push may be helping to launch the career of a future gold medallist; but equally he may be setting a youth off down a path to nowhere.

But, again, I simplify: the process is two-way and black kids contribute to their own general lack of success at school by manifesting little desire to learn conventional subjects. Over the past chapters, I have sought to show how the combination of broken homes, disturbed domestic backgrounds and lack of a full understanding of the needs and implications of formal education create a family environment unsuited to the requirements of black youth in British education. As Winston McLeod expressed it: 'Black kids have special problems,' referring precisely to these factors. These allied to an apprehension of the uselessness of qualifications anyway – blackness being seen as the immovable obstacle to career progress – produce a situation in which black kids are receptive to alternatives, to different life plans. Enter the teacher: he supplies the means through which black kids can elevate themselves, become fêted at school and, most importantly, achieve.

The cost of sporting involvement may not, in most cases is not, realized during early phases, but, on reflection, many black sportsmen believe their academic results are badly affected by an overconcentration on sport. Yet, a large number go on and eventually do reasonably well academically, the implication being that sporting involvement may not be so detrimental to education as it might appear. A volte-face? No, I believe the two sets of findings are reconcilable. Black youths may feel that their participation in sport has a negative effect on their other school pursuits and it may; but this does not mean that their academic lives are burnt out by the fires of sporting commitment. Sport, I will argue, can have a most stimulating, uplifting impact on the participant and instil in him a fresh thirst for achievement in sporting and other circles.

Even if, to the youth, 'living was more important than education', engaging in competitive sport can bring home the new realization that achieving results in education can be important to living. Sport is a positive, exhilarating force in the lives of those whose attentions and commitments it commands; but the complexity of the force is sometimes lost on its practitioners and observers. In the next chapter, I will attempt to sort out the way in which it feeds back positively into education.

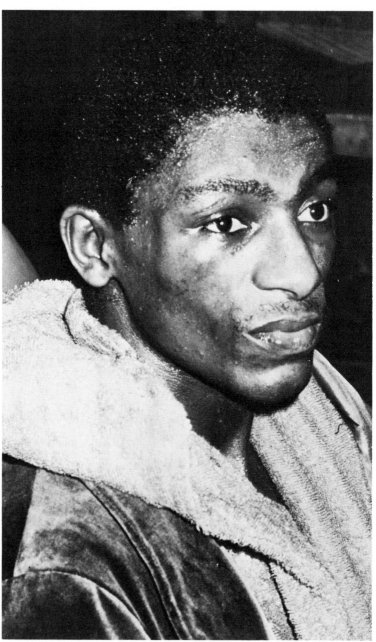
Herol Graham. Photograph courtesy of Fred Cicharski

HEROL GRAHAM
commitment and trying

Born: Nottingham, 1959; father: Jamaica; mother: Jamaica; occupation: professional boxer – formerly, meat porter, barman, diesel mechanic, sheet metalworker, industrial painter – and others.

In 1948, Graham's family migrated to Nottingham where they brought up their seven children. Herol was to be the most famous, winning the British light-middleweight title from Pat Thomas in an all-black contest in 1981 to complement the Amateur Boxing Association title he had won in 1978. His celebrated boxing career had strange beginnings.

I was 8 at the time. A mate of mine and I were roller-skating by a local boxing club and these two white guys were hanging out of an upstairs window and shouting abuse at us. 'You black so-and-sos,' they shouted. There weren't many blacks in our areas and, really, it didn't register; they didn't seem to mean it. But they said, 'come up here!' and we did. Well, they had some gloves and the one guy, I suppose, thought he'd give me a beating. We put the gloves on and shaped up and I hit him in the stomach and that was the end of him. Anyway, the guy who ran the club saw it and asked me to stay, so that was the start of it really.

Prior to that I'd been too scared to go to a boxing club. I'd watched Muhammad Ali on the television, but I suppose it was the insults which really got me going. There was only him [Ali] for me then 'cause he was black and there was racialism. I didn't hate the whites but resented them. So, 'cause Ali was black, I used to base myself on him.

His sporting interests were split in two, sprinting occupying much of his energies. He acquired the nickname 'Bomber' because of his explosive style and was encouraged in both sports by teachers.

All the time, teachers used to say 'come on – let's train. We've got an important match.' Even if you were doing your work, like revising for exams, they'd still want you to go training.

On one occasion, he refused to train, preferring to study and the teacher, he reckoned, 'got really vexed'. He concluded: 'They wanted us for sport not for exams.'

> There was quite a clash of interests between sport and normal education. I went all the way through school before I realized it was too late. It wasn't until I was in the fourth year that I realized and there was only one year to go.

At this stage, he gained a very clear perception of the pattern cut out for black youth: as good sportsmen who were to be encouraged, but as bad scholars who were to be ignored. One teacher used to ignore him quite literally after he refused to train:

> If I wanted to speak to him, I'd have to go through the headmaster. It wasn't just me, but the other black kids I used to hang around with as well. We resented it, actually.

By the age of 14, his interest in athletics had faded as the boxing trophies began to accumulate, and, by the time he left school, his commitment to the sport was strong. He had established a reputation as the school's sportsman *par excellence* and his boxing achievements were celebrated: 'My friends used to put me on a pedestal; they used to worship me.' He had started his boxing with the Nottingham School of Boxing but left to join the Retford Club. This proved an unsatisfactory move.

> There was this guy at the club who kept calling me a 'black this' and a 'black that'. He used to resent me, especially as I used to do the flashy stuff like Ali. So I went to this other club and had only one fight in one season. Then I had another argument there. There used to be a joker, but it was a serious joke with me. It used to be 'come on you idiot', or something like that with everybody else. But, with me, it used to be 'come on, you black sod'. It got me down so I had to leave there and went back to Retford. . . . They started building me up for the Schoolboy Championships. I was 13 when I won my first title – that was 1973 – and I went straight through and won everything. . . . By the time I was leaving school, I wasn't even thinking about careers. I didn't want to work 'cause I wanted to train. Of all the jobs I had, and I had about twelve different ones after leaving school, none of them suited me: they all clashed with my training. I'd got five 'O' levels and the rest

CSEs, moderate grades, 1s and 2s, and I didn't know what I wanted to do. My mother wanted me to stay on at school or go on to college and I should have done, but I preferred to leave. But boxing was, by then, my main interest and, because they were clashing with the training, I ditched the jobs.

The vision of a possible future as a full-time professional boxer began to get sharper as his amateur achievements mounted with international representations and national titles.

But I was scared of the pros. It's a harder game altogether. I was going well in the amateurs at the time. But I won the ABA title and I was looking forward to getting picked for the England team for the European championships. Well I didn't. To this day I don't understand 'cause I'd beaten the guys that they were putting in ahead of me. At that time I met Brendan Ingle [a Sheffield-based pro trainer] and he invited me to go up and have a look at the set-up.

He was 17½ when he first moved his training base to Sheffield and his parents objected to his leaving home, especially his father, a Pentecostal Church lay preacher ('I go to church myself, but I'm not committed,' said Graham). But the break was made and it was an important one.

That's when I decided I could really make a career out of it. When I was in Nottingham, I was training myself more or less and all the others were interested in going down the pub and that sort of thing. In Sheffield, Brendan knew what needed to be done and I thought, 'this is serious now.' When I moved up here, my career started [1978].

His commitment paid dividends in the form of sixteen straight wins and in his seventeenth contest, he took the British light-middleweight title from St Kitts-born Pat Thomas. The win established him at the forefront of the 'new wave' of black sportsmen and he had well-rounded views on why he and others like him grew to prominence in the 1980s.

Blacks have been known as bad-tempered in a way. They're sharp to react to things. Playing football, I've seen them and they're dead cool with the ball, relaxed, sloppy, flicking the ball around as if they're not bothered. Now, they're realizing their mistakes. They've got to be hard tacklers as well as being creative. Now, they're starting to push themselves. Most of them have come from the West Indies and there's a happy-go-lucky sort of thing there: you live life as it comes and that's how they live – on a day-to-day thing. They take things easy as if nothing's going to happen – if it does, it does. But that's not enough.

If a black kid said 'how come you've got so far?' I'd say 'through commitment and trying. If you don't train and just want to play, nothing will happen. And, if that's the sort of attitude you've got, you're not going to get very far.' If they say, 'I might do,' I say: 'It's four times as hard not two times as hard. So you've got to try and keep on trying.' Because they're black they've got to try four times as hard as the white guy. The white people control and I think sometimes they can't accept that blacks are coming up and they've got to live with them. This makes it tougher for the black guy to make it.

Chapter Seven

MAKING IT in and out of sport

It's down to attitude: they [sportsmen] have an adjusted attitude. They aren't dropping out of school or anything like that. They're working at getting on and they can't separate the two sets of attitudes to life and sport. They reflect each other.

John Isaacs, athletics coach

The American studies

Considered in isolation, the comments in the last chapter would give bountiful gifts to the critic of sport. Those wishing to denigrate the part played by sport and hoping to reveal the way in which too much involvement in sport interferes significantly with other aspects of education would look at my examples as support for the view that sport is over-emphasized in schools and the effect this has on education standards is, overall, negative. To many this has become a self-evident article of faith, particularly as many black kids fare well in sport but not in other academic areas.

To cull some of the reflections of black sportsmen on their academic performances and how these were perhaps distorted by too much involvement in sport, I can present three points of tension. The first one is obviously time: students devote much of their time to any number of sports. Garth Crooks was comparatively single-minded in playing soccer so many times a week, but when three or more events are participated in, the pressures on time are extreme. Even three sports, such as javelin throwing, sprinting and soccer, kept Birchfield's Andrew Jarrett busy six nights a week plus Saturdays when he was 14, though he promised: 'Next year, I've made my mind up; I'm going to get down to more school work.' (Twelve months later, he was still spending six evenings a week in sport.) Unless involvement is very casual or ephemeral, sport is a rather costly business in terms of time and it could be argued, as it was once by Arthur Ashe (1977), that time spent on a playing field could be more profitably spent in the library.

Second, it could also be argued that sports, certainly the ones for which blacks show a distinct preference, are physically demanding and, therefore, serve as a drain on energy resources. Exhausting training sessions could leave the physically maturing youth with depleted reserves, leaving him wanting when it comes to other pursuits, including intellectual ones.

The third point of tension concerns status. At school, success in sports brings prestige. When Birchfield sprinter Des Deans moved to a new school in Tamworth and 'cleaned up' the sports events, he became a minor celebrity. Shortly before he had showed his form on the field, he had felt an outcast as he was the only black student in the school. Sports success is a rich source of prestige and can be used as an alternative to success in academic subjects. So much so that ambitions can be phrased in terms of sports rather than academic success. Herol Graham's achievements in boxing were made visible by the presentation of trophies in front of the whole school. Sporting achievements are valued by both the school staff and students and the ever-present threat is that kids will abandon academic goals and the less obvious status they bring in favour of the pursuit of sporting glory.

Debate over such issues has been rife in the USA for practically the whole of this century and the question of whether involvement in sport injures educational performance has been batted back and forth like a ping-pong ball. After eighty odd years, there is still no unanimity in the research findings and, after a protracted sequence of claims and counter-claims, the central problems remain. However, it may prove instructive to run over the various contentions put forward over the years and see if it is possible to tease out some pertinent insights.

Education in the United States with its grading system lends itself quite conveniently to quantifiable research. So much so, in fact, that Davis and Cooper were, in 1934, able to review a total of forty-one studies which had been conducted and they drew the general conclusion that the school performance of non-sportsmen was consistently better than that of sportsmen and that sportsmen tended to do better after the conclusion of the sports season.

Twenty-seven years elapsed before this view was given enormous backing by the publication of James Coleman's influential work *The Adolescent Society* (1961), a comprehensive study, in which it was argued that the heavy emphasis placed on sport in high school diverted the energies of participants – and, for that matter, non-participants – away from the academic studies. Coleman found that achievement in athletics was valued more highly than academic achievements or social background by high school boys, the majority (44 per cent) expressing a wish to be remembered as an athletic star rather than a brilliant or even popular student.

In 1968, however, two independent studies, one by Emile Bend, the other by Walter Schafer and J. Michael Armer brought forth broadly similar results which suggested that, contrary to Coleman's findings, high school athletes achieved slightly better grades than non-athletes:

> Not only does participation in sports generally seem to have little or no effect on a student's scholarship, but it seems to actually *help* certain students academically – especially those students from the poor and disadvantaged groups that usually have most trouble in school

argued Schafer and Armer (1968, p.21). They found that higher scholastic achievement was especially striking amongst athletes from working-class and deprived backgrounds who were not more or less 'earmarked' for further education after secondary schooling and conclude that athletics has what they call 'a democratizing or equalizing function . . . it represents a vehicle for upward mobility' (1968, p.61). Though, in their conclusion, they maintain that: 'we know that sports is an important channel to success for many Negroes, but we do not know *how* important' (1968, pp.61–2).

The overall thrust of the study is to argue against the conventional wisdom about sports having a negative effect on other aspects of education by presenting data to the contrary, while opening up a number of speculations as to why involvement in sports improves performance academically. Whether the idea about sport as a vehicle for upward mobility, that is a means of achieving social success greater than one's background would indicate, holds any sway is open to doubt. Certainly, in straightforward terms, it does provide a means of gaining social status – but only for a small minority. But what Schafer and Armer suggest is that kids from deprived backgrounds, particularly black kids, see sport as 'an important channel to success' (1968, p.61).

Schafer has been an active figure in this field of research and, in another study, this time with Richard Rehberg (1970), he found that for youths from disadvantaged backgrounds there was an association between involvement in sport and high expectations of educational achievement. Amongst those youths from better-off backgrounds, involvement in sport had no effect on their other aspirations, presumably because they were already predisposed towards high educational achievement by virtue of their upbringing.

H. G. Buhrmann takes up this point in his comprehensive study, published in 1972. He, too, found that 'athletics may be the most important means for these lower socioeconomic status students to gain social recognition and acceptance, and through it, greater academic aspirations and higher scholarship' (1972, p.127).

Steven Picou and E. W. Curry (1974) expanded the relationship further by reporting that athletes from underprivileged backgrounds who received little or no encouragement from parents to do well in further education held higher aspirations educationally than similarly situated kids who had no involvement in athletics.

Not that all the American results were consistent in their dismantling of Coleman's contentions: William Spady (1970) argued cogently that participation in sports can stimulate greater academic aspirations but without developing the requisite scholastic skills. The consequence was that, if inflated aspirations were solely due to involvement in sports, then that involvement was dysfunctional in the sense that the student aimed higher than he could reach.

Following up this research, Elmer Spreitzer and Meredith Pugh (1976) qualified the argument by stating that the unrealistic and inflated educational aspirations of Spady's sportsmen may have been limited to schools where sport rather than pure scholarship was the primary source of status and heightened aspirations. They found that the positive relationship between participation in sport and high expectations was strongest in schools where the sports specialist was given a great deal of status and prestige. It was weakest where status was regarded as being earned through scholarly achievements.

In a similar vein, L. B. Otto and D. Alwin (1977) suggested that the influence of sports participation on educational aspirations is mediated in three ways. (1) By participating in sports, athletes may acquire 'interpersonal skills' that can be utilized outside athletics; (2)

involvement in sport may serve an 'allocations function' that increases the visibility of sportsmen and labels them as successful individuals; (3) because of their participation in sport, they may experience 'interpersonal networks, contacts, and information channels that are beneficial in establishing careers.'

Another intervening factor was described by Rehberg (1969) as the need for achievement, a somewhat vague psychological concept, which was criticized by Susan Birrell (1978) who found evidence to support the idea that achievement motivation performs a significant role in the relationship between sports involvement and educational aspirations. More recently, the early debate on whether there was a positive or negative effect exerted by sports participation on educational aspiration and performance, has been replaced by the more complicated discussions on the intervening factors in the relationship. All the findings support the idea that a relationship of sorts does exist between sport and education and that the relationship is most pronounced amongst groups from working-class or deprived backgrounds, for those who go to schools where sports are highly valued and maybe for those who achieve a degree of status from their peers because of their sports successes. It seems that these factors combine in some way so that youths who would not normally be inclined to continue into further education, possibly because of an absence of encouragement from parents, inflate their educational aspirations more so than others from similar backgrounds but with no interest in sport. The drawback is that the heightened aspirations may not be in line with their intellectual ability or their previous life style and so lead to disappointing failure. (For a partial summary of the USA studies up to 1970, see Phillips and Schafer, 1976.)

Unfortunately, there is no comparable tradition of research in the UK, only a couple of studies which conclude rather tentatively that participation in sport results in improved academic performance (McIntosh, 1966; Start, 1967). Nevertheless, I have come to believe that there is foundation for suggesting that sport can serve a positive function in cranking up educational aspirations, fixing more firmly orientations towards qualifications and, by implication, aiding the attainment of those qualifications by black kids. Exactly how sport functions will be the concern of the rest of this chapter.

Spill-over

One of the assumptions implicit in the work so far is that a meaningful division can be made between the physical and the mental. I have written in terms of sports participation and educational achievement as if they were separate and discrete categories; this implies that physical and mental spheres do not necessarily mix, when, of course, they do. We 'box clever', we 'play intelligent ball', we 'run thoughtful races'. Sport is not simply about brawn but it is also a cerebral activity. Early acknowledgements of this indivisibility were given by the Greeks: Plato, in particular, championed an education which incorporated a synthesis of the mental and physical. The idea here was that a healthy mind stayed in tune with a healthy body, so the condition of both were emphasized.

In a similar vein, James Michener (1976) reported on how he used to train rigorously before and during the writing of a book. The view that exercise purifies thought processes as espoused by Bernard Shaw, who wrote his last play at 83, is supported by Ron Lawrence of the University of California in Los Angeles. His research indicates that there is a positive link between exercise and the central nervous system (O'Connor, 1981). Though it sounds an appealing notion – especially to those of us who strive to stay in shape – the rather scanty research on this particular relationship only indicates that there may be a significant relationship between physical efficiency and cognitive ability, between brawn and brains. Mostly, the studies have been done on young children and two in *Research Quarterly*, by Chasey and Wyrick (1970) and Thomas and Chissom (1974), suggest that if physical movement is directly related to cognitive development then its influence is confined to very early stages in life. In straightforward terms, there was no support for the belief that participation in sports or other physical manoeuvres would improve intellectual performance. On the other hand, there are no studies which indicate that sport actually interferes with cognitive development. Further, there are a number of not immediately obvious ways in which developing physical prowess and technique can have an indirect positive bearing on intellectual expansion.

Serious involvement in sport is nothing if not an earnest business. It is not uncommon to find schoolkids around the age of 15 or 16, leaving school to go directly to the gym or the training ground three or four times per week and every Sunday, summer and winter. If top flight sport is approached, for example representative athletics or boxing at county or even national levels, training can occupy six, sometimes seven days. Idleness is not a property of any sportsmen: participation in sport means competing against others holding similar commitments and so success is attained by striving to achieve that little bit more on the field or in the ring, but, equally as important, working steadfastly and unremittingly during training sessions. As Mike MacFarlane put it, invoking the 'Battle of Waterloo was won on the playing fields of Eton' idea: 'This [the training track] is where races are won and lost; here night after night – not on the day of the meeting.' His view is endorsed by practically every sportsman I spoke to – with the notable exception of former British welterweight champion Kirkland Laing, who was so confident in his 'pure ability' that he preferred to train only the minimum in order to win: 'I can beat virtually anybody in the country without doing any training at all.' Such an attitude was not a popular one, but there again, Laing was never a popular man. However, very few sportsmen of even the most modest ambition would agree with Laing and most would concede that the key to sporting success is 'graft', sheer hard work for long periods.

Sport is less about ability, more about commitment to tasks, ambition to succeed and willingness to persevere. It is about learning – the hard way. Extremely few sportsmen can dispense with demanding training schedules. Haringey coach John Isaacs speculated that an unprepared sprinter may blast off a single 100 metres successfully, but the exigencies of continual competition, including heats, make long-term success contingent on 'good conditioning'; in the sports idiom, it's impossible 'to get away with it' for long periods.

Abilities and skill are not gifts with which we are born: they are acquired, learned and practised. Anybody who believes the Brazilians are naturally talented footballers should watch participants of all ages play hour after hour on the devitalizing beaches of Rio; the talent is hewn out by day-to-day, year-to-year practice. Even George Best, to many the most outstanding 'natural' in British soccer since the war, learned his skills kicking makeshift balls around the backstreets of Belfast (though of course there are odd examples of late starters in sport, for instance Steve Heighway). To view sporting ability and success in any other way is misleading and leads only to mystification not clarity.

Accomplishment comes through the efficient allocation of time and the economic expenditure of effort. It comes through completing a day's work and ignoring one's exhaustion to go to the gym or ground and start all over again. It means foregoing other, possibly pleasurable, activities to sink more hours into preparation. It means facing unpleasant conditions and never letting the elements disturb a pre-set programme of training. It means following the often perplexing instructions of coaches and withholding doubts about the ultimate aim of them. It means, most of all, breaking pain barriers, pushing oneself to the utmost limits and then beyond, dredging up the reserves of endurance when collapse is imminent. It means, in other words, disciplining oneself. And then, on the day of the match, the performance is produced – and it all looks so easy to the spectator, just like natural ability, in fact.

But it belies what decathlete Fidelius Obukw called 'going beyond the crack-up point', a process in which the sportsman has to conquer a body and mind synthesized but ready to break apart:

> It's mental and physical in combination. You think you can't take
> it any more, your body and your mind won't stand any more
> pressure and that's the crack-up point. But the problem is
> reaching it and conquering it and that's not a physical thing, it's to
> do with attitude. You must stretch yourself mentally to be able to
> master yourself physically.

It involves the acquisition of what another athlete called 'mental strength', that critical ability to drive oneself on, pretending the body does not hurt. Resilience comes with practice.

The point I am leading to here is that, in contrast to my opening remarks about sports absorbing too much time which could be more gainfully spent in the library and requiring too much energy which could be channelled in intellectual directions, sport may instil in the participant characteristics and properties which are of the utmost importance in conventional academic pursuits: steadfast work, persistence, optimal organization of time and sensible distribution of energy. Involvement in sport could intensify, even develop, these characteristics and, in so doing, lead to improved chances of success at school. 'To stretch yourself mentally' is a prerequisite of success in sport as it is in academic subjects. No one gets away with it for long in either realm.

It seems feasible to suggest, therefore, that the attitudes forged on the anvil of sport, which imbue the sportsman with discipline and control, can be carried into the classroom where they provide the student with the basic requirements of academic success. If he approaches school work in the same frame of mind as he does sport, then he is on his way to good performances. So, there is at least a potentially positive impact that sport can make on education.

Extending this argument a little further, Derek Anderson, who coached at Birchfield as well as competing for that club, reckoned of the schoolkids in sport:

> They get used to the idea of winning physically on the track and field and then they try to do it mentally. Their attitudes become centred on winning, on achieving. This was the process with me and it's happening to a lot more black kids.

Anderson calls it a 'spill-over effect': winning in one sphere, sport, gets to be a preoccupation and the youth lets it spill over into his academic work. If he achieves things in sport, he achieves things academically.

Obviously, the equation is not as simple as Anderson suggests, but the basic idea that success at sports generates an achievement orientation is persuasive. My interpretation of his idea would be that black kids, even those who do poorly in regular academic subjects, once into sport, become exposed to the possibilities of winning: they glimpse what it is like to succeed, even if that concept has been strangely alien to them up to that stage. Results at school may spell failure and point the way only to disappointment, but, once a measure of success is attained, the youth enjoys it and seeks to make it a general habit. Success promotes success and the spiral goes into motion.

Sport provides one, probably the first available, context in which blacks can achieve success, even limited success. If the black child has gone through his early school years without managing much distinction, and for a variety of reasons mentioned earlier, is not prepared to achieve anything in terms of examination results nor expects to achieve anything, then he may be pleasantly surprised to find that success is a lot more accessible in sport. His successful experiences in sport help enhance his sense of self-esteem – 'I am a winner, after all' – and, generally, his impression of himself undergoes a slight adjustment from an all-time loser to a sometime winner. I detect that black kids do have a pronounced success orientation when it comes to sport, more so than is conventionally thought. The reasons for this stem from the perception of limited opportunities in occupations reinforced by tales to this effect transmitted from elders; sport is one area in which advancement is untrammelled so they are prepared to make their efforts in that area thinking, perhaps unreasonably, that opportunities to succeed are unrestricted. As a consequence, there is a craving for success of any order. Results feed back a positive response, self-esteem inflates and this translates into an achievement orientation which is invaluable when it comes to approaching academic work.

It is no more than an interpretation, a version of what might happen: sport has this potential. There are, it must be stated, several drawbacks which may leave that potential unrealized. For all the visibility and ostentation of winners, sport conceals its losers: it provides a context for ignominious failure as well as celebrated success – and it has to accommodate a great deal more of the former. The adage 'Everyone wants to know a winner' holds sway in sport as solidly as anywhere. As a voluntary activity, sport cannot hold the interest and commitment of a participant through any forcible means. Unlike school attendance, which is compulsory, sport retains its practitioners by a tenuous thread of success. While you're winning, you carry on; repeated defeats make you think of quitting.

Certainly, with most black kids, success is vital: they hunt for it with voracity and, when it is not found, their appetites go unsatisfied and the likelihood that they might fall away completely or look for another avenue occurs. Des Deans, in competitive athletics since the age of 14, summed up the general ethos of black youth in sport when he reflected on what fixed his interest in sprinting: 'Winning. I like the feel of power, when style and technique come together as you cross the line. I feel good in myself.' Javelin thrower Phil Jarret summarized the sentiment: 'It's not so much the trophies now so much as it was to start. Now it's the winning that's important.' Coventry City footballer Garry Thompson reiterated this idea saying that his commitment was sealed by a desire 'to make myself number one'.

With Leroy Jones, on the other hand, it became increasingly obvious that he was never going to be a number one at any sport: 'I've tried other sports, football, cricket, running, but couldn't make it in any of them; now, I'm trying in boxing to be a success at least at one thing.' Winning for him was a prerequisite of continuance and, when it did not come, he disappeared from boxing. Another Leroy, this time a sprinter was similarly unsuccessful and he also transferred commitments, in his case to weightlifting: 'I couldn't seem to quite make it in sprinting. All the time, I was near winning but never quite there.'

In many cases, of course, a string of defeats does not lead to retirement or transfer of commitment, but, by and large, with blacks, the probability of maintaining enthusiasm and steeling oneself for the shame and embarrassment which failure brings is low. Unlike white youths, to whom defeat is not so severely terminal and whose parents can provide support and maybe encouragement 'to try again', blacks face only pressure or neglect. Mickey Morris's parents mocked him following a defeat and, though the instance is extreme, the general trend is for parents to fail to recognize either success or defeat: neglect is the norm. Coupled with an urgent craving for success which is founded on the perception of sport as one of the few uncluttered roads to prosperity and status, it severely taxes the black kids' resolve when the expected success is not forthcoming. Whilst not wishing to distort the impression, it seems that black youths are rather less likely to return from protracted adversity than whites. This may be because they lack the motivating influences of parents or that they brook no arguments in favour of deferred gratification. As I have argued in previous chapters, a combination of family indifference and an awareness of limited opportunities predisposes black youth to crave success in areas which they recognize as accessible.

At the outset of the research I was told by Birmingham City ABC's head coach, Frank O'Sullivan, that: 'Black kids come in here full of themselves and they want to be champions in a couple of weeks. They've only got to lose one or two fights and you'll never see them again.' Virtually every coach reinforced the idea of black sportsmen lacking the resilience and purposefulness to assimilate failure and respond positively rather than 'swallow it' and opt out.

Blacks are so plugged into succeeding in sport that failure has a profound effect and may mean the premature termination of a sporting career. And one is then forced to consider what impact this might have on their educational outlook: if the achievement orientation gained through success in sport can build up self-esteem and then transfer to the classroom, what might resignation to failure lead to? It is regrettable that 'born losers' are not born at all but are those who have, through a variety of circumstances, been made to accept defeat and incorporate this into their ideas about themselves.

Quite possibly, the youth may take his defeats in sport to mean that his real abilities lie in conventional educational realms and make success in these his new targets by way of compensation for sports failure. The potential of sport then lies in two, and possibly three, directions: it can encourage and sustain a general achievement orientation, it can foster a defeat or failure orientation or it might prompt a reaction to failure in the form of a new-found positive approach to education.

The other side of the touchline

The spill-over of success orientation is one aspect of sport's potential in education and, although it has particular relevance to black youth, the effect can also work in relation to whites. Another manner in which sport can operate to the benefit of education was outlined by Leroy 'Chalky' White, a Birmingham-born triple jumper, educated at Handsworth Grammar School where he gained ten 'O' levels and three 'A's which enabled him to take a mechanical engineering degree at the University of Birmingham. He reckoned that the importance of sport for blacks was that it constituted an arena in which they were able to mix without sensing that their colour made them different. Adding this dimension to the spill-over interpretation, he said of the role of sport:

> The way it works is that kids come to the ground at around 14 or before and there's no racial problem at all. Black and white kids mix and so do Asians. They have to get on with each other in sport, so they realize that it's possible to get on, no matter who you're mixing with.

This critical realization, White believed, counterbalanced the injurious views formed in day-to-day life: 'They use that experience in sport in life generally to see that they can get on with whites. From there, they translate from sport into everyday life. If you achieve in sport without racial conflict, then you can in life, too.' Of course, the theory suffers from the same kind of weaknesses as the spill-over theory and failure at sport may set the tenor for everyday life. But there is a way in which, success or failure apart, this realization can prevent the kid from using his blackness as an excuse:

> There are kids who blame everything they do on to the fact that they're black. But it's an excuse. The kids coming down here [to the ground] start winning things and making progress and they see that it can be done elsewhere so they go out and try. Even if they don't win anything great they still can't use colour as an excuse.

'You can't allow yourself to think that being black might harm your chances,' Noel Blake told me, suggesting that, in sport, it is simply counterproductive to entertain any thoughts about how being black might harm long-term chances. He was, of course, referring to soccer, by nature a team event requiring coordinated team work and a high degree of reciprocity. But sports generally exist amidst an atmosphere of interdependence: blacks and whites need each other to spar with, to pace each other, to monitor each other's moves, to offer advice, support, even constructive criticism. All sportsmen at every level, whether world champions or untutored novices, rely on each other. There is simply no room for doubts about colour. Even at the Repton Club, situated in the notoriously right-wing Bethnal Green area, one can see black kids sparring and working out with self-confessed members of the neo-Nazi British Movement. What enmity there is has to be subdued for the sake of preparing adequately. As black middleweight Wendell Henry, himself quite used to tangling with the skinheads of the area, pointed out:

> When you come here to do your work, you have to forget about the others; even if you spar with them you don't think about their beliefs, you just get on with what you're here for. We never have any trouble here, but we know we all have different opinions.

The East End of London is, at least according to its inhabitants, a unique area, housing as it does a multi-ethnic population plus a heavy phalanx of reactionary quasi-political groups, the skinhead-supported British Movement being the fastest growing in the early 1980s. But the area might also be seen as a caricature of other districts in which sports clubs have grown and attracted large numbers of black kids. Birmingham City ABC is located in the centre of a city which has become almost the 'capital' of British race relations;

Birchfield stands alongside Handsworth; Haringey and Islington (the home-base of Continental FC) are districts rich in ethnicity and political faction. In its own way, each has developed and, indeed – judging by results alone – prospered in the face of sometimes quite intimidating racial hostility, most particularly in Bethnal Green and Handsworth. Each area is representative of the type of situations arising in working-class districts where large black populations congregate: concentrations of deteriorating houses and flats mostly occupied by immigrants and their offspring, ghettos, increased crime rates and police attempts at their curtailment, and right-wing backlash groups, all making for what are frequently tension-filled atmospheres.

It would be unreasonable to surmise that both blacks and whites are able to rid themselves of such tensions as they step over the threshold of the club; it is not some paradisical oasis untouched by the kind of problems that beset the rest of the area. Yet, the sports club is a place used for instrumental purposes, initially at least; kids go there to improve their physical capacities, increase their power, sharpen their reflexes, perfect their techniques and generally get better at their event. They are too occupied in getting through six repetitions of 200 metres or eight rounds on the heavy bag to bother about racial problems. As a result, problems are not given the opportunity to occur – and they don't. Blacks and whites get on with their jobs. At least the impression of consensus is given and the impression is so lasting that racial situations never surface and blacks and whites work together and assist each other. What is more, they achieve and, to repeat White, 'if you achieve in sport without racial conflict, then you can in life, too.'

In this perspective, sport is an interfusion: people of differing backgrounds with maybe conflicting outlooks, interests, ambitions and contrasting futures blend together for the expressed purpose of achieving. The idea has a pronounced Utopian ring about it though, and as I will argue later, sport is by no means unaffected by racism. But I am not entirely dismissive of this perspective; sport *is* an arena for learning not only technical or event-related skills but also social skills: how to suspend judgments on others, to dovetail one's own interests with others', to combine one's own weaknesses with others' strengths and vice versa – overall, to mix.

Learning certainly does take place in the gym or on the training field but one must be cautious about whether the social skills learned there are assimilated sufficiently to stick once the carrying bag is packed with the sweat-sodden tee shirts and track suit and the showered youth steps once more into the 'other reality' where mixing may not come so smoothly. After all, the 'marriages' at the gym are ones of convenience: what goes on outside the sports centre may be quite at variance to what goes on inside. A black kid and a white may spar together on Sunday morning; in the afternoon the black may be listening to reggae music with his black friends and the white following Mr Michael McLaughlin to Paddington for a street rally. The instance is colourful, but exemplary. Mixing in the gym does not mean you mix in the streets.

There is also a second problem and that is that those who do combine their efforts in sport to integrate and are accomplished street-wise are maybe those who already had predilections to mix with whites in the first place. This might even have accounted for their initial entry into sport. Their backgrounds and school experiences might have predisposed them to entertaining stable relationships with whites and so what appeared to be an effect of participation in sport was, on analysis, one of the causes behind it.

White, himself, would be the first to concede that his experiences at school were not flavoured by racist undertones. He referred to himself as 'well-balanced': 'I was the only black kid in the form on the day I arrived, but eventually all the kids wanted to know me. It was because I was different that I was popular, I think. So being a different colour helped me mix – which isn't the usual experience.' Being the only black made him something of a celebrity amongst his school peers and, he reckoned, 'it became the thing to know me. I was good academically and good at sport, so it became "in" to know me and the group [mainly white] I used to hang around with.'

White's 'in-crowd' sounds reminiscent of the 'leading crowd' of James Coleman's study, that group whose members have, through their excellence in sport, acquired high status and the approval of their peers. Through his involvement in such a group, White bootstrapped his way up from a working-class background in Handsworth (his father was a semi-skilled manual worker at GKN) to university and third place in the AAA under-20s long jump in 1980.

It is an interesting idea that sport presents a kind of model of harmonious race relations and black kids learn from this how to mix with whites, a lesson they can apply to their experiences in the 'outside' world. But the problem which persists is that the youths who acknowledge that sport does work in this way are usually the ones who were, in White's term, 'well-balanced' anyway: in other words, the fact that they were good mixers with whites facilitated their entry and continuance in sport. Leroy Atz, a Continental footballer, gained four 'O' levels from a school in which he 'got on all right'. He has held a simple philosophy since his schooldays: 'I'll listen to any man. I'll entertain anybody's ideas without necessarily agreeing with them. I've always had many black friends and many white friends in school, in football and out of football.'

Newtown Warriors' striker Ricardo Watson echoed this point:

> I get along with everybody. I've got so many friends, not just
> black guys, but whites and Asians too. I can go anywhere in Aston
> and people will say 'Hi, Rick!' If you talk about blacks and whites,
> to tell you the truth, I prefer to play with a mostly white team.

These are the type of kids likely to view sport in the Leroy White perspective: in other words the type of kids who mixed freely with whites prior to their involvement in sport (both Atz and Watson began seriously in sport within two years of leaving school). Another side of the story is presented by Guyana-born boxer Brian Johnson, who identified with blacks while admitting at the same time that there is no overt racialism in the gym: 'But that doesn't mean it's disappeared. It happens at school and it happens in the street – just looking around tells you that being black makes it tougher for you.'

Sport may provide clues and pointers about what can be achieved in spite of being black; that blackness is not necessarily a basis for failure in all spheres. But it would be rash to suggest that black kids seriously balance off their experiences in sport against the experiences they go through outside the walls of the gym or on the other side of the touchline.

Having considered and retained a degree of dubiety about the previous two interpretations of the potentially positive impact of sport on conventional education, I want, finally, to consider the pressures from within the school or institution of higher education which might contribute to the sportsman's doing well at school subjects. Many sportsmen are cognisant of their academic successes being contingent on their sports progress whilst at school. Mickey Morris's belief that, 'I was only acknowledged for my sporting ability' was reinforced when a PE master asked him to go to a football match when he was otherwise engaged in geography tuition.

His refusal to cooperate met with a not-so-subtle threat from the master: 'He said that I'd let the school down and it would go down badly in my report.'

Herol Graham had almost exactly the same encounter with a school teacher: 'If we didn't do the sport, he'd give us a bad report.' Now, I chose these two examples because Morris did only modestly well at his London school, picking up only one CSE Grade 1 before continuing what was to become a successful academic and occupational career in the Civil Service. He grew to resent being used and refused to cooperate. Graham, on the other hand, kept up his sporting interests at his school in Nottingham and gained five 'O' levels and 'a few other moderate grade CSEs'. Without reading too much into these cases, it seems that preferential treatment may be metered out to pupils willing to devote their time and efforts to the pursuance of sports goals.

In their American study, Schafer and Armer speculated: 'Perhaps athletes are graded more leniently, because teachers see them as special or deserving' (1968, p.25). Lenient grading would not ultimately reflect in good examination results, but favourable attitudes from teachers leading to encouragement and support in all spheres of academic life may. No teacher I contacted would acknowledge this, of course, but it might be worthwhile considering whether teachers may be a factor in lifting up the sporting student's examination levels. They are certainly responsible for urging black kids into sport and, in many cases, are the spurs behind significant careers in sport; it seems that they may also operate to improve the sportsman's life chances generally – providing the pupil is prepared to stick with his sporting endeavours.

Another way in which sport might uplift the youth's educational performance is by exerting a 'holding' influence: at school-leaving age, the student may realize that being jettisoned into the occupational world will mean a severe limitation on time normally spent training or competing, and so opt for continuing his education; as such an option necessitates qualifications, he might work more energetically at achieving these, not so much because he believes in the value of them so much as he sees in them passports to the furtherance of his sporting career. Both Des Deans and Lincoln Asquith admitted that, when faced with the prospect of leaving school in 1980, they chose to work towards reasonable examination results in the expectation that they would be able to carry on in a school life which afforded them ample time for training. (Deans got five 'O' levels, Asquith three.) Such cases are common to both black and white athletes.

Lastly the student may be given preferential treatment in academic realms because of the kudos he achieves in areas distinct from regular school work. Meanwhile the student regards sport as the vehicle through which he can pursue goals which may have no direct bearing on his academic work. Contradictory tendencies perhaps; but both may lead to achievements academically.

I have expressed my reservations about the way in which experiences in sport might translate into higher expectations and achievements in school. The idea that a broadening awareness of the way in which healthy relations with whites can facilitate progress in the world outside the sports arena was seen to be fraught with special problems, not the least of which was that the more conforming, ambitious, 'well-balanced' youths maybe more inclined towards sport in the first place: they would not so much learn about harmonious race relations in sport as have their ideas confirmed. Those kids who were not so 'well-balanced' and had not entertained such good relations with whites or who identified strongly with blacks – or both – were less likely to extract much apart from sporting expertise and fitness from their endeavours.

The other element, however, is more stimulating, the idea that achievements in sport can spill-over into the rest of life bristles with prospects. If a black kid who is, for the most part, depressed in his expectations about what he can achieve from life can enter sport and start to glimpse himself as a winner, he can gear up his ambitions generally. He is also attuned to hard work, discipline and the persistence necessary in sports, qualities of value in education.

The contrary effect is also possible: the ambitious orientation may not spill-over, but siphon off all ambitions elsewhere. Sport may become a total preoccupation; winning in sport may become an obsession distracting attention away from academic pursuits. My own view is that this 'siphon' effect is less prevalent than the spill-over effect. Sport, I contend, is an uplifting, exhilarating experience which can do much to enhance the self-esteem and provide the participant with a positive image of himself; and these are important qualities in any sphere of life, in sport, education, and anywhere else. There are, of course, many losers in sport, but even those are usually exposed to success at some level, either in minor local league athletics, Sunday league football or inconsequential boxing tournaments; everybody in sport is capable of winning something and that I take to be vitally important to the spill-over effect.

Sport can work as a sharpened instrument that cuts like a tool, making patterns to be employed beneficially elsewhere, rather than a weapon that incises destructively. Whatever the dubious reasons for getting involved, the immersion into and experiences wrought out of sporting involvement can have a positive effect on the youth's view of himself and therefore, on his efforts elsewhere. Such a dovetailing is not meant to disguise the structured social inequalities reflected in school, inequalities which give rise to the social phenomenon of the modern black sportsmen. It does, however, point up some of the possibilities offered by sport for evolving attitudes and postures conducive to higher aspirations. Whether the black youth is able to translate these into actual achievement is, of course contingent on social circumstances and, overwhelmingly, such circumstances seem to militate against progress. The majority of black sportsmen are drawn from the ranks of the working class and their opportunities are not wide. Hence, to many of them, sport is a method of creating more opportunities which may eventually lead to escapes from what they regard as rather one-dimensional lives. In effect, they see sport as a priority in their lives.

Daley Thompson. Photograph courtesy of the *Birmingham Evening Mail*

DALEY THOMPSON
not black

Born London, 1959; father: Nigeria (deceased, was a cab-driver);
Mother: Scotland; occupation: full-time athlete.

'I don't know what you want to talk to me for,' said Daley Thompson on our first meeting, 'I'm not black.' Though he was not
resistant to cooperating with my research, he was puzzled by my
interest in him, as he clearly did not regard himself as a black
sportsman and, indeed was rather derisory in his remarks about a
great many black athletes who used their blackness as a point of
identification: 'They're just immature; they'll have to come to grips
sooner or later with the fact that you can't go through life thinking
about your colour.' His opinions served to alienate him from other
black athletes and he was – and is – disliked by many blacks. (On
one occasion, I stood with a group of black athletes as Thompson
walked by; one of them announced mockingly: 'Hey, look at me!
I'm standing on the spot where Daley Thompson's arse just passed!')

His parents were divorced when he was aged 7 and he was moved
from Lambeth to a private ILEA school in Haywards Heath. It was
here that he received a degree of insulation from the kinds of
experiences encountered by most black kids and so failed to develop
a consciousness of being different.

> Even though all the other kids at school were white, I never sensed
> I was different at all. I never ever thought about my skin colour. I
> suppose I was protected from many kinds of the pressures on
> black kids because of my schooling. Having mixed parents
> probably had a lot to do with it as well, even though I never had a
> lot of contact with either of them.

He cultivated sporting ambitions some time before leaving school,
though his aspirations had no adverse effect on his studies; he gained

nine 'O' levels and two 'A's. Essex Beagles was his local club and he joined it.

I never thought about any other career except one in sport. All I ever wanted to do was sport. At first it was soccer and then athletics. Never anything else. I had a trial for Fulham but I think I would have done better in an old-style team where you can express your individualism. Nowadays, they work with defensive units and I'm more of my own man; I don't work too well in teams.

My teachers were all right about my sport; they left me alone and left me to do what I wanted to do, which suited me. They never bothered me in regard to sport or academically. I knew that, if I did the work, they couldn't say anything to me, so I did the minimum. After I left there, I went to Crawley Technical College for a year to do some 'A' levels and an HND. But I didn't do any work; I wasn't interested in it; I used it as a vehicle. I'd decided I wanted to do sport and going to college gave me time to train. Later I got a sponsor, but even if I hadn't, I'd have still carried on with my athletics.

I had no influences on my career: no idols or friends who were in athletics and I didn't see my coach that much. I just worked at it myself. I feel no obligation to anyone at all. It's not as if I'm in a sport where I have to sell tickets. I don't depend on people. They never used to come to see me when I was doing decathlons earlier – I used to get about ten people come to watch me!

Those ten increased to several millions in 1979 when, as British representative in the Commonwealth Games, he took the gold medal and with it the adulation of all television viewers. After the success at Edmonton, he was offered training facilities at San Diego State University where he spent three months in 1979 and four in 1980, the year in which he briefly held the world decathlon record and won the Moscow Olympic gold medal. Returning to England after his success, he resumed his austere, isolatory training programme, splitting the decathlon disciplines into two sets of five and practising each set on alternate days. But his extreme isolation did not prevent his speculating on the causes of black kids' problems:

I reckon they stem mainly from the family background. The families give the kids unrealistic ideas about the world, about it being different for them if they're black. They'd be better off ignoring it. I'm not unsympathetic about black kids; it's just that you can't resign yourself, you've got to confront things.

When asked how he would react to a situation in which he and a white youth, who also had two 'A' levels, both went for an interview and the white guy got the job, he answered, 'Then I'd go away, think out why and then come back again.' And if it happened three more times? 'Then I'd go out, get a degree and then go back to the job which required two "A" levels!' Such is Thompson's determination to succeed regardless of what odds are stacked against him. He refused to let the fact of his blackness retard his progress and his tactic was simply to refuse to recognize it.

When the first blacks came over here, they didn't expect to have hard lives in this society. But they did. And so they grew ideas about being black and they've passed these on to their kids. So they've got these ideas too. They don't want to take a positive attitude towards society and try to achieve. I do.

Thompson is an unusual case in many but not all senses. Like many black sportsmen, he established sport as his main – in his case, sole – priority at about 17 and oriented himself towards sporting goals. In every way, he was an almost obsessive achiever. Though he refused to identify, associate or even sympathize with blacks, his continual rejection of blackness belied the way in which he forced it to the rear of his consciousness in an effort to remove it as an excuse for failure – which, he felt, is how it was used by a great many black kids. He knew he was black but realized failure was more easily assimilable with that knowledge. Failure to him was unacceptable on any terms.

Chapter Eight

CHANGING PRIORITIES from work

Sport – Amusement, diversion, fun.

The Concise Oxford Dictionary

As a career, the only thing I'm really good at is triple jumping and so I'm channelling all my energies into it. I've been athletically-minded since I was about 9 years old and, even though I've just finished my apprenticeship [at British Leyland], I'd have to be honest and say that I'd give it up to concentrate on athletics if I could get a sponsor or something.

Eric McCalla, athlete

The way out

There is a time in the morning of the black youth's sporting career, somewhere between leaving school and winning a relatively significant – to him, at least – event, when he begins to see his future as structured around sport. Like a butterfly breaking from a chrysalis, the youth discards his work role and sets himself loose to discover his real prowess as a sportsman. No longer does he struggle with the constricting contradictions of having to subdue his fanciful interests in sport because of the more earthly possibilities offered by the world of work. He sees the limitless horizons of sport, a realm in which expression is encouraged and is, indeed, necessary. It beckons; he responds.

Sport assumes primacy as the source of ambition: thoughts of the future turn about winning, then winning again. His own qualities are viewed in the light of sporting assets. Quickness of movement and thought, dexterity, power he recognizes and wants to capitalize on. His character he sees as composed of such elements as determination, persistence and courage.

Maybe the flight into sport will be episodic. The reinterpretation of his biography might lead only to struggle and successive failures, compounded by injury or the non-materialization of promise. These combine to force the youth to return to more mundane levels. Sports careers are frequently long on promise but short on delivery and initial successes may have little lasting effect. They may constitute brief holidays, but coming home is inevitable and may be more imminent than at first thought, as in the case of Leroy Brown, who had his at first unshakable sporting ambitions demolished after a desultory series of defeats. He resigned himself to his work as a carpenter in the same way as many would-be superstars resign themselves to careers as electricians, postmen or shop salesmen.

Conversely, the excursion might be extended; new possibilities not entertained before might reveal themselves. Winning declines in importance for some sportsmen and the involvement itself becomes the adhesive. After a moderately successful amateur boxing spell in which he gained Young England representative honours, Rupert Christie turned professional and had what those in the fight game euphemistically call 'mixed fortunes'. Yet he never doubted his priority: 'I'm a boxer and this is what I am. My life is boxing. The missus goes mad at all the time I spend in the gym and that, but she's realized now how much it means to me; it's more or less my whole life.'

For Christie, his work had lost significance just after leaving school with three CSEs in 1973. As his affiliation with the sport and its practitioners intensified, he came to find boxing less a diversion, more a preoccupation. 'To me, boxing comes first; before anything.' Sandwiching nine hours as a carpenter between 4 miles roadwork at 5.30 a.m. and a gym session at 5.00 p.m. and carefully controlling the intake of food so as not to exceed the 175 lbs light-heavyweight limit were not even inconveniences to Christie: he was a boxer and boxers do such things.

Some sportsmen are less committed, but the nature of boxing itself dictates that anyone entering the ring, whether for sparring or competition, must be honed mentally and physically. Bluntness of reflex in such a brutal sport is manifestly dangerous. Athletes and footballers too, if they are serious about their sports, need to acquire dedication and commitments which often result in abstemious existences. And, as the youth pours more into sport, he takes more out, not simply in terms of trophies and medals, but in terms of pointers to what he considers his true vocation.

The gym or the sportsfield is the place where the sportsmen go not to earn their livings, to sell their labour for the best return they can get, but to develop personalized relationships with others who have similar outlooks, to rub shoulders with seniors who have risen to a level of sporting excellence and command respect because of it and, generally, to find support and gratification. Thus the nature of the relationships with other sportsmen and coaches is a feature of no little importance as they see it. The extent to which the kids form close interpersonal ties at work is very limited indeed; close friends at work are something of a rarity and, in some cases, hostility is cited. Newtown forward Ricardo Watson left his work with the GPO because he was uneasy in the racialist atmosphere which he felt permeated his department. (Not a single black sportsmen I contacted claimed a 'close friend' amongst his workmates; experiences and relationships in the workplace were not valued highly.)

In contrast, sport generates new bonds: friendships formed at the gym seem to lead on to friendships outside. Sometimes friends cultivate compatible sporting interests which lead them to the same club. On the other hand, they might not see each other from one session to the next, and their out-of-sport interests may not be even remotely similar, but, in sport, their views matter.

Quite obviously, there is nothing magical about sport which makes its participants give themselves over, possibly to the detriment of their work. Indeed, it is a recent phenomenon that sport is seen at all as a career, a vocation rather than a trivial pastime, a purely leisurely activity. The professionalization of sport has meant that people can possibly earn a living out of sport, but the chances of actually making sport the yielder of 'bread and butter' are extremely small. There is no noticeable lack of awareness of this among black youths; they know the opportunities of getting into sport in any meaningful way are limited and the chances of being successful are about as remote as winning the football pools. Yet, this does not serve as a deterrent, only as a reminder.

Undeterred by the narrow gaps they see ahead, black kids plough their energies into sport, strive for perfection in their chosen sphere and continue to aspire to greatness. At 16, only months after leaving school, Godfrey Amoo asserted he was on his way to his first million – earned through boxing, as his DHSS job certainly would not pay that much! Amoo did not see himself as a clerical worker for the rest of his life: 'I want to make some progress and get promotion, but I'm *going* to succeed as a boxer.'

So, what is it about sport that attracts black youths' interests on such a scale and with such intensity, captures their imaginations and monopolizes their career ambitions? The question has been partially answered by the finding that black kids see sport as one of the few unblocked roads to success in an otherwise congested maze of occupational culs-de-sac. As a consequence, they apprehend sport as a way out, a passage from the limited, menial existences which they anticipate (particularly in view of their parents' lowly occupations which they might use as guidelines). In the perspective of the black youth, sport looks a good bet. So he gambles and puts a sizeable portion, if not all, of his chips on sport. It invites, but offers nothing special unless the very highest strata are approached: a few tawdry trophies, worthless medals, maybe a mention in *Athletics Weekly*, on the surface, there is little to be gained.

Whereas many kids enter sport on a casual basis, preferring to see it as a leisure pursuit or a hobby, a pleasant and intrinsically rewarding alternative to work, blacks see things the other way round. As Aston Moore, employed as an arc metalworker, put it: 'Work is nothing to me. Triple jumping is everything.' To suggest to a black sportsman that his football or athletics is a hobby is often tantamount to insulting him: 'You try slogging it out five nights and one morning a week, fifty-two weeks a year and see if you think it's a hobby.' The term seems very shallow when applied to boxer Robbie Smith, living in Morden but working in central London; the distance meant he had to rise every morning at 6.00 a.m. and travel directly from his job to his gym after work, so limiting his opportunities for road work. After two successive losses, he reflected that his lack of running had left him wanting in stamina over later phases of contests, so he resolved to get up an hour earlier. 'But that will mean getting up at 5.00 a.m.,' I reminded him, to which he replied: 'If that's what it takes, it has to be done.'

Clearly, sport has a meaning for black kids which it does not have for whites: they feel the need to develop it into a career much more urgently. Leslie Stewart, at 20, varnished wood for a living; he left school with CSEs in metalwork, woodwork and art – 'they weren't much use to me.' Just after leaving school in London, some friends introduced him to the Repton Club and his horizons expanded: 'Boxing I saw as a way of doing something different with my life, which, apart from boxing, is everyday, you know, ordinary.' His immersion in sport brought him to see the constructive components: 'I can make something of myself through boxing; it's if you like, my way out of everyday life, a way of distinguishing myself.'

When a hobby is a way out of everyday life, when a leisure activity is a way of distinguishing oneself, there must be something happening in relation to sport which compels attention. To understand why sport becomes the source of aspirations, ambitions for the future, gaze must be diverted away from the gym, the track or the playing field and towards those dominating areas of everyday life, the family, the school and the workplace, for it is the experience of home, school and work which moulds the commitment to sport and influences what it is to be expected from it. It seems reasonable to suppose that, if one spends all day stacking bottles in a pop factory with no immediate, or even long-term promotion prospects, little apart from tea and lunch breaks to interrupt the dulling monotony and only the incentive of 'all the lemonade you can drink' to spur you through the eight and a half hours, then a couple of low key sprint victories will be more than mildly stimulating.

The example is not mine but that of a 16-year-old sprinter from Birchfield Harriers, a youth who, frankly, was a little slow in learning skills and only moderately faster on the tartan. The effect that an unexpected 200 metre win at a West Midlands junior league meeting had on him was revelatory. Almost immediately, he began to envision a future as a track competitor, he found in himself an ability to 'dig in' as never before, he equipped himself with new spikes and track gear and his whole approach became suffused with confidence. When faced with the alternatives of sportsman or bottle stacker, his choice was clear-cut – as mine would be. Watching this young man wander disconsolately from the Alexander Stadium after a training session, prepared for only a night's sleep before another several hundred bottles, I was forced to reckon with the potency of sport as a restorer of purpose and resolve; in a none too perfect world, sport compensates somehow for the realization that the working life is often empty and meaningless, devoid of principle and full of arbitrary rules.

The view was put forward stridently by Mitch Daley, who, in the

late 1950s, travelled from Guyana to London where he started the
Continental Football Club, which he managed:

> The reason for the magnetism of sport is that kids here have a
> chance to show themselves as individuals; it's self-expression.
> They don't get this in their everyday lives and they don't get it at
> school. There, they're made to conform, work to rules.

Well, of course, anyone familiar with sports realizes that serious
involvement implicates one in a whole new set of rules. Sports
competitions are bound by rules and training regimes sticking to
often tedious schedules. Success is contingent on effectively organizing one's life around rules of one kind or another. And, if the rules
are not laid down, then the sportsman has to invent his own. No one
sanctioned Rupert Christie if he did not get up for his 5.30 a.m. run;
he lost pay if he was late for work. He voluntarily surrendered
himself to the rules of boxing.

Andrew Jarrett found his school unacceptable: 'I don't like it. I
don't like being told what to do or being bossed around by people.'
Yet he did not object to being subjected to training schedules by his
coach at Birchfield. His case is revealing because, at only 15, he had
set his sights on a sports career, but was not seriously concerned
about regular employment: 'I suppose I might become an electrician
like my brother . . . I'm going to be a top javelin thrower, definitely.'

Rules in themselves are not despised by black youths; indeed,
many sportsmen submit themselves to regimes of rules imposed by
coaches, trainers, managers and even senior sportsmen. They are
certainly not devalued for the overwhelming majority of sportsmen
believe that adherence to some sort of disciplined schedule is a *sine
qua non* of eventual achievement. It is not the imposition of rules at
school which black kids find objectionable, for they organize their
sporting lives around rule-hemmed programmes. It is the purpose
and meaning behind such rules to which they react. The worth of
school work is brought into serious question, especially as the stories
filtering down from peers and older brothers and sisters do not
depict the world of work favourably and the examples of parents are
not inspiring.

Few black youths find school an intrinsically worthwhile experience. Often it is quite debilitating: it loses its point somewhat when
cast against a background of prospective unemployment. Why get

the qualifications in the first place? Compounding this perception of pointlessness is the limited scope black kids feel that school offers them when it comes to creative self-expression. Daley's assertion that sport gives them 'a chance to show themselves as individuals' has relevance here because school and work are thought to deny such chances. One consequence of this is that sport assumes the main priority: it becomes the focus for ambitions; it becomes the central interest in life and displaces other concerns.

Obviously, early success might lend a hand here. The seeming invincibility of Lincoln Asquith in his late teens almost certainly had a mighty bearing on his adoption of athletics as his priority even while still at school in Handsworth Wood. Reflecting on his father's work, he said: 'I'm not sure what he does for a living but I know it involves lifting.' He had two older brothers; 'One of them has just come out of the army. He can't stand it . . . the other's got a factory job, I think.' Having joined Birchfield in 1979, he accumulated AAA Youth titles in 100 and 200 metres and assessed his future thus:

> Well, my education has suffered already because of all the time I put into sport. There's been a clash when it comes to exams. I wouldn't say sport dominates my life, but it is the most important thing at the moment and it could get even more important.

He found his school life dull and unchallenging; but what lay ahead of him was not attractive either. His perception of the unsatisfactory working lives of his father and brothers, added to stories from his peers, gave him an insight into what work might be like. Life in sport for him, on the other hand, had been punctuated with honours at the highest levels; he made his choice.

Asquith is, in my opinion, one of the two outstanding teenagers who are poised to become forces in British athletics in the 1980s. The other is Enfield's Hugh Teape who, though also at school, has fairly clear career ambitions: 'I'm working towards the decathlon eventually. It takes a lot of training, time and hard work, but I think I can be the next big one after Thompson.' In fact, Daley Thompson himself is another sportsman who had his aims fixed obdurately whilst at school: 'I only ever wanted to be a sportsman. Sport is all I ever wanted to do. . . . Never anything else for as long back as I can remember.'

Of course, many kids at school go through phases when they entertain sports ambitions. Very few have the equipment physically or the perseverance to follow through. Black kids seem to be more intent on realizing their ambitions at this early stage, especially would-be footballers like Carlos Francis who combated his parents' discouragement: 'I was single-minded; I knew there was only one thing I wanted to do with my career before I left school' (he went to Orient and Chelsea before signing professionally for Birmingham City in 1980). Or Garth Crooks who, at 14 and playing representatively for Stoke schoolboys, came to a realization about his career: 'Football was the only way. I was determined to do well. I had the confidence. I knew one day I'd make it. I was too involved in football, too single-minded to think of anything else.'

None of these had ever been to work before fashioning their orientations about sport. All were imbued with the same sense of destiny allied to purposeful ambition which enabled them to perform well enough to make it as sportsmen. Perhaps Mitch Daley was right when he pointed to the school's lack of facilities when it comes to creative self-expression. (I will have something to say about this in the final chapter.) Having been exposed to the alternative of sport and, at least in the above cases, found success, they opted for channelling their efforts into sport, they became 'single-minded'.

Quite obviously, Thompson and the others were exceptional in that they eventually made it on a scale most other schoolkids only dream of. But they were unexceptional in the respect that a great many other black kids bump up their sporting aspirations after or during a meaningless school life. They do so because they anticipate the dreariness of a future at work.

Working lives

Given the types of work most sportsmen – apart from the fully professional – are engaged in, it does give cause for astonishment to realize that many regard sport as their main priority. Most are employed in skilled, semi-skilled or unskilled manual occupations or sometimes clerical jobs. For example, Cyrille Regis was an apprentice electrician and qualified with a City and Guilds certificate only weeks before he signed professionally for West Bromwich Albion; Courtney Smile worked behind a post office counter in Handsworth but travelled 15 miles to the Wolverhampton and Bilston Athletic Club immediately after work four times a week; Prince Rodney Noel worked as a labourer on a building site in Halifax during the day before drifting into the world of pro boxing every evening. Labouring would seem to be the perfect foil for a sporting orientation: heaving bricks around, pushing barrows and humping cement bags might be viewed as an extension of training. But it is limited in its scope for self-expression; it is not the place, in Leslie Stewart's words, to distinguish yourself. Sport apparently is.

Nor do the more skilled occupations provide such facilities; for the most part, they are elements of the 'ordinary life' sportsmen seek to get away from. Even the higher grade occupations afford only slightly better opportunities for the worker to express himself totally. Despite being part of a bank management training programme, entry to which required a minimum of two 'A' levels (which he had), goalkeeper George Bates was, in his words, 'attracted to sport 'cause it's such a contrast to boring, flat, everyday life.'

Bates, who both played himself and managed another soccer team, generalized his feelings to those other black youths of his age (22) and younger: 'A lot of these guys work in jobs or are unemployed and sport is exciting, competitive. That's why they got into it.' The view was endorsed by Peter 'Danny' Lawrence, who, at 24, was a qualified electrical engineering estimator with a firm career orientation and had the responsibilities of a wife, three children and a mortgage to enforce this. A broken ankle just after leaving school effectively quashed what he thought might have been a football career – he was approached by Alvechurch FC – but he continued his involvement, devoutly creating and masterminding with two others an all-black football club.

Even those who find their work a source of aspiration and gratification reveal a need to allocate some portion of their lives – and often a considerable portion – to sport. Work to these people is not monotonous, boring or fragmented but absorbs their interests and energies. Yet that urgent need to get involved deeply in sport still manifests itself. The sense of this I take to lie in the simple observation that it is not so much the nature of the work itself which influences the proclivity of the worker to seek alternative forms of self-expression, but the way in which the work is experienced. What is evident about the way in which black sportsmen experience their work, whether unskilled manual or 'white collar', is the generally low level of satisfaction they derive directly from their work tasks and roles. Only the minority, like Bates and Lawrence, find the work they are involved in rewarding, while, for the most part, sportsmen find their work a necessary evil: 'boring', 'not interesting', 'a doss' are typical descriptions of work.

Factory work, with the physiological and psychological rigours normally associated with process work, accounts for the severest forms of felt deprivation. Working at Dunlop, for instance, could be stultifying, as footballer Emerd Penley attested to: 'It's the same thing over and over again and you lose the point of it. I've got no interest in it: this [football] is my main thing.'

Physical demands made by work are not a problem, but repetition is, as Repton boxer Jimmy Dublin, a slinger in a wood yard, evidenced: 'I've held the job for over three years, now, so I'm used to it. I'd been a storeman before that, but was no good. This is all right; it's just that it's got no variety.' Asked if boxing was at the centre of his interests, he answered: 'Oh yes. This is the way for me. It's not an easy way out, but you can do it through sport. It's hard, but it's worth it.'

Birmingham's Tony Campbell took up boxing 'out of boredom' with his job as a postman. Aston Moore gave up athletics for twelve months, only to return after 'an empty year' metalworking. There is most definitely a repulsion factor at work; sport offers a contrasting compensation. Towards their everyday jobs they have an instrumental orientation – the majority of sportsmen are tied to their jobs by the wage packet – but sport has an intrinsic fascination.

The types of work engaged in by black sportsmen clearly limit the opportunities for the exercise of judgment, initiative and, in most cases, skill. With supervised work, such as in industry, the display of individuality is tightly restricted; and even where there is little supervision, the work is likely to be subject to a routine. Ricardo Watson's work in a GPO sorting office was done under the auspices of a senior; Tony Campbell also worked for the GPO but, even though unsupervised, delivering letters was highly routinized. Both were outstanding individualists in their respective sports, Watson as a striker for Newtown, Campbell as a stylish welterweight for Birmingham. They went into sport where their activities would contrast sharply with what they did in their everyday lives.

Neither this pair nor any of the other black sportsmen dislike their work; it is simply that work does not command their attention; they are not interested in work except as a way of earning money. Their efforts are motivated by the extrinsic reward of payment. And somewhere in the future lies the realm in which they will dispense with their work about which they are avowedly indifferent and make ends meet by putting their sporting expertise on display.

The paradox is, of course, that a good 80–90 per cent of the time devoted to preparation in sport is composed of strictly supervised, rigidly scheduled and often cripplingly routinized training. But, for ninety minutes, three three-minute rounds, or even ten and a half blistering seconds, they set themselves free and become self-expressive sportsmen, unshackled by the restricting exigencies of work. These short moments are effectively the pay-off and, for these, sportsmen are prepared and willing to withstand arduous hours of exhausting training. Tedious, sometimes mechanical, occasionally frustrating experiences at work are relegated to the margins of concern.

My suggestion here is that sport provides the possibility and, for black kids, the probability of compensating for inherently unsatisfying work by supplying: (1) an area in which the building-up of rewarding relationships with other sportsmen and coaches can be done on a regular basis; and (2) a perceived outlet for self-expression where the restrictions and limitations of everyday life do not apply. In consequence, most black youths involved in sport adopt a view of their employment as a means to an end – money. Work is the realm of the necessary and is fairly sharply set apart from the realm of relative freedom in which the satisfaction of needs of an expressive and affective kind can be properly pursued, even if in a highly disciplined way.

Even the anticipation of what work might offer in comparison to sport can register, as it did with Steve Medstone, a half-miler who left school with five GCE 'O' levels and, at 20, was near completing a TEC diploma which might have gained him access to university:

> I'm bored with it, now and I can't really face the possibility of doing this all my life. It affects my running. . . . If I was pressed for a choice and could only do one of them, the work would have to go. My running is my main thing. That's where I see my real ability. But I suppose we all have to work.

The changing priorities in which sport displaces everything and becomes the central interest in life are usually, but not always, formulated sometime after leaving school when the reality of work is discovered. The greyness of the working day becomes a backcloth against which to set the colour of sport. The possibility of elevating oneself from fellow workers, of seeing one's name in the newspapers, of exhibiting the spoils of competition become incentives. Sport has a rich supply of imagery to stimulate aspirations.

Despite the wide variety of work engaged in by black sportsmen, all show a consistency in their priorities: sport, one; work, somewhere down the order. Whether working as carpenters, welders or clerks, in jobs offering no promotion prospects or genuine career possibilities, black sportsmen, to a great degree, rate their sport as the priority. Given the range of work and working environments, it seems that the decisive factor at work is not so much the work itself, but how the youths define their own working situations, the particular wants and expectations they have in regard to their employment. And, crucially, how they compare these with the requirements and apprehensions they have of sport.

Of course, white working-class kids have such perceptions too, but even those seriously into sport are cautious about allowing their sport to assume primacy in their lives. Either their parents deflate their more exotic ambitions or they learn to adjust. Adjusting is more difficult for the black youth, if only because he sees his colour militating against his progress in work spheres.

Not that sport is given priority status by all black youths in sport: for most, I argue, it does, but there are exceptions. Mickey Morris, for example, at 22, agonized over the problem of pursuing his sporting commitment or his career, but refused to let his sprinting 'overwhelm' his career: 'My dedication is split. I just look at them as two separate areas. I've got to have a good job and be good at running. I want the best of both worlds if I can have it.' Derek Anderson, while studying for his Masters degree, held similarly divided dedications and claimed he competed in decathlons 'just for a laugh, nowadays'.

As he approached his late twenties, Repton's Frank Edwards found his ambitions in boxing fading and his work as an electrical components salesman taking on increased importance: 'I decided to stay with the amateurs and make my ambition to win a major championship, preferably the ABAs. But, I've got a reasonably well-paid job and I can take care of my family' (wife and daughter).

It is a measure of the attraction of sport, however, that these are exceptional cases of 'splits'. The vast majority of blacks in sport see their main priority as winning medals, trophies and money from their sport. School or work is, as I have called it, a backcloth against which to set such ambitions and sport is set sharply in relief; it has a clarity and definition lacking in school and work.

Orientations to school and occupations range from negative to neutral; in them black youths find little meaning or purpose. Only occasionally, when a job with career prospects is secured – as in the case of Morris or Edwards – does work take an equal split. For most black kids, 'everyday life' is a means to an end, while sport is a means to something infinitely richer and more satisfying.

The worlds of school and work tend to lose relevance for the black sportsman: they are seen as restrictive and tightly bounded to the point where they limit his opportunities for self-expression, for creativity. All this is not to romanticize sport, for it is fraught with stifling rules and tedious routines carried out to the point of exhaustion in frequently unpleasant conditions. There is precious little to attract on the surface, but that little is enough. Once beneath the surface of sport, the sportsman begins digging for something else.

What exactly sport offers, what the diggers expect to get and often do get from their sporting involvements, I will attempt to answer in the next chapter. For the negative reactions to work do not adequately account for the sustained interest in sport demonstrated by young blacks. They may account for the initial encounters, but sport must surely have something more deeply rewarding about it – even for those who never make it to a major championship – to maintain such a level of commitment. What do sportsmen dig out of sport in the course of their careers?

CYRILLE REGIS
the absorber

Born: French Guyana, 1958; father: French Guyana (labourer);
mother: French Guyana (seamstress); occupation: professional
footballer – formerly, electrician.

In February 1978 Cyrille Regis was an electrician working in London. In March he was a professional footballer playing in the West
Midlands. He is probably as deviant a case as one gets, in footballing
terms. At 19, he had no particular ambitions as a footballer: in his
words, 'I just enjoyed playing that's all.' Hayes, the Isthmian league
team for which he played on a semi-professional basis, were
approached by West Bromwich Albion and Regis found himself 120
miles north playing first division soccer. Scarcely had he completed
his City and Guilds examinations before he switched worlds. But,
within weeks, he became, with his team-mates Laurie Cunningham
and Viv Anderson, part of the vanguard of new black footballers.
'Black Power' and 'Black Magic' were newspaper phrases which
regularly headlined reports of his matches; but 'black bastard' was
the more familiar phrase from the terraces.

> You just have to learn to absorb those kind of things. Most black
> guys, if they get called a 'black bastard' or whatever, they'll get
> aggressive. But, personally, I've learned to absorb. I hear it from
> the terraces a lot, even now, but it's nothing new to me; I've been
> hearing it from my school days. The old man used to try to prepare
> us telling us about the hard times, always saying, 'get your
> education; I've never had any.' So he let us know how tough it
> could be being black.

As a unit, the family was broken for a period of one year.

> We went through a bad patch when I was about 9 or 10 when we
> couldn't get anywhere to live. My dad was over in Ladbroke
> Grove, my mother was in the East End with the Salvation Army,

Cyrille Regis. Photograph courtesy of the *Birmingham Evening Mail*

me and my little brother were in Aldershot, in a convent, and my sister was in Neasden.

He reckoned it did not affect his education.

Eventually, when I left school, I took seven CSEs; two grade 2s and the rest 3s and 4s. I wasn't heavily into soccer at the time: I just loved to play it. I wanted to do an apprenticeship really. I found a job as an electrician very easily and I still used to play football Saturdays and Sundays. The guys I'd played with at school, we started a team between us to play on Sundays. We'd played together for three or four years. Mr Marsden, one of our teachers, had organized us into a good team and we stayed together. Then, somebody watched me and said, 'would you like to play for Mossley in Surrey?' and I played for them for about a year. Then somebody else watched me and I went to Hayes for another three years.

I loved playing the game but there were big temptations. The guys I used to hang around with – they were mostly black – we tended to drift away from the white guys soon after leaving school, or it might have been just before; they were going pickpocketing, to parties, going to blues and staying out all hours. But I couldn't do that. I didn't feel I was missing out or anything 'cause I enjoyed playing. There were outside distractions, though, especially when I had to give up Tuesday and Thursday nights to go training in the freezing cold and Saturdays when I could have been earning more money working.

For the three years after leaving school, he divided his interests between his apprenticeship and football. People at his club circulated rumours about football league clubs' scouts attending the matches, but Regis tried to subdue his sports ambitions.

I thought that, at 19, I was a bit too old to make it as a professional so I was shocked a bit when Albion came along. I didn't have any doubts about the choice as I'd taken my City and Guilds and, anyway, my firm said I could have my old job back if I didn't make the grade in my first year. The old man just said: 'Cyrille, do whatever you want to do.' So, at the time I signed for Albion I was finishing my City and Guilds and that's all I wanted to do. I saw it as a gamble.

The gamble paid off quickly and within weeks of moving to West Bromwich, he was in the first team. So impressive was he that he retained his place in the WBA attack and graduated to the England 'B' team. Not that his presence was approved of by all West Bromwich fans: racialist chants were rife and peltings with bananas were regular.

> I think they were rebelling against me cause I'd taken a white guy's place in the team. On the field, I can only recall about two occasions when racial remarks were made. . . . At Tottenham, Chris Hughton and I were running for a ball and he's black as well, well I think he's got one black parent. Anyway, I heard somebody in the crowd shout 'you black bastard!' I thought I must be mistaken cause he's black too and they're supposed to be his supporters!

Despite reservations about some supporters, he had no hesitation about appearing in an all-black versus all-white testimonial in 1979. 'A great atmosphere,' he declared. Regis is not a flamboyant character though he is convinced of his own ability and says: 'I've never suffered from lack of confidence.' As one of the first important black footballers, however, he remained aware of his responsibilities.

> I like to set a good example on and off the field for all the young black kids. I've never been in trouble and I don't do the Muhammad Ali thing. My philosophy is to let my actions do the talking; I'm never big-headed.
>
> I know there's a lot of problems black kids have got and its easy for them to go off the straight and narrow. This is because of a combination of things: pushy parents, getting hassle at school 'cause you're black, not getting on with the teachers there – you think they always pick on you 'cause your black. A lot of it stems from what the parents tell their kids. The kids will go home and, the box is on and the old man is watching and will say something like 'get the black bastard'. The kids are bound to pick up what the parents say. I think prejudice is handed down; you get the feel of this even in primary school and so black kids and white kids drift in two different directions.

His career is atypical in so far as his priority up to the age of 19 was completing an apprenticeship. He had no hesitation in accepting WBA's offer, but the qualification he had gained afforded him a cushion, 'something to fall back on, if I failed.' Blackness was seen not as an obstacle by him but as 'a fact of life'. His early years after moving from French Guyana were spent in a variety of London boroughs and he acquired a sponge-like capacity to soak up remarks about his colour without responding vigorously – though he did add that his muscular barn-door frame might have dissuaded many from being too open in their comments!

Chapter Nine

MOMENTS OF REVELATION about identities

When I was about 14, I guess I decided I wanted to be a footballer and so I started to tell everybody I could, 'I'm going to be a footballer definitely.' But you know, deep down, I wasn't really convinced myself. I suppose I did it in a way to put pressure on myself, to get other people to respond. Anyway, people did start to take notice. My friends, scouts, trainers and the media – they all started saying, 'This kid's going to make it' and the rest of it. And I think eventually it got through to me: I began to think: 'They're right, I am going to' and before I knew where I was I was a pro footballer.

Justin Fashanu, footballer

The alternative solution

The attempt to account for why so many black kids fall under the spell of sport has led me to a situation in which the black youth is seen as approaching school-leaving age with pessimistic views on his possible progress in the occupational world, a pessimism wrung out of his perception of blackness as a retardation. At the same time, images of success register in the shape of black sportsmen and sportswomen and these together with the encouraging parts played by some school teachers help push the youth towards attempting a sporting career. Without exaggerating their feeling for sport, it is possible to say that many black kids come to regard sport as their central life interest and other pursuits are relegated to peripheral zones. Sport becomes a momentous force in their lives, superseding work and, sometimes, school in terms of aspirations and ambitions.

Superficially though, there is not a lot to sport except whipping one's body into a healthy physical condition, mastering techniques, learning when to use them and then bringing them to bear in competition. There is nothing so extraordinary about this; they are basic, primordial human behaviours – elaborated and refined maybe, but still primordial, basic, fundamental. Yet sport is often demandingly complex and intricately subtle even when played most belligerently; in this, it reflects some of the deep-rooted aspects of social man – a sense of challenge backed by resourcefulness and purpose. To view it as any less profound is to miss the point about black youths' sporting involvement; it is not because sport offers them scope to develop their physical capacities and skills; it is the conflation of challenge, resource and purpose which grips the collective imagination. Aston Moore expressed it this way:

> It's about your mind more than your body. Obviously, the physical thing is important, but not so much as the mental. Every time you train or compete, you have to work with your head, setting new challenges for yourself and pushing yourself towards them. The body might not feel like it and so you have to work mentally, pushing yourself towards the target, ignoring the body.

The insight is similar to that of Fidelius Obukw whose parents returned to their native Nigeria, leaving him in London at the age of 16. He reckoned 'crack-up point' had to be approached in order to release full potential: 'The problem is reaching it and conquering it . . . you must stretch yourself mentally to be able to master yourself physically.' He believed: 'You discover yourself through your sport. When you're training, competing, especially in the decathlon (his event) where you're in isolation a lot of the time. You get near yourself and find out about yourself.'

With Moore, he agreed that, 'it's not only physical, but mental too', and gave the example that, on occasion, his body had felt that it could not withstand any more pressure: 'That's not a physical thing, it's to do with attitude . . . you really get to know yourself as a total person through sport.'

Sport becomes a process of excavating fibres of the self buried beneath the surface, digging through the outer layers and finding the 'total person'. To participate in sports means to struggle, often bitterly, to find one's limits. It may involve sacrifice, compromise, commitment, at times, boredom, but there is a willingness to pay the price because the rewards are not just medals and trophies, they are a knowledge of one's self and possibly, according to James Michener, even more: 'Sometimes in the process of a game, a man or woman will experience a moment of revelation about either himself or his opponent, or even about the nature of life' (1976, p.445).

Light-heavyweight boxer Leslie Stewart put it similarly: 'It's a way I can really find myself. I think you can find yourself, your true self through boxing, and that's exactly what I'm doing.' The distinct theme here is the way in which sportsmen express the need to search for and find their true selves, their identities, through sustained involvement in their particular discipline. Identity, the image we have of ourselves, our perception of essential characteristics, is inevitably linked to role and if the youth sees his role as a sportsman as the dominant one in his life, his image of himself is bound to reflect this. Given, as I pointed out in the previous chapter, that black sportsmen usually locate their central life interest in sport, it is not surprising that they also believe their true identities lie in that realm; therein lies the challenge to find themselves.

When asked his reasons for immersing himself in sport, pro middleweight Hugh Johnson answered in a definitive way: 'Because I am a sportsman, that's all.' He identified himself essentially as a sportsman; his involvement was a process of defining himself in a specific way and acting on that definition. Losing his job as an engineer in 1980 meant less to him than wrenching an arm muscle during a bout in the same year.

Sport is a source of identity, a medium through which the youth can establish a definition of himself, a definition which is seen as positive both in his own eyes and those of his peers. While sport means different things to different groups, it certainly constitutes a generator of self-concepts to black kids and, though it can offer no guarantees, the uncertainties of the alternatives make it an attractive proposition.

The reasons why black kids need to generate positive identities have to a degree been implicit in the preceding chapters. But to understand fully, one has to turn black sportsmen back into the community from which they came. They have to be seen as part of the generation of working-class blacks which became such a problematic phenomenon in the 1970s and 1980s.

Basically, the drastic difference in the life experiences of first and second generation Caribbeans in the UK lies at the heart of the dislocation which left black kids restless, invariably aimless and often penniless. To offer a simplified scenario: the first wave of blacks came amid a period of relative prosperity in the 1950s, leaving behind the despair and struggle of post-war West Indies. They were content to settle for what were often menial, lowly-paid and unpleasant jobs simply because they compared favourably with what they had left behind. Racialism was something they may not have expected and it made life unpleasant, but material factors outweighed other considerations and they came to accept their positions passively, opting for low profiles and, generally, showing no collective sense of disapproval with their conditions.

The second generation had no recourse to the kinds of comparisons their parents could make: the UK was their world. Even those born elsewhere would have had some education in England. They came to expect to play a full role in society, to be accepted as equal. As I have documented, the perception of being black, being different and being at a possible disadvantage because of this generally becomes obvious to the black youth as he approaches school-leaving age. The idea that they, as blacks, share a common destiny, is a powerful one and social arrangements are organized accordingly. As Cyrille Regis put it: 'We [black kids] tended to drift away from white guys soon after leaving school, or it might have been just before.' This results in a clustering together of black kids and initiates a process of what Mickey Morris calls 'learning to be black'.

Without implying that black kids form a homogeneous group, I want to suggest that, despite huge variations (occupationally, attitudinally, politically, etc.), black kids are unified by their perception of problems that are unique to blacks. Winston McLeod called them 'special problems'. These stem from the disjunctives in family life – and there was ample evidence from sportsmen to suggest that a high proportion came from unsettled families if not broken homes – conflicts at school and tensions in trying to enter the employment market.

Let me here enter a caveat: black kids are not just the recipients of pressures at home, school and work which force them to the disreputable edges of society; they contribute to their own 'special problems' in a number of ways. Often they do not develop attitudes suited to progress in education or work and they aid their own social estrangement. Most certainly, there are processes at work in society that militate against the black youth's advancement, what many call 'pressure', but the kids themselves are not impotent; they feel bitterness, rancour and so respond, thus reinforcing the sense of antipathy.

A multitude of factors lie behind what I have called the 'crisis' of black youth (see Cashmore and Troyna, 1982). The upshot of them is that black youth in the 1970s were existing amidst what they considered to be a social contradiction. They grew up believing themselves to be part of society, yet in adolescence had the awareness that they would not be accepted as such shaken into them and matured, often prematurely, with a full recognition that the positions they were to occupy in society were marginal ones. The apprehension of marginality fed feelings of insecurity and doubts about identity: who exactly were they? They were not Caribbean, like their parents, for many were born in the UK and the others at least had some education in England, but they were not 'English' – not in the cultural sense of the word, at least.

Let me reiterate that this simplifies, even to the point of distortion, the position of black kids in contemporary society and it would be careless to neglect the many that had intact home lives, perfectly satisfactory experiences at schools, gratifying jobs and adequate domestic arrangements. For the most part, however, black youth was in turmoil, disjointed, estranged and neutral, if not negative in their feelings towards the wider society. A glance at the bare statistics alone indicates that they were achieving less than whites and Asians at school and were disproportionately unemployed – and excessively hit by the impacts of rising unemployment (see Runnymede Trust, 1980). In certain high immigrant areas, they were opting for crime as a temporary 'solution' (see Pratt, 1980, ch.7). Running the risk of caricature, I would suggest that black kids were generally insecure, without workable definitions of themselves.

There were various modes of coping with such social crises, one of the most dramatic being the Rastafarian movement which surfaced so vigorously amongst black youth from the mid-1970s. Here was a creative, collective response, uncompromising and totally against any kind of sustained contact with whites or other representatives of 'mainstream society', what they called 'Babylon'. Rastas sought to transform their identities, redefining themselves as, at roots, Africans to whom positive evaluations should be attached. They celebrated their disaffection and projected it through their vivid imagery: prayer sticks, Ethiopian colours and long, coiled dreadlocks. Theirs was a movement developed as an effort to construct a new definition of the black man; one in which blackness was upgraded. In this, Rastas attempted to develop an alternative identity to the ones they perceived to be on offer. The enterprise was about exchanging old identities for new (see Cashmore, 1979, for a full account).

Sport can be seen as another mode of response, one of a very different texture. Participants in sport are not necessarily resentful of society (though some are), they do not wish to estrange themselves, nor do they strive to form a collective following organized around specific principles. Sportsmen are not in confrontation with society as are Rastas, for, as footballer Kenny Mower put it:

All the guys like Rastafarians have lost interest in society and have dropped away from it. People who have been successful in sport have had a different attitude; they thought, 'Well, I'm either going to give way or overcome it.' And they had the determination to overcome it.

Whilst not agreeing that the difference is due merely to determination, there is a sense in which sport is a method of adapting to similar problems. Black kids entering sport may not feel the crisis as urgently as do adherents of the Rastafarian movement, but they do feel the contradictions in society and in their personal lives, as Maurice Hope remarked reflecting on his childhood in London just after migration (when aged 9):

I was a child but I saw it, the black and white thing; it was a reality. Not that it came to me just thinking; I realized it at school. Most of my schoolmates were black, though I had a few white ones. . . . there were a few of them put it straight at me. . . . I remember a fellow spat in my face and called me a black bastard. . . . Now that I'm somebody, they don't say it to my face. . . . Now they say things behind my back. And I'm an English citizen.

The implication of Hope's view is that, even though a degree of honour and prestige had been attained, the contradiction still existed; he stopped getting spat at in the face and started getting called names when his back was turned.

The point I am using Hope's example to make is that black kids, at a crucial stage in their lives, recognize that there is a contradiction in their roles in society and that this recognition forces upon them questions as to their identities. Sport, I see as a response to solving such questions. Whereas some elements of black youth turned to more overtly political organizations, attempts to change labour and property relations, others turned to improving themselves through sport, an individual, sometimes solitary endeavour, lacking any kind of commitment to change at a societal level, but demonstrating a concern with individual attainments. In this, sport is a narcissistic endeavour: the interest of sportsmen is not with the general uplifting of everyone, with changing circumstances that affect the lives of others, but with examining and exploring one's own personal features, to re-use Obukw's phrase, 'getting near yourself'.

The emphasis given by black sportsmen to such things as mental stretching, physical mastery, finding their true selves tempts me to compare their involvement in sport with what Christopher Lasch terms 'a cult of expanded consciousness, health, and personal "growth" ' (1976, p.5). All these features are of vital importance to black sportsmen for, as I pointed out, medals, trophies and even money are not the only orders of the day. Sport is much more a challenge, expanding one's self-awareness often without too much regard for notions of others outside sport. Ultimately, sportsmen, even the highly skilled, have a reliance on their coaches for they are the victuallers of the basic techniques and therapies. But, 'you have to help yourself in this game,' Mike MacFarlane contended, a view that was endorsed with only minor alterations by every black sportsman. 'I'm a loner and always have been,' Noel Blake analysed himself. 'I've always been able to cut myself off and work for hour after hour with just a football against a wall.' Paul Morris of Birchfield described himself as 'an isolate': 'I come down here by myself and do my training before Kev [his coach].' Contact between Daley Thompson and his coach was extremely limited: 'I see myself as independent with no influences. I know myself and I know what I have to do to train myself.'

In agreement with this, middleweight boxer Winston Davis speculated: 'I think you can learn so much from people and then stop; then you have to carry on searching.' Boxers, generally, tend to be slightly more acknowledging about their dependence on coaches, but the long, stamina-accumulating road runs are done in isolation and the nature of the sport itself necessitates a strong sense of independence, for boxing is perhaps the ultimate one-against-one combative sport. (As Wally Swift once put it to me, comparing boxing with other sports: 'It's the only game where, when the bell goes, every other fucker moves backwards as you go forward!')

Even in football, a truly team game, players tend to view their contributions at an individual level rather than part of a team effort. Mitch Daley saw no tension in this: 'These guys play in a team, but they are individuals within the team and they can express themselves as such.'

There is a distinct pride about athletes, boxers and footballers whose achievements they adjudge to be their own. And this pertains not only to black but to all sportsmen. Comparisons lead me to conclude that blacks lay more accent on their independence and self-control, but whites also take dignity from what they believe are their own personal achievements – summed up sweetly by Joey Singleton who won the British light-welterweight championship and resented his manager taking the credit: 'I won that title with *my* brains and *my* bottle!' Black sportsmen are insistent that they assume full responsibility for themselves. Competing, as such, is the outcome of a search for purely personal gratification: 'When I get on the runway, I'm jumping for Aston Moore, not for Birchfield or England.'

One of the strong themes which comes across from black sportsmen is that their pursuits, in essence, do not involve other people. Coaches, trainers and managers are not devalued or underestimated, but the real work on which achievements are based is done by the individual. No coach can discover or conquer the 'crack-up point', but individuals, in the last instance, cause their own pain, then push themselves through it. Reiterating the sentiments of many others, Romel Ambrose, from Antigua, said: 'I always try to work up to and then through my own pain barrier. Nobody else can do that for you; that's up to yourself.'

Most black sportsmen are, when pushed, advocates of extreme individualist positions (and carry their ideas into politics; many of the older ones favour no particular political party). By implication, this is a rather conservative tendency in so far as people are seen to create their own pain, take responsibility for their own achievements, and make any struggle individual rather than collective. To stretch the conception of sport as problem solving at an individual level, I can recruit the examples of black sportsmen who consciously used their sport as a means of ridding themselves of frustrations – even if it was a purely cosmetic cover-up rather than a penetrating solution. Mickey Morris' initial encounters with the track were therapeutic: 'to get off my frustration . . . run out my aggressions.' His was, as he saw it, an alternative to the other strategies available to blacks: 'Ordinary kids might go around robbing or beating up old ladies. I used to come down here.'

Also contrasting sport with 'street corner' pursuits, boxer Brian Johnson, born in Guyana but brought to Birmingham when 10 years old, said: 'Boxing? Well, it's doing *something*.' In other words, sport was a constructive solution to felt problems rather than a destructive one. Garth Crooks coined sport 'the alternative solution'. In a general way, it is possible to see sport, or at least sport in the way it is viewed by black kids, as a transferral of problem solving from the day-to-day world of frustration and identity vacuums to a world of fewer 'pressures'. Sport is the pursuit of purely personal satisfactions.

To recapitulate the argument this far, black youth, when faced with the problems of occupying marginal positions in society without clearly specified identities, have a number of ways of responding. Sport is one of them. Politics and social movements are others. I am not trying to draw exact or even inexact parallels between the methods of response, but merely wish to point out the ways in which each can serve a similar purpose in totally different ways. The purpose they serve is in the provision of new identities.

Glaziers and looking-glasses

As with the identity-conferring social movement, sport provides a context separated from the expectations and roles defined by work, school and the family. The processes through which the identity is gained are quite similar. Peter Berger argues that: 'in a sociological perspective, identity is socially bestowed, socially sustained and socially transformed' (1967, p.116). Simply put, this means that sociologists are less concerned with the inner mysteries of the source of identities, more with the ways in which identities are learned. The stress is on learning because the identity is seen as reflecting the views, attitudes and opinions of others, what Charles Horton Cooley (1964) called the 'looking-glass self' to bring out the way in which we experience ourselves and the world through an awareness of other people – at first, fathers, mothers, brothers and sisters and, later, members of important groups at school. Our involvement with other people enables us to get impressions of how they see us and so we organize our self-conceptions in broad alignment. There is, therefore, an intimate dependence upon these other people, in relation to whom we feel pressing needs, fears, pleasures and joys: they are significant to us.

The child first takes the conceptions of these significant others, whose attitudes are decisive for the formation of his conception of himself. His identity does not emerge spontaneously but is bestowed in social encounters. This view does not disregard the fact that an individual is born with certain characteristics that are carried genetically despite the social environment, though the exact balance of influence between biological and social factors is a matter of some debate (see Wells, 1980).

But, even with the biological problems unsolved, it is fair to suggest, as does Berger, 'that to be human is to be recognized as human, just as to be a certain kind of man is to be recognized as such' (1967, p.117). A child who grows up without the care and attention of adults and is allowed to roam free in forests is likely to become almost inhuman, like the wild boy of Aveyron who, in the early nineteenth century, was abandoned and lived wild for about eight years surviving as best he could (see Shattuck, 1980). Whereas a child who receives respect comes to respect himself.

If, at school, a youth is told repeatedly that he is an imbecile, he will come to see himself as one and become one (of interest here is the view of Bernard Coard, 1972, who, in accounting for the overrepresentation of Caribbean children in ESN schools, pointed to low teacher expectations, teacher stereotyping, cultural bias and the low self-esteem of black children). A youth treated as a naturally endowed athlete will begin to think of himself and treat himself as is appropriate to such a figure; he merges his identity with the one he is presented with in these expectations, hence my emphasis on the role of teachers in chapter six.

The importance of this is that identities, as well as being socially provided, must be sustained by others; it is not possible to hold a particular identity all alone. The self-image of the sportsman as a sportsman can be maintained only in a context in which others are prepared to recognize him in this identity. Where the recognition of significant others is not forthcoming, the identity supports are missing and the structure of the self-image crumbles. I discerned this process at a Birmingham boxing gym where an aspirant failed to attract the requisite attentions of the coaches and other boxers. Devotedly, he went to work out, but did his session in an almost detached way and received no encouragement from the others. After a couple of months, he drifted away from the sport. Some time later I ran into him and he recounted: 'I thought I would do something as a boxer, but I had to come to terms with the fact that I'm not really a sportsman.' In the absence of others in his immediate environment confirming his identity as a sportsman, he found the image impossible to maintain in his own consciousness.

Almost synchronous, at the same gym, another would-be boxer, Howard Henlan, was treated by all the significant people at the gym as a 'natural'. Physically, he resembled the indomitable triple Olympic heavyweight champion, Teofilio Stevenson, having the same colouring, height, build and weight. Quality heavyweights being at a premium, he was given encouragement and told by his coach: 'You can go all the way, you've got everything going for you.' Consequently, he took stock of this and other comments and came to view himself as others viewed him. 'I'm feeling stronger and better since I started coming up here,' he said. 'Now, I've started to feel like a real boxer. I'm really going to make it. I know it.' Henlan saw himself not as an engineer for Addressograph office machines, but as a boxer.

Obviously, once away from the gym or on 'the other side of the touchline', the youth is stripped of his identity props. Office workers and Addressograph staff are unlikely to hold the same kind of images and expectations as gym personnel or fight buffs. And here the importance of the changed priority emerges. We live with many identities, each appropriate to specific contexts; each identity requires very specific social affiliations for its survival. Dennis Givans may have been surrounded by glaziers all day and conformed to his workmates' expectations, but, once his working day was over, he was a footballer and recognized as such by his fellow peers and footballers. His motions during the day were perfunctory, done merely for the sake of getting through his working day; his central interest in life was football and so he chose his associates in such a way that they helped maintain his self-image. They treated him as a footballer and based their expectations of him on that; he responded positively to their expectations. In other words, his affiliations in the priority area were the significant ones for him. The conceptions of fellow glaziers were not important compared to those of other sportsmen.

The process of manipulating affiliations so as to strengthen a specific identity which gives a level of satisfaction is a common one amongst sportsmen. As they immerse themselves in their chosen sport, they tend to opt for friendships from within the sport. Pushing the looking-glass analogy, I might say that the youth seeks out those who hold mirrors whose surfaces allow him to see a sportsman. These observations are not intended to expose sport as a perpetuator of fantasies or ridicule the sportsmen for allowing themselves to be sucked into a hoax. There is no sense in which the youth is really an Addressograph engineer or a glazier and only deceives himself that he is a boxer or a footballer. Biographies are multifaceted and there is often no continuity between those facets. To take, as many theorists have, a conception of society as a drama, one can see man as playing many dramatic parts in the total play. He not only plays those parts: he is those parts. His identity is moulded by the requirements of each part, the important ones usually being decided by the audience. Engineers or glaziers may demand different things to sportsmen, so the youth fashions his performance accordingly. Indeed, he may feel as if he is acting in some parts, particularly at work, but he is always what he is playing.

Sports identities, then, are precarious, for once the supports, or significant other people, are gone, the identity may collapse. That is why the interests and concerns of coaches, trainers and the other sportsmen are so vital. It is through continual contacts with the others that the sportsman is able to sustain the preferred image of himself. So conversations, for instance, add greatly to identities. Sportsmen use an argot, a common language, with specific terms not used outside a sporting context. Thus an athlete who cannot talk in terms of 'pb's', 'splits' or 'differential 300s' is unlikely to have much support for his sportsmen's self-image from other athletes – any more than a would-be boxer without a vocabulary which includes 'thinking-distance' or 'hooking-off-the-jab', or a footballer who does not know the meaning of 'laying-off' or 'lying-deep'. Sporting contexts ripple with sometimes very esoteric language, for the ears of sportsmen only. Athletes talk casually in terms of fractions of seconds as boxers do about pounds and ounces. But, if the youth is to identify himself with sport, he must identify with the sport's linguistic tradition. If he is articulate, then his conversations will enhance his feelings of belonging to an enclosed group and reinforce his identity.

One is left then with the almost paradoxical conclusion that black sportsmen, though believing themselves to be on individual missions exploring physical and psychic dimensions of themselves, 'getting near themselves', in effect rely on the responses of others to sustain their images. Sport becomes what Stanley Cohen and Laurie Taylor (1976) would call 'a battleground on which to fight for a separate identity' and because black sportsmen feel the battle they fight is a personal one, their dependence on coaches and others is heavier than they care to acknowledge. Like Narcissus, the youth of Greek mythology who fell in love with his own reflection, black sportsmen tend to be preoccupied with themselves rather than others. But, those very reflections are gleaned from others who feature significantly in their sporting lives. It is they who hold the mirrors whose reflections depict the youth as a sportsman. Their image is his image.

Sport seems a rich, promising area for black kids; here they establish for themselves a basis for a positive self-image separated from the often mundane routines they have to carry out in their everyday lives. Herein lies the attraction of sport. The period of time spent in the sport may be short, but for those years, an alternative script can be performed outside the pressures of work or even school. In that script black kids can find an identity which separates them from the expectations and roles and rules imposed upon them by the family, school and work; a way of distancing themselves from what Cohen and Taylor call 'the flywheel of habit and the nightmare of repetition' (1976, p.69). Fixing in windows, servicing addressing machines, performing clerical duties or similar routines are not regarded by black youths as the loci of identities.

The view is by no means unique to black kids. It is more prevalent amongst them than other groups, but, certainly, a great many whites also feel themselves to be 'really' sportsmen. Like blacks, they devote inordinate amounts of time and energy, physical and psychic, to their sport. The general pattern, however, suggests that whites are more able to maintain distinctions between bread-and-butter existences and sport.

Black kids, for the reasons I outlined earlier, have little meaningful commitment to or investment in contemporary society; they feel, in some senses, rejected by it. One consequence of this is that they feel denied an identity. Thus, the alternative offered by sport is attractive. Appreciating this need for identities is one of the keys to understanding the continued, deep involvement of black youth in sport. They can get out of sport far more than they may appear to. As such, my conclusions are that sport is a positive force in the lives of many black kids. They believe they can get near themselves and who can question them? Because it is positive at a personal level, however, does not lead me to conclude that sport makes an ultimately positive contribution in a social way. I will explain why in the following chapters.

Cornelius Boza-Edwards. Photograph courtesy of *Boxing News*

CORNELIUS BOZA-EDWARDS
fulfilling the prophecy

Born: Kampala, Uganda, 1956; father: Uganda (fireman); mother: Uganda (pub-owner); guardian: England (sports administrator); occupation: professional boxer.

'He's had virtually no recognition at all in this country and yet in all the years I've known him I've never heard him once mention the fact that he's black,' said George Francis of his protégé. Arguably the least-heralded British-based champion made not the least suggestion of a complaint about his lack of acclaim and he attributed this to his adolescent years of turmoil. Born Cornelius Boza he first became interested in boxing at the Kampala Boxing Club and was encouraged by Jack Edwards, a British tea planter who fled the country in 1973 after the ascension of Idi Amin, and from whom Boza was later to take his name.

My parents split up when I was a little kid and my mother couldn't handle me by herself so she sent me to a boarding school. I was there for about three years and when I came out – I guess I'd be about 12 – I went back to the club and started boxing again with Jack. My dad had got married again so we didn't see much of him. . . . After Jack left, he wrote to me to come over and I followed him in 1974. I went to live with Jack and he more or less acted as a father to me. He took me to the New Enterprise Club [in North London] and I started boxing again. But, you know, I couldn't settle down in England. I didn't go to school and I couldn't get on with the kids 'cause the language was hard for me to understand; the Cockney was real hard for me. Anyway, I wanted to go home after a year, but Jack told me: 'There's nothing for you over there; you might as well stick it out.' So I went to Harrow Technical College and got on a course doing GCEs and carried on boxing and things started to get better.

Whilst at college where he got five 'O' levels and one 'A' level, he met a London girl and, at 20 years of age, he felt sufficiently settled in the new environment to get married. His boxing career had blossomed and he had turned professional under the management of boxing mogul Mickey Duff.

When I got married, everything was going smooth for me. I was just setting myself up in a boxing career and doing everything right the way I planned it and then my wife died – she had kidney failure six months after having our daughter. And then I was going to pack up boxing and, at the same time, forget about everything. Then I realized my kid was there and boxing was the only thing that would bring me back to life; every time I'd step in the ring, I'd forget about everything. When I got out of the ring and went back to my place, I'd sit there and the tears would roll down my face and I didn't know what the hell was happening to me. 'Cause life was just beginning for me, it was just starting to build up and I'd found someone and, then, someone was taken away. I just couldn't believe it. But I recovered from it.

He had been beaten only once (on injury) in two years boxing professionally before his wife's death, but was unknown outside boxing circles and had concentrated from 1978 on campaigning abroad.

I was winning fights all right, but I'm not a ticket seller and promoters need boxers who can sell tickets to their mates and that, so I fought mostly in support fights in Europe and Africa and the States.

Having Duff as a manager ensured him constant work abroad and, in 1980, he gained an unexpected breakthrough at world level. Triple world title-holder Alexis Arguello needed a late substitute and Boza was able to step in. Although he lost – in his opinion he was not in top condition – he gained credibility and, in his next couple of contests he established himself as a contender for Rafael 'Bazooka' Limon's world superfeatherweight championship. On 8 March 1981, at Stockton, California, he took the title from Limon and, within months, made a successful defence against Bobby Chacon in Los Angeles. He saw his triumphs as confirmation of his trainer George Francis' prophecy.

As soon as I came in the gym and did a few exercises and a few rounds, he said to me: 'You've got it kid; you're going to be world champion.' I thought it was bullshit 'cause so many people had told me that and I'd compared myself to other fighters, but I never really believed that I'd make world champion. But George used to say 'you're going to be a world champion' every time I used to come here [the gym] and that made me believe in myself.

Not that Francis was the only prophesier.

Jack had been telling me I was going to be world champion since I was 12 years old, when we first met. Now, he's more of a father to me. I've lived with him since my wife died and my mother-in-law looks after my daughter. Every time I fight, Jack's on the verge of a heart attack!

Even on fulfilling the prophecy, however, Boza remained almost unknown in the UK. Like a great many other black sportsmen, he did not find this a great disappointment but said he was able to assimilate it.

If you can take it in the brain you can take it outside too. You can take all the hassle outside the ring, the racial thing you suffer – they call you whatever, outside – and then you come along here in the ring and respond.

I've been beaten up in Uganda and seen people shot. Then the wife died and for nine months I used to go to hospital every day after training. No way was it smooth for me. I was going to kill myself, but I survived. Now, if I can take that shit, why can't I take a few punches? You're creating something. So I'd say it to all the black guys in the street: if they can take all the shit, they can do something with themselves.

Chapter Ten

TWICE AS HARD for blacks

I began to realize at the age of about 14 or 15 how a lot of black kids moved with other black kids and very seldom mixed with whites. There were problems they had and they were problems I had to cope with being a black person. But then it dawned on me that this was a situation that wouldn't do me any harm if I was going to be a footballer. You see I remembered all the stick Clyde Best used to get from the crowd and other players when he was the only black player about. I knew what he went through and I knew then that I was going to have to face that and I thought: 'If I can't face what I'm having now, there was no way I could put up with what he was getting.' The only way was to be really determined and get on with it. I suppose being successful was my own way of getting back at the whole system, a way of proving myself.

Garth Crooks, footballer

The reptile's lair

Confronted with the possibility of only limited chances in a labour market ravaged by seven digit unemployment in the 1980s and attracted by models of success, black youths tailor their ambitions to suit sport, an area in which they are encouraged by teachers and coaches and a site where, in contrast to everyday life, self-expression is encouraged and new images of the self can be formed.

Because of the highly visible minority of successful black sportsmen and the competitive but rule-governed structure of sport, the black youth regards sport as one of the realms in which his colour will not prove a disadvantage. Possession of skills plus requisite application are, ostensibly, the two main criteria of sporting achievement. This is not necessarily the case in other areas of endeavour. What is more, these criteria are specifiable; goals scored are counted, track times are recorded, results are tabled and on-target shots are accumulated. Even allowing for 'bad decisions', application of skills and determination should bear fruit. But, as the sportsman discovers, the fruit is not always readily available and, in the event, he 'finds this supposed Garden of Eden overrun with reptiles' (Michener, 1976, p.145).

Whatever his illusions before changing his priority to sport, the black youth finds that his chosen area is not so different from the rest of society. It is not an insular area somehow separated from and untouched by the wider social influences. As Harry Edwards observes: 'sport manifests the same racist tendencies towards discrimination that are extant in the larger society' (1973, p.204). Footballer Danny Thomas said of sport: 'It's the same as the rest of society. If there are two people of equal ability, the white man will usually be given the opportunity.'

As such, being black introduces unique difficulties, probably ones which were not anticipated before the change in priorities. Sport comes to be seen as just one element of a wider social complex, as footballer Danny Lawrence reflected:

> I knew when I started just after leaving school that it was going to be tough for me as a black person. Sport is no different from the rest of life. I knew that it was going to be harder for me to get on so I was very determined to make it. If you're black, you have to try twice as hard, be twice as good.

Such a perception is the organizing theme of this entire book. The idea that being black makes the going tough in sport in much the same way as in the rest of society inspires budding sportsmen to redouble their efforts. Being capable is often not enough; excellence becomes the only guarantee of success. James Michener confirms that, in the United States, 'the black has to be so much better than his white competitors that he is forced to be almost a superstar' (1976, p.373). Extending this, Edwards reckons that this is a contributory factor in the 'black domination of sports by eliminating less skilled black athletes from participation' (1973, p.205). In other words, discrimination in American sport has the effect of 'weeding out' those of modest proficiency: only those outstanding sportsmen can ride out the discrimination so that, when they surface, they *are* 'superstars'.

I do not want merely to transfer the American arguments, plausible as they are, to the situation in the UK. There are certain parallels, though, and a glance at the American research into discrimination in sport may be an instructive beginning. The critical American studies on racism and sport which took shape in the 1960s and 1970s were, in part, reactions to the sanguine and rather romantic statements of people like Robert Boyle (1963): 'Sport has often served minority groups as the first rung on the social ladder. As such, it has helped further their assimilation into American life.' The view was endorsed by Martin Kane, who wrote: 'Sport is a way out of the despair of the slums, a route to social prestige among one's peers and sometimes a way to quick wealth' (1971, p.83).

The common assumption underlying these statements is that sport represents one sector of society where members of minority groups – most particularly blacks – are given equal opportunities. Sharing this general assumption are Richard Thompson ('the most important contribution of sport to race integration in the United States is, perhaps, the opportunity for Negro sportsmen to be seen by their fellow players and spectators as individuals and good football or baseball players or athletes rather than as Negroes'), A. S. Young ('Negroes approach closer to the democratic ideal in the world of sport than in any other facet of American life') and B. Quarles ('the participation of the Negro in sport has been a significant development in bringing him into the mainstream of American life') (all quoted by Coakley, 1978, p.275).

Such naive views were taken to task by Jack Olsen whose cogent repudiation of the view of sport as immune from racism included the simple but perspicuous comment:

> Negro athletes are almost unanimous on one point: They have to be better than their white team mates. 'A white kid can make five or six mistakes and stay in. . . . We make one and we're on the bench.' And, if a black player and a white player have equal ability, the white player is much more likely to start. The Negro athlete has to be what Muhammad Ali once called himself: 'Superspade' (1968, p.155).

Though few studies were to criticize more bitterly than Olsen's acerbic account, many were interested in documenting precisely the often subtle ways in which exclusion tactics worked to disadvantage blacks in sport. John Loy and Joseph McElvogue, for example, related discriminatory practices to the centrality of playing position: the more central the position, the greater the likelihood that the player would be white (1970). So, in American football, the quarterback berth, popularly regarded as the position requiring thought, judgment and leadership from its incumbent, was not likely to be occupied by a black player. He was more probably in the positions needing speed and power. Joseph Dougherty followed up with a later study which lent further support to the idea that blacks were being diverted into non-thinking positions (1976).

The soccer equivalent of the quarterback is the midfield player, often the 'general' responsible for organizing players, strategies, directing movements and keeping the team cohesive. At the highest level, there have been very few black midfield generals in the English Football League and I propose that this is partly due to coaches' and managers' stereotyped views of blacks' intellectual capacities (and my research indicates that a great many officials entertain profound doubts about blacks' intellects) and partly due to black youths themselves. In soccer, the black youths look at black forwards such as Crooks, Cunningham, Fashanu, Regis. If they look at black midfield players, they find only Remi Moses and a few other lesser known figures. The same principle holds firm for athletes. Blacks in Britain predominate in the sprint and jump events. As most locate their role models (overwhelmingly from the USA) in such events, black kids organize their own sporting aspirations around such disciplines.

Historically, the reasons for the concentration of blacks in certain events and sporting fields are rooted in the availability of resources. Access to boxing, athletics and, later, soccer, was not as restricted as it was to some other sports, for instance tennis or golf, so the first inroads were made in those areas. After that, the cycle continued. (In view of the general argument of the book, it would be ridiculous to posit the idea of black underrepresentation in such areas as swimming or middle distance running as due to 'natural abilities'; indeed, I anticipate black swimmers and middle-distance men in abundance after the initial breaks of pattern are made – probably at the behest of an imaginative coach whose vision is uncluttered by historical stereotypes.)

Although there would appear to be a process at work in the UK whereby blacks are assigned to specific events or positions, a segregation known in the United States as 'stacking', it is by no means an inexorable one. Racist conceptions by officials believing blacks to be equipped for certain disciplines only will undoubtedly contribute to the perpetuation of such classifications, but black kids will vary their appetites in sport and officials will realize that the scope for potential is far wider than presently envisaged.

The other major strand of American research has been coined 'unequal opportunity for equal ability' by Norman Yetman and Stanley Eitzen (1972). Blacks, it is suggested, have to outperform whites to gain equivalent rewards; or, to repeat Olsen: 'They have to be better than their white team mates.'

There is a plethora of evidence from the USA indicating strongly that the black sportsman must demonstrate a greater degree of proficiency than his white counterpart if he is to make commensurable progress. In baseball, for example, 'on average a black player must be better than a white player if he is to have an equal chance of transiting from the minor leagues to the major' (Pascal and Rapping, 1970, p.36). And studies in football (Scully, 1973) and basketball (Leonard and Schmidt, 1975) indicate similar patterns. One important consequence of this is that those blacks who do make it successfully in any of the above sports will have to have achieved an exceptionally high order of competence. To gain and maintain an equal footing with whites, the black sportsman must have distinguished himself with playing performances. This is the meaning of the assertion that the black player has to be 'Superspade' (see Justin Fashanu's career in profile for his impressions on this).

This form of racialism is of far more significance to British sport than stacking or segregating principles, even if, given the structure of sport in Britain, it is virtually impossible to nail down. The aforementioned American sports have unambiguous performance criteria; it is possible to measure baseball batting averages and pitching statistics. In American football, where the emphasis is very much on collective endeavours, single performance factors can be identified as yards gained and passes completed. The indices of scoring in basketball, points scored, field goals and free throws, transfer neatly into statistical tables.

In contrast, the assessment of performances in boxing and soccer and, to a lesser degree, athletics, is much more subjective, requiring interpretation and inference more than linear measurement. The referee's or judge's discretion determines how a boxing performance will be rewarded (scoring criteria can only constitute guidelines). The number of goals scored is sometimes accepted for measuring the effectiveness of a soccer forward but is not always applicable, particularly in the modern game. In athletics, times and distances are the most available methods of assessment, but, of course, an athlete's recordings are subject to huge variations depending on weather conditions, magnitude of occasion and quality of opposition. Times and distances are only elements of a much wider complex of variables which have to be considered when teams are selected. There is no precise way of analysing whether blacks have to out-perform whites for equal rewards in British sport in the same way as American sports can be analysed.

Whether or not systematic racialism actually exists in sport as in other areas of society is not the issue, however. The thrust of this chapter is to document whether black sportsmen themselves believe it to exist, how they apprehend it and, crucially, how it affects their orientation to and performance in sport – and, indeed, in life. 'If men define their situations as real, they are real in their consequences,' was the maxim of W. I. Thomas (1966); and, applied in this context, it translates into: if black sportsmen define their situations in life as determined by racial characteristics and if they believe, rightly or wrongly, that their progress will be retarded because of others' feelings towards blacks, then their conduct will be affected in a most severe fashion. It affects their goals, ambitions, attitudes towards other sports people, postures towards society generally; it shapes their identities and ideas. Whether or not their definitions of reality are based on delusion or not, is, in this sense, immaterial, for what matters is that their social destinies are influenced massively by their beliefs.

Now, obviously, this is not the whole story: lives are not guided solely by our definitions, but also by groups which may hold quite contrary beliefs. Groups holding power and resources provide limitations on how we lead our lives and formulae for the ways in which we understand the world. Black kids are no less urgently affected by power than other groups. Their lives are, to a large degree, regulated by others and a key factor in this regulation is blackness. They do have greater difficulty than non-blacks in obtaining worthwhile employment and they are adversely – and disproportionately – affected by unemployment. Their parents do get a raw deal in the housing market and stand in an ambiguous position in relation to social services (see Karn, 1977; Runnymede Trust, 1980, chs 4 and 6). But, what is of interest here is not so much if such processes impinge on their lives, but how they see them impinging and what they do about it.

A black sprinter may believe that, as a black person, he has no chance of making an England representative team, but this belief could be totally erroneous. However the researcher does not dismiss this belief as produced by the sportsman's ignorance and chuck in his analysis, for this is only the beginning. His task is to uncover why the black sportsman believes this and what consequences it will have on his subsequent behaviour. If Maurice Hope had thought his route to the World Boxing Council title would be smooth, well-lubricated and untouched by prejudice, he would, in all probability, have seen no necessity for equipping himself with additional strengths and techniques which would place him above all his contemporaries. In his case, he did not believe this to be true; early in his career, he became aware that this 'black and white thing', as he called it, could be destructive. He had to devise ways to combat the pestilence; his solution was simplicity itself.

Black bastard

'If anything, blackness was an inspiration. It gave me the impetus to go out and get things done,' reflected Ainsley Bennett, born in Jamaica but based in Birmingham from the age of 12.

> I'll never forget this: the very first day I went to school in England, this white kid said to his mate 'another black monkey for our school'. Now, that really hurt me. I didn't do anything about it; in fact, I never told my parents. But something like that affects you. I think about it even now. I think, 'well, he was ignorant to say it, but he hasn't done any harm to me.'

The perceptions of being black worked in a similarly inspirational way for pro footballer Kenny Mower:

> I felt left out, being one of the only black kids around; nobody really wanted to know me. So I chose sport as a way of proving myself as good as they were. I thought that, if I could, they'd accept me. That's still what it is now.

An almost duplicate experience came from Garry Thompson:

> I felt shut out; us black kids had to do our own thing. They [white kids] wouldn't let us play football with them. But I played a few games eventually for the school and scored a few goals and people

were still taunting me, calling me names. I knew that I had to play better all the time to win them over.

The spark in Herol Graham's boxing career was ignited by racist malevolence:

I was roller-skating by a local Nottingham boxing club and two guys – both white – were hanging out of the window and shouting abuse. 'You black so-and-so,' they shouted. They said, 'come up here!' Me and the guy I was with went up there to them and I put some gloves on and started boxing with this guy who had been shouting at me. I hit him in the stomach and he went down and that was the start really. I was 8.

The examples are illustrative: many black sporting careers were primed by the perception of being black and the feeling of being excluded. When exposed to sport, the youth would consider seriously the opportunity of transcending racial barriers by achieving in an area to which high status is attached. Acceptance was thought to follow success. And for many it did to an extent. Mower, for instance, reckoned that: 'Everybody I went to school with seems to accept me, now. I don't get the stick off them like I used to.' But, it was not so straightforward, for, even when he made it to the first team of Walsall FC, enmity continued to surface. 'I couldn't figure out why but I was the centre of attack for our own fans. They'd say, "Mower, you're a black bastard and you're lucky just to play for our team." '

Most professional footballers found their receptions, from both home and away fans, a mixture of hostility and derision. Regis and company were continually pelted with bananas at West Bromwich and racist chants reverberated around most stadia where black players were present in the late 1970s. George Berry devised a strategy for coping with this: 'I blow kisses at them when they get at me. I can see 'em bursting at the seams.'

'Offputting' crowd reaction could be, but Bob Hazell, at one stage a team mate of Berry's at Wolverhampton Wanderers, believed it could be turned to an advantage: 'The barracking makes you concentrate as hard as possible 'cause you know that if there's one slip, the crowd's waiting to get at you for anything at all.' Similar sentiments were echoed by many black footballers who expected such taunts and responded to them simply by concentrating all their attention on their sport.

In view of the relative novelty of black soccer players and the traditional reactionary elements of football crowds, from which the neo-Nazi British Movement reaped a rich harvest of recruits in the early 1980s, it is perhaps not surprising that those footballers were objectives for vilification. The black presence in boxing, on the other hand, is more entrenched historically and crowd reaction is less predictably hostile, which is not to suggest that it does not exist. Indeed, if the testimonies of black boxers are guidelines, hostility is prevalent.

Boxers, no less than footballers, are susceptible to its effects, as Maurice Hope detailed:

> In the ring, you find your punches and go a few rounds and maybe get tired; and, all of a sudden, you'd hear someone outside the ring make comments about your colour and you raise your enthusiasm as if to say, 'I've got something to prove' and this comes as a blessing in disguise many times 'cause I needed that sort of boost, like a kick in the arse. So it helped me. The next thing I know, I've won the fight because of it, and it helped me in that sort of a way.

Other black boxers underwent similar experiences, including Kirkland Laing to whom 'nigger' and 'black bastard' were signals for gearing up efforts.

Because of the historical tradition I traced in chapter two, boxing tends to pride itself on an absence of discrimination in any manifestation. But if any event showed this up as an illusion it came on 27 September 1980, when Britain's Alan Minter lost his World Boxing Council middleweight title to the black Bostonian Marvin Hagler. On the announcement of the fight, Minter proclaimed: 'I have spent many years reaching the world title. I have no intention of letting a blackman take it from me' (London *Evening News*, 21 August 1980, p.36).

Minter's intentions were laid to rest as were other things, according to *Boxing News* editor Harry Mullan:

> The long-dead myth of British sportsmanship was finally buried at Wembley as a cascade of beer bottles and cans showered the ring and a racist mob howled obscenities at the black fighter who had taken Alan Minter's world title and at the black referee who had stopped the fight after 1 minute 45 seconds of the third round (3 October 1980, p.2).

John Street, writing for the *Tribune*, commented on the 'riot': 'The root cause was not alcohol nor bad habits picked up from the football terraces, but racism' (3 October 1980, p.4).

Much less obvious but as destructive in its impact on the sportsman is interior racism, shows of discrimination from other people in sport which are invisible to the spectator but vivid to the sportsman himself. 'Being a footballer, you know you're going to be called a black this or a black that once or twice, even lots of time,' Cyrille Regis anticipated. Bob Hazell found it equally as predictable: 'People always get to you on the field; the racial thing just gives them a bit more ammunition to hit you with.' Whereas Regis usually absorbed the bullets, Hazell reacted: 'I respond to taunts on the field. If someone says "you black bastard" I say something equally as personal and that subdues them.'

Birchfield's international triple jumper Conroy Brown remembered how: 'On one occasion, a guy came up to me and said "you black bastard" and I turned round to him and called him a "white bastard". He looked a bit stunned and said, "Oh I'm glad you didn't take it the wrong way!" ' Such a right of reply was absent when Bunny Sterling won the British middleweight title in 1970 for his antagonists were anonymous. 'I kept getting threatening letters calling me a black bastard and the rest of it,' he remembered. His manager George Francis was also abused: 'I kept getting letters saying, "you fucking traitor, letting a black man win the British title." It was the same when Conteh won his; the letters were nobody's business.'

Even if sportsmen had not anticipated racial hostility inside sport on their entry, they were soon jolted into awareness. Maurice Hope was spat at regularly by his own Repton team mates. On his arrival at Birmingham City FC, Carlos Francis was given 'a bad time' by the other players. 'They used to call me nigger and even my own team mates used to come in hard on me.' He also was spat on in changing rooms. Garry Thompson almost had his career wrecked when he was thrown into a pool by fellow club members just after he had had plaster removed from a broken leg: 'I was sure it was 'cause I was black. I still think so.'

Between the crowd and the players lie coaches, trainers and managers. This group, while certainly not implementing racialist practices, occasionally leak views about black sportsmen which suggest they might be 'just a little bit different' as one coach put it. Apart from the personal theories about black sporting proclivities stemming from, amongst other things, natural talent, coaches, trainers and managers often allude to the fact that blacks lack 'bottle'. Deriving from the rhyming slang 'bottle and glass' (for 'arse') it refers to that part of the person's moral character that impels him to abandon hesitancy and disregard pain in the pursuit of a goal, in this case winning. 'They've got no bottle' is the oft-repeated assessment of black sportsmen. Even when confronted with examples clearly at variance with their assessment, coaches stand fast. 'There are one or two who do show courage and are prepared to take stick, but in my experience generally, no,' Birmingham's Frank O'Sullivan opined. 'You get a white kid and he'll grit his teeth and get stuck in; but give a black kid a tickle on the chin and he'll swallow.'

'Lazy' is another adjective used liberally to describe blacks. In all three sports, coaches are, for the most part, in agreement on the preparedness of whites to 'graft' or work steadfastly without any palpable reward, but on the reluctance of blacks to raise their efforts above the minimum required to accomplish the task at hand. This may well be related to the belief in the black sportsmen's inability to accept deferred gratification and their need to seek immediate rewards for their endeavours. I made the point earlier that winning is often a prerequisite of continuing in sport for black kids. Often, the first few results will play a decisive part in determining whether or not the youth will continue. For reasons I went over in chapter seven achievement is desperately sought after and a lack of it in the initial phases of involvement can foreclose a possible career in sport.

Quite obviously, I am not in the best position to dispute what might seem grossly unreasonable claims. A coach, trainer or manager forms his opinions through sustained, involved contact with his protégés. The relationship is tailored to clearly defined ends: high performance and winning. As such, coaches' relations with sportsmen are of a different order to mine. I have witnessed what I consider extremely courageous performances requiring plenty of 'bottle' on many occasions. I have seen black sportsmen and white compete with a ferocity that takes them to the brink of exhaustion. So sports club officials apparently work with different sets of criteria.

Yet it is interesting to note how the sportsmen themselves are aware of the general belief. Boxer Tony Campbell said of coaches: 'They think black guys don't have a lot of bottle, but you can't argue against it; you just have to try and show them they're wrong when you're in the ring.' Garry Thompson found it offensive that his coach (then Ron Wylie) accused him personally of cowardice and then added: 'All you people are a bit cowardly.' 'It succeeds in one thing, getting me going when I get on the pitch,' said Thompson. Mike MacFarlane responded in a similar way: 'Bottleless? Well, it makes you want to destroy the opposition when you hear that kind of remark.'

Whether or not black sportsmen are lazy or short on bottle is not my concern; nor, for that matter, is whether their mentors seriously believe it or use it as a ploy to provoke or liven up their protégés. What is important is how black sportsmen apprehend this; they think that others regard them as idle and undercharged in determination and so respond in their performances.

The pattern continues. Sportsmen subjectively experience a form of prejudice from their audience, team mates or coaches and react to it, not through retreatism or dropping out, nor by rebellion or vigorous repudiation, but by trying to improve actual performances. Being black or, more specifically, feeling black works to aid the sportsman in reaching new levels. Critically, in reaching those levels, he recognizes that blackness, though a sufficient cause of retardation, is not a necessary one. Put another way: blackness may be a disadvantage if you accept it as such, but, if you respond positively to it, it should make only a slight difference. Or, in the words of Leroy 'Chalky' White:

> There are black kids who blame everything they do on the fact that they're black. Everything comes down to the fact that they're black. But it's an excuse. You have to get on with it. The kids who come down here [to Birchfield], they don't sit around and mope about it; they get on and win something.

Far from regarding it as an encumbrance, sportsmen use blackness as a source of inspiration, taking from it reserves needed to cope with their futures which will often involve facing rejection and hostility. It may be a rare competence in blacks generally, but there is an abundance of it in sportsmen, as Kenny Mower summed up:

> All these guys like Rastafarians have lost interest in society and dropped away from it. People who've been successful, like Crooks, Hope, Thompson, have had a different attitude. They thought: 'Well, I'm either going to give way or overcome it.' And they had the determination to overcome it.

Because sportsmen do not make a submission and, as Mower put it, drop away from society, but make their blackness a challenge, does not imply that sport 'whitens' them. Many feel that their sporting achievements give them more leverage with whites (the dissipation of a potentially explosive encounter with the police with a simple 'I'm Garth Crooks' was not an unusual type of story). But the activity of their awareness of being black is not stopped by the involvement in sport. Mickey Morris, for example, admitted that, in his formative years after leaving school, he became embittered: 'I was using blackness as an excuse, being black and not getting on. But then I realized that you can't; if you want to get on, you've got to drop it.'

As a result, he 'mellowed a lot' and, at the age of 23, was able to reflect:

> If you'd come to me when I was 18 or 19, I wouldn't have spoken to you. I've changed because of a combination of things. To get on I couldn't have been the way I was; to get on in a white society, I couldn't have been as rigid in my thinking. I knew I had to change it.

Yet Morris was a man with a sharp perception of racial inequality and a firmly contoured black identity: 'Being militant, being black and identifying with blacks makes me stabilized.'

In possessing a blend of assertion and stability without the open aggressiveness of juvenility, Morris seemed to embody the central characteristics of many black sportsmen. He had, in his language, learned to be black in adolescence but recoiled at the prospect of resignation or dropping away. Coach John Isaacs, a Jamaican, offered his general view on black sportsmen: 'They haven't broken away from society, but are very much part of it. It's down to attitude. They have an adjusted attitude . . . yet they're still conscious that they're black.'

Nineteen was a critical age for Jackie Jackson. Brought up by her Jamaican mother in a middle-class, predominantly white, district, she felt at no particular disadvantage because of her colour. A relationship with a white boy turned sour after his parents had objected to his having an affair with her. 'That incident transformed my attitude to life', she recollected. 'After that, I became blacker.' Elaborating, she added: 'You can be black and you can be really black; there are *degrees of blackness.*'

It follows that the more resentful or embittered experience a high degree of blackness and structure their lives accordingly. Most sportsmen do not; although many vacillate, as did Mike MacFarlane, who confessed that, during his mid-teens, he 'almost went completely black' and considered finishing with athletics and immersing himself in 'street life'. As sportsmen, however, blacks have to come to terms with white society; the overwhelming majority of coaches and other officials are white and relationships with them are the important nexus. Most sportsmen do not reach a high degree of blackness. Boxer Leon Young, for example, assessed himself thus: 'I'm not as black as a lot of these guys you see around today. I am black but I'm not that black, if you see what I mean. I've got a few white mates and get on with white people no problem.' A Barnardo's child, Young knew only the birthplaces of his parents (Jamaica) and demonstrated no animosity towards whites. He is not exactly typical, but then no one is. Each sportsman has his own orientation to whites and, for the most part, they are not negative, but far from neutral. Even this is a simplification. There is no meaningful way to encapsulate the feelings and emotions about and postures towards white society. The best I can offer is a distillation. It seems that most go through periods when, like most other black kids, they sense that they are black. There follows the acquisition of black traits, modes of dress, musical tastes, generally a style of life. But the pressures exerted by sport introduce strains. If for no other reason, sport demands a great deal of time and physical energy and going to parties or discos erodes that time and depletes the energy. Also, sportsmen are forced to stitch together close, often personal, relationships with whites, frequently extending beyond the gym or sportsground; this can be another area of strain. Some, like MacFarlane, manage it with Janus-faced tactics: 'I have two ways of life – Hackney with my mates and Haringey with the athletes. I keep them separate.'

The experience born out of adolescence leaves lasting, maybe permanent impressions and, although the sportsman might 'mellow' and entertain relationships with whites, and even dilute his acidic views on society, he is unlikely to lose his sense of being black – and this inevitably flavours his future. Such an awareness is cumulative in nature; it builds up as the child develops in later school years, prompting him to see himself as different. In the illustrations I have provided it can be seen that he feels the blackness impinging on him at school, at work, then in sport where both spectators and fellow sportsmen may remind him forcibly that he is 'different'.

Blackness as an excuse becomes bankrupt in sport and the participant is forced to recognize that he must hold in abeyance any ideas of being 'completely black', to use MacFarlane's phrase. The futility of using blackness as an explanation of failure or even an excuse is clear to sportsmen; they realize that no one will listen to their protests. So, they bring themselves to their mettle in order to achieve good performances and demonstrate their worth. Not that this dulls their perceptions of racism, the belief, and racialism, the practice, at virtually every level of sport, from the face-to-face, as documented by John Skeets – 'They [whites] acted as if they didn't want to know me' – to the international level, where, if Mickey Morris is to be believed, 'I think they [the selectors] would prefer to give a white guy a run. . . . I wouldn't tell a black kid this 'cause he'd probably already know it.'

The accumulation of such apprehensions takes effect on the blacks' sporting performances, even if they are reluctant to admit it has any direct bearing, like Bingo Crooks of Wolverhampton, perhaps one of the most underrated boxers of the 1970s: 'I'm not saying the rough times I've had are because I'm black; but the black man's got to fight harder, I don't care what no man says.' Bunny Johnson called it 'that little bit extra the black man must have.'

Being made to feel excluded at school, made the object of racist taunts by spectators, cast in the role of outsider by team mates and provoked by competitors, accused of lacking courage, determination and effort by coaches, and denied the kind of access open to white sportsmen of comparable proficiency – these are the kinds of experiences which determine or at least influence strongly the black sportsman's outlooks generally and his approach to sport specifically. They gel into a recognition that, for blacks, the route to success is a tortuous one. Sport for some may be a Garden of Eden, but the reptiles are most certainly rife and there is only one simple strategy for insulating oneself from their venom. I can do no better than to close this chapter with Maurice Hope's version of this strategy:

> Black people have been known to be fighting for their survival all their lives. They've been in that condition for centuries. So fighting comes naturally. So you have to have perseverance, ambition and dedication. If you don't, you don't survive.

THOMPSON AND THOMAS
in the two-tone city

Garry Thompson – born: Birmingham, 1958; father: St Kitts; mother: St Kitts; occupation: professional footballer.

Danny Thomas – born: Worksop, Nottinghamshire, 1962; father: Jamaica (miner); mother: Jamaica; occupation: professional footballer.

Coventry is the birthplace of two-tone, the music of the early 1980s which was played mainly by young bands composed of black and white members, and which numbered amongst its aims a unity between black and white kids. The city's football club had two top black players. For one, the passage into league football was turbulent, for the other, relatively smooth. The eldest and first to arrive was Thompson.

> GT: I've got three brothers and three sisters and they're athletically inclined, really, even though our parents never gave us any encouragement. My dad never came to watch me until he knew I'd got something. At school, they kept ramming it down your throat how important football was. It was predominantly a white school: there was eight coloured guys when I was there. Because we were in a minority, we were all trying to be big shots. If we were good at sport, then all the kids would look up to us. The other kids wouldn't bother with you unless you had something to offer.

He felt 'shut out' at school, especially after he was told by a group of white kids that he could not play football with them because he was black. His response was 'to get so good that they had to let me in'. Thomas, who had five brothers and sisters, underwent exactly the same experience:

> DT: I went away and got my own ball and started a game with the other black guys and the whites who weren't prejudiced against us. Our games were so good that eventually we formed a team and

Danny Thomas. Photograph courtesy of the *Coventry Evening Telegraph*

played the others. And the thing was we kept beating them, so they wanted to mix the teams up. That was the start of the integration!

Thomas' parents also showed no interest in his sports, but were unremitting in their insistence that he should do well at school: 'That was the main reason they came to England,' he said. He achieved six 'O' levels to complement the honours he took from football, representative honours for his town, county and England at schoolboy level. His pedigree guaranteed the interest of first division clubs. His older brother Val was already at Coventry City so he joined him; Val had joined some years before, just prior to Thompson's arrival.

GT: I went straight into football from school. When I was in the third year at school, Coventry said they were interested and I made my mind up there and then. Val Thomas was the only other black guy on the staff when I started and we used to get it rough from some of the other players. Alan Dugdale was the worst but, in training, some of them used to take it out on me; there was John Craven, 'Kingy' (Bryan King), Jimmy Holmes and 'Hutchy' (Tommy Hutchinson). It was because I was black. I almost took a crow-bar to them once.

Thomas, at this stage, was 15 and still at school in Nottinghamshire. He admitted:

I didn't put an awful lot of work into it. You see as soon as I knew I was going to Coventry, I had a job, it didn't really matter to me if I got my 'O' levels or not. If I hadn't got something to fall back on I would have gone all out. But Coventry told me I would get apprenticeship forms virtually as soon as I signed and my work started to suffer from then on. I still did do my homework and worked hard at school. . . . But even when I joined, my mother insisted I went to night school otherwise I couldn't come.

His progress in soccer accelerated and reserve team football was achieved quickly. Unlike Thompson, who had faced opposition from both spectators and other playing staff members, Thomas found no comparable pressures.

DT: I had it a little bit easier for me. There was him [GT] and Val and I signed with another black guy, David Barnes; everybody knew me as Val's younger brother. I was called all the usual names that you get called, black this and black that. When I was at school I'd fight

Garry Thompson. Photograph courtesy of the *Coventry Evening Telegraph*

anybody who called me that but not now. There were just a few of us at Worksop and I exploded every time they called me names, but my popularity grew eventually because I was a good sportsman.

In the 1980/81 season, Thomas joined Thompson in the first team but not before he had encountered a little resistance.

DT: Initially, to make the breakthrough, it's very difficult for black people. It's the same as the rest of society, if there are two people of equal ability, the white person will usually be given the opportunity; he'll progress whereas a black man won't. I for a while thought I was playing as well if not better than another player in my team, but he had more experience than I did. He wasn't playing well and they kept playing him and wouldn't give me a chance. And I really started to believe that it was simply because I was black. But Garry was in the team so I kept telling myself it couldn't be. But I couldn't help thinking: Is this a racialist thing? I just kept dismissing it. But my brother reckoned Ron Wylie was colour prejudiced and said that Garry was a one-off thing. Ron liked him because he was really aggressive, the type that Ron likes. That was Val's explanation. Even now, I'm very distant with Ron; I speak to him but I never ever go to see him if I've got a problem.

Thompson also had friction with Wylie.

GT: He used to say to me, 'I don't think you're aggressive enough.' One day, he called me over and said: 'I think you're a coward. All you people are.'

It is, of course, possible that Wylie was merely 'winding up' Thompson, trying to motivate him into being more aggressive; if so, it worked. Thompson, according to his team mates was transformed from a 'gentle giant' into an aggressive forward. The point is, however, that Thompson took him at his word and believed him to hold racist views. 'All you people are' was the tell-tale remark.

'Nigger, nigger lick my boots' was a chant Thompson had learned to live with and was somewhat innocuous compared to the comments in letters to his wife, a white girl. 'The barracking is nothing now', he mused. 'I even take it as a sort of compliment.' But even so he was shocked at the reception he and Thomas received at West Ham when they played in a League Cup semi-final in February 1981. The East

London supporters set in motion a ceaseless barrage of racist chants and lobbed the almost mandatory bananas at them. Thomas was unnerved just once.

> DT: The ball went into the crowd and, as one guy went to throw it back, he said 'Here you are, nigger!' Then threw it hard at me. I went for him, but fortunately, the linesman stopped me.

Though the incident occurred within days of a meeting of the Commission for Racial Equality about such matters, the two footballers seemed the least concerned. They did not find such receptions intimidating. Thomas's lapse was momentary and he felt equipped to ignore them. Thompson dismissed them mockingly: 'I don't know why they call both of us black. Danny's more of a mahogany colour.' In their way, they offered another version of two-tone to the city!

They present a useful example of the first and second phase of blacks' incursions into soccer. Thompson, as a forerunner, had troublesome times encountering opposition inside and outside the football club. His resilience was tested and he emerged creditably. By the time of Thomas's arrival four years on, people in and around soccer were beginning to recognize the contributions to be made by black players. As a consequence, his progress was less cluttered by the kind of obstacles which lay in the way of Thompson.

Chapter Eleven

THE BLACK SPORTING LIFE without future

Athletics is the only thing they [two of his protégés] can do. They have literally nothing else in their lives. Their days consist of getting up, going to the job centre – no jobs, of course – going home, playing some music, coming down here, training and that's it. These two are good at one thing: athletics.

Derek Anderson, athlete and coach

Can't do anything else

At 22 years of age, Lloyd Hibbert had established himself as a leading contender for the British welterweight boxing title. After turning professional boxer in 1979, he had progressed smoothly, almost effortlessly, winning all his contests and raising the level of his performance with each successive bout. Yet he was the butt of often severe criticism, not the least of which came from his own manager. His commitment to sport was constantly called into question as a series of injuries exacerbated an obvious dislike of training. A protracted absence from his gym prompted a threat from his manager to disown him and allow his apparent potential to go to waste.

Born in the traditionally working-class district of Aston within yards of the Villa Park football stadium, Hibbert grew up in a broken home, his Jamaican father leaving his Banbury-born mother so early that the boxer recalled: 'I don't remember ever seeing him.' His mother had, he reckoned, little influence on his childhood and he went through his school years without meaningful aspirations, accepting the empty advice of careers masters. It was in his later school years that he was introduced to boxing by a white school friend who had taken up with a local amateur club.

After a couple of false starts, Hibbert began training in earnest and accumulated an impressive collection of trophies. Most of his successes came after he had left school at 16 without any qualifications and with few ideas about a career. He took the first job he was offered, as a sheet metalworker, but found it restricting and soon 'jacked it'. 'After that, I went through about twenty jobs, none of them any good,' he estimated. 'A lot of the time, I was on the dole.' But Hibbert was a quixotic fellow: 'Even at that stage, I had my mind set firmly on the pros. I knew then that all I ever wanted to be was a professional boxer.'

In 1979, the year in which he forsook his amateur status, he married and became a father. In January 1981, therefore, when he was matched with Joey Singleton in a contest he seemed certain to lose, he had a wife, child and one source of income – boxing. Singleton, a white former British champion and a boxer of considerable experience and guile, was ranked as number two in Great Britain and so posed what in boxing circles is called 'too big a jump in class'. Hibbert eclipsed his previous performances to win handsomely on points. After the victory, he admitted to his lapses in training and lack of conviction, but resolved to strengthen his purpose and pursue his sporting career with more determination. Why? He answered: 'I've got to keep in boxing. I can't do anything else.'

The Hibbert case is by no means typical. I use it to illustrate a single point which provides the clue to understanding why so many black kids will continue to swarm into sport and why so many will succeed: lack of alternatives – 'can't do anything else'. It seems plausible to expect, by the end of the decade, half the England football side to be black, over five out of Britain's ten boxing champions to be black and all the international athletics sprinting and jumping positions to be occupied by blacks. They will do so because of the complex of reasons I have set out in previous chapters and because the social conditions in the UK in the early 1980s are permissive of a continuing enthusiasm for sport. In prospect is what I have called 'the black sporting life' (Cashmore, 1981a).

Those conditions of seemingly unrelenting rises in unemployment, social service cut-backs and deteriorating housing add to the circumstances unique to black youth in the family, home, during school years and after leaving school. They combine in manifold ways to yield not just a deepening depression, but a variety of responses. Black youth's propensity to carve out careers in sport is but one.

Blacks are poised to become a more or less permanent lower

working-class group. As a highly visible, increasingly large minority with an initially low occupational status, blacks face a competitive disadvantage compared to other groups in the labour force (Lee and Wrench, 1981). As the debilitating effects of unemployment reach further, blacks will suffer inordinately. The intensity of anti-black feeling manifested in such groups as the National Front and the more youth-oriented British Movement is evidence that the optimism of the assimilationist 1960s was ill-founded. There is a clear relationship between disintegrating material conditions and racialism as there is between material conditions and the types of disturbances witnessed in practically all major English cities in the summer of 1981.

For most black kids face a wageless existence or low-paid occupations, possibly the more unpleasant types, and there is a sense in which all attempts to improve their life chances with research hopefully leading to understanding are futile. The forces which critically affect the futures of blacks and, for that matter, whites are beyond the scope of influence of those interested in improvements.

Accounting for the numbers of black youths entering sport and achieving success in their disciplines has exposed a number of pressure points: the families' inadequacies in playing supportive roles in education; the school teachers' willingness to encourage black kids in sport but, often, not in other aspects of education; the black kids' perceptions of only narrowing opportunities available to them after leaving school; all black kids' feelings of being at possible disadvantages because of their blackness. Although the focus of this book has been on black sportsmen, those issues effect in some measure the lives of all black kids in modern Britain. The vast number of kids zealously clambering to get into sport and steadfastly trying to make careers for themselves tells us something about the general condition of black youth; sport is not separable from the society of which it is part any more than black sportsmen are separable from the ranks of working-class black youth from which they emerge.

All this is not to put forward the idea that sport is the special domain of blacks. Its attraction to both black and white youth, particularly in the 1980s, suggests that sport speaks to a general condition, a most important feature of which is a widespread loss of confidence in the future. Throughout the late 1970s and into the 1980s the sanguine conviction that things would improve and stability would be restored was shattered. Articulated most stridently by the punks, the conception of what the Sex Pistols called 'no future' grew amongst working-class youth, black and white. Of punk, Dick Hebdige comments: 'It issued out of nameless housing estates, anonymous dole queues, slums-in-the-abstract. It was blank, expressionless, rootless' (1979, p.65). And of the punk followers themselves: 'They were bound to a Britain which had no forseeable future' (1979, p.65).

The punks of the late 1970s shared an affinity with black youth organized around the vision of a common, void destiny. The period was one of pessimism, resignation, social torpor. And, as the realization that things were in decline set in, a variety of other responses sprouted. Most sinister was the re-emergence of the skinheads, racist in their original 1970s form, but, in the 1980s, more urgently political with very strong links with the British Movement.

Another revival group was the mods, who were ostensibly apolitical but, in thrust, liberal with their connections with West Indian ska music; two-tone bands with black and white members played a new brand of the Jamaican forerunner to reggae and their music decried racism, insisting that black and white kids were united in a web of hopelessness. The Coventry band, the Specials, pioneers of two-tone, articulated the mood: 'I know I am black, you know you are white. . . . We don't need no British Movement, nor the Ku Klux Klan. It makes me an angry man.'

A total detachment from the flat, mundane everyday reality of the 1980s was the all-consuming objective of the New Romantics, an essentially white movement though with black adherents. These kids were into 'blitz'; the imperative was simply to appear as extraordinary as possible, the more outlandish, exotic, asexual the dress, the more acceptable. The theatrical ostentation was part of an attempt to place distance between themselves and the ordinary world in which they had to spend eight hours or more of their days. They were peaceful peacocks indulging in highly narcissistic pursuits with few ambitions which did not centre on dress.

These were the stylistic options available to youth in the first years of the decade; they were, as Mike Brake puts it: 'dramaturgical guerilla forays on the main body of a culture', which he elaborates as 'a response to the combined experience of primarily a location in the labour force and in social class, and in the experience of a reality mediated by education, neighbourhood, generation, leisure, social control and dominant values' (1980, pp.176–7).

Though writing of an earlier set of 'youth subcultures', Brake's suggestion is that movements, from the skinheads to the New Romantics, can be seen as efforts by young people to create for themselves an existence 'outside the stark reality of industrial society', which is episodic and always fated to terminate with the onslaught of age. They are ways in which youths establish their difference to the rest of society.

A life in sport is, for all its demands, an alternative to the 'stark reality' of everyday working life in the labour force. In chapter eight, I tried to bring into relief the contrast between the somewhat flat, routine working lives and the undulating, exhilarating experience of sport. Coming in the main from working-class backgrounds, their parents without exception in manual occupations, the would-be sportsmen see little likelihood of an interesting, fulfilling career and have this confirmed by the perception of being black in what is to all intents and purposes a white society.

Sport is another option available to young people. It presents an area where new dimensions can be explored. Expression is valued, even encouraged; self-improvement and achievement are key goals to be aimed for. What is more, black kids are adequately equipped to excel in sport. The teachers prepared to guide and support them in their sporting endeavours play no little part in providing the equipment. Black youths plough their energies into sport in the often pointless pursuit of their role models, conspicuously successful black sportsmen, and are often encouraged to do so by well-meaning teachers. Blacks' links with sport, therefore, cannot be extricated from their material lives with the limitations of home, school and work. Sport offers one of the very few alternative routes of progress accessible to blacks – in their eyes, at least – and it also offers a space to explore different modes of self-expression, and a site on which to develop new identities. In all these ways, sport exhibits parallels with the more obvious youth cultures: it satisfies similar appetites.

Though not necessarily a 'foray on the main body of a culture', involvements in sport of such intensity reflect a general state of disaffection with the future. If sport is regarded – as it is – as an important channel of advancement, then it shows how restrictive the alternatives must be. Continuing involvements, in this way, are a disguised critique of the existing structure of opportunities available to blacks. When, at 22, a black sportsman says his motive for continuing in sport is 'I can't do anything else', he makes a pertinent comment on society. Sport as a vocation may be, for some, rewarding and a means to material well-being; but, for many, it may be a route to nowhere.

Going nowhere

Black sportsmen are making incisive statements on the condition of black youth in modern Britain. But to try to make some conclusive sense out of their statements, let me organize systematically the main points of the general account. I have argued that tensions between home life and school life leave the black youth somewhat under-nourished in the stimulation so critical to a fulfilling educational experience. Caribbean families value education highly and, in a great many circumstances, migrated to Britain in order that their children could benefit from the educational provisions available. So emphatic are they in their commitment to British education that Caribbean parents often impose disciplined regimes to ensure their children's dedication. Education is regarded as essential to the child's development, but, crucially, it is seen as the responsibility of the school; the school alone is the domain for education.

Although they are very ambitious for their children, often setting for them impossible objectives ('the ten foot wall'), they do not accept that they too have a part to play in the general education of their children. A policy of non-interference is frequently adopted.

Lest I be criticized for stigmatizing the Caribbean family, let me temper this view by adding that, in many cases, the pressures on the family militate against the parents' taking a more active part – even if they wanted to. A great many sportsmen come from backgrounds where family organization has been disrupted by the loss of one parent, either through marriage splits or death. Further, blacks seem more likely to occupy jobs where working hours are awkward and demanding. Hibbert had four brothers and three sisters for his mother to cope with in his father's complete absence.

There are many exceptions where families encourage and even inspire their children to do well at school; but the general pattern suggests that Caribbean families, whilst valuing education and attempting to instil this in their children, fail to play supporting parts and leave their children in vacuous domestic situations.

Disorganized family backgrounds and parents unsympathetic to the educational needs of children do not help the black kid in school, but they do not adequately account for the continual failure of many blacks educationally. It is impossible to understand why so many black youths go into sport without considering why so many disengage themselves from school and underachieve. All sorts of reasons have been advanced for this pattern of black underachievement and, after surveying some thirty-three pieces of research into this, Sally Tomlinson concludes:

> The explanations offered for these research results range through disadvantage, socio-economic class, migration shock, family difference and organisation, cultural factors, child-minding, school and teacher expectations, stereotyping, female dominance, self-esteem, identity problems, and racial hostility (1980, p.227).

With such an embarrassing richness of explanation available, it seems pointless to try to draw out any precise, meaningful statement on why black kids fail; there is very little agreement. Some point to the family, others to the school; some to the school personnel, others to the whole educational system. Whatever the specific reasons, one thing is certain and that is that the cycle has a self-perpetuating element to it: as more black kids fail to achieve, they tend first to reject the means society provides for access to goals, then they reject the goals themselves, then they transmit their ideas to those younger than themselves. The end result is increasing numbers of black kids ending their school years in failure.

In a way, this is central to my argument on black sportsmen because it is at school the kids are encouraged and persuaded to take up their sport and intensify their involvements, often at the expense of other academic work. The black family does contribute to the failure of the child at school, quite unwittingly, but black kids undergo experiences at school which work to disadvantage them in straight academic subjects but benefit them in sports. Clearly, there is something amiss and my research indicates that the imbalance of interests stems from the behaviour of teachers.

Two interpretations, weak and strong, emerge. The weak suggests that teachers have slightly lower expectations of blacks than whites and so, maybe not consciously, tend to organize their attentions around these expectations, possibly teaching them in unstimulating ways. Black youths react to such expectations with poor achievements and poor behaviour, thus reinforcing the expectation. Scholastic endeavours are ignored and the child tends to react positively only to high expectations (see Jellinek and Brittan, 1975; Brittan, 1976). The teachers, believing blacks to be more capable, even 'gifted' in sport buoy up their expectations about blacks on the sports field. The stronger version would hold that teachers consciously discriminate against black children, relegating them in disproportionate numbers to lower forms in secondary schools and using them only for the purpose of bringing prestige to the schools with sporting achievements.

This is, of course, a blanket generalization and I do not intend to point accusatory fingers at teaching staffs by suggesting that they channel black kids into sport designedly. It is, however, important to realize that black sportsmen, almost without exception, feel that they had been urged by teachers to compete in sport and that this had, in some way, eaten into their chances of being successful academically.

I defined the teachers' impact as the 'push' factor: encouragement supplies the impetus necessary to instigate and sustain the interest in sport. But, while most sportsmen believe their academic pursuits suffered as a consequence of sporting involvements, there are grounds for arguing that such involvements have a leavening effect, transforming the youth's understanding of his own capabilities and inspiring him to greater objectives in other realms. This 'spill-over', as Derek Anderson called it, refers to a process in which the spirit of achievement gained through participation in sport enters other spheres of the youth's life. Once exposed to the possibilities of achieving, the youth seeks to habitualize success. The achievement orientation spills over into academic life.

The idea is by no means new and was perhaps refined most memorably by Jean Jacques Rousseau in his treatise on education, *Emile*, first published in 1762, in which he demonstrated the connection between physical and intellectual development: 'Give his body constant exercise, make it strong and healthy in order to make him good and wise' (1974, p.84).

One of the thrusts of this argument is that sport can have an invigorating effect on the youth and can promote motivation in 'pure' academic spheres. A coach once told me: 'It isn't hard to win something in sport; to start with, at least. It gets harder when you try to keep on winning.' At the lower levels of sport, there are plenty of winners and even losers get medals and trophies. At the critical stage in later school years, if the youth can glimpse success as often happens in modest competition, then he can use this vision to energize other pursuits.

Generally, black sportsmen do not express bitterness towards the educational system and society; unlike a great many black youths in the 1980s, they do not feel resentful. 'You can't afford to', reasoned boxer Curt Nisbett. 'It gets you nothing if you do take that attitude.' Most go for what Garth Crooks called 'the alternative solution'. But solution implies a problem and there are many problems unique to the black kid in the world of work. Quite apart from the racist attitudes, evidence about which is available, there is systematic discrimination against blacks (see McIntosh and Smith, 1974; Lee and Wrench, 1981). This surfaces in the area of employment and, because career opportunities are less available to black kids, they often have to settle for jobs with more limited prospects – or, in an increasing number of cases, no job at all.

Work is the next phase in my account. For most sportsmen, it does not occupy the central position in their lives, sport does. Even if sport is approached more casually at first, as it was by Cliff Gilpin, born in Telford and brought up along with four sisters by his Jamaican mother, it takes on importance as more commitment is called for: 'I always used to think of my work [as an electrical engineer] as the most important thing in my life. But just recently, I've begun to see boxing as my career and I think I'd have to say that it's taking over my life.' (He was 21.)

The world of work, for black youth, lacks the facility for self-development, interest maintenance and expression. Coming in the main from working-class families and schooled in working-class areas, the would-be black sportsmen face broadly the same kinds of working futures as whites from the same backgrounds. For white youths, the transition to work brings with it what Paul Willis calls 'insights' about 'the blank necessity of work', a commonsense understanding which 'supplies an overpowering feeling that the way of the world is the way of work' (1977, p.162). Willis' analysis of white working-class kids' movement into work locates the source of such views as in ideologies which are not so much imposed by dominant institutions but 'arise very often from internal cultural relationships' (1977, p.160). Ideas about the inevitability of work and the inherent limitations of manual labour are generated in the 'counter-school culture' and gain concreteness through the direct experience of work. In other words, through involving themselves in anti-school activities, the 'lads' reject academic, mental work, oppose official authorities and repulse notions about self-improvement or self-realization. In the process, they prepare themselves for a future of routinized labour. By the time they reach the factory, they are quite familiar with boredom, time-wasting, finding futile ways of resisting authority; they do not want to conform, but are faced with the necessary task of earning a living. So they accept the official view of how the world works, the *status quo*.

Black kids are less resigned to their circumstances and the investment many have in sport indicates the extent to which they crave some alternative to work. I am not suggesting that the whites' enthusiasm for sport, especially football, is not a reaction to more restrictive material worlds of work, but there is a sense in which whites see sport as occupying a corner of their lives, an important corner maybe, but very much away from the preoccupying zones of everyday life. Even those who have achieved an appreciable amount of sporting success, like Paul Brice, are reserved in their commitment to sport: 'Athletics is very important to me at the moment, but, of course, there are more important things to consider: a career must come first.'

How starkly such a view contrasts with the general outlook of black kids in sport to whom work is often a dull, uninspiring backdrop against which to conduct the real drama of their lives. Certainly, the tyro black sportsmen are not resigned to the blank necessity of work. They aspire to the fuller promise of a different world, a world in which they labour routinely, discipline themselves regimentally, train monotonously for the chance to express themselves, to develop their virtuosity, to strive for enhancement. In real terms, the pay-off in sport is very, very small, but the investments are made on a grand scale.

The tendency for blacks is, as Cyrille Regis put it, 'to drift away from white guys', either in later school years or, in Regis' case, 'soon after leaving school'. The drifting away usually begins before leaving school, sometime after the third year (age about 13). At this stage, black kids could be seen as splintering off from the main counter-school culture and this could have the effect of affording them some insulation from the forces which prepare whites for submission to working life.

The cultures into which many black kids move are founded on the perception of having a future which will be affected considerably by blackness. Being treated differently, possibly excluded from certain activities or made to feel disadvantaged combine with ideas transmitted from elders about the problems endemic to blacks and so add force to the drift away from whites into black cultures. Getting blacker for many accompanies the transition from school to work and a concomitant of this is a feeling of indifference.

Whereas white kids may house an anti-school orientation which eventually equips them for manual work, black kids may be dis-interested in school and fatalistic about their futures at work. Getting into sport can mean starting from a basis of indifference, nct being interested in school work and feeling destined about employment, but can result in a more positive orientation not so much towards school but towards achieving. The idea is captured almost perfectly by Herol Graham: 'In the end, I felt nothing particularly towards my school. I didn't owe it anything. But I was trying to get something out of it in terms of qualification for me and me alone' (he got five 'O' levels).

Once in the world of work, or, as is increasingly the case, the world of unemployment, the black youth is introduced to the lack of possibilities: the scope to develop productively, to maximize poten-tialities is limited. So having experienced sport and maybe sensed the potential it holds, he becomes more heavily involved, promoting the involvement to the prime interest in life. Sometimes, the sport is so central to the ambitions of the youth that it guides him for the next several years after leaving school. Success will reinforce the interest until he arrives at the point when, like Lloyd Hibbert, he has no alternative but to continue.

As his attachments to the world of work weaken, he undergoes something resembling a metamorphosis: even moderate success in-duces a change in self-perceptions. He may have to work in order to exist, he may even have to pick up his Social Security giro cheque, but he sees himself as, in essence, a sportsman. In his eyes working or signing on may be temporary measures to make ends meet. His real identity is that of a sportsman and his efforts towards maintaining that are important tasks.

Throughout this process the black sportsman derives sustenance from the examples of other blacks with whom he identifies and who have made sport their vocation – with conspicuous success. These figures provide tangible evidence that black people can make material gains in at least some sectors of society. Sport is an obvious sector. But, of course, beyond all this one is forced to reckon coldly with the fact that the number of black kids who will make it in sport and be able to attain and keep a standard of proficiency high enough to earn them a living in sport are few. Less than a hundred blacks in the UK can claim to be earning a full-time living from sport (at the time of writing). Proportionately, the statistics for successful blacks will probably be impressive in the years to come for, as pointed out in chapter two's opening quotation, 'desire and dedication are easier to

come by when the alternative is a one-way ticket back to the ghetto.'
Many kids may end up with little apart from precisely that ticket.

Searching questions have to be asked of involvements in sport. In
this book, I have tried to account for the reasons, historical, social
and, to an extent, psychological, for the vast numbers of blacks
entering sport and the high quality of their achievements. I have also
ventured to appraise the functions of sport, believing it generally to
fulfil a positive enriching role in the lives of black youths. But, for the
majority, the involvement with sport, however intense, will be
ephemeral; it will last only until a coach slips his arm around the
youth's neck and earnestly informs him: 'You're going nowhere, son.'
In fact, he may well be going somewhere on his one-way ticket.

Involvement in sport has its costs and its benefits. They are not
always obvious. Weighing them up will be my final task and I attempt
this in the concluding chapter.

Chapter Twelve
CONCLUSION

At most, sport has led a few thousand Negroes out of the ghetto.
But for hundreds of thousands of other Negroes it has substituted a
meaningless dream.

Jack Olsen, American sports writer

I've had enough of athletics. I won't be running again, I don't think.
My speed didn't improve and the coaches didn't seem interested in
helping me. I haven't been down the club for a few months and I
can't see me ever going back now. Anyway, I'll be able to
concentrate on my job [as a carpenter] with the extra time I'll save.
. . . Some mates of mine have been down to a boxing gym; I might
give that a go.

Leroy Brown, ex-sprinter

Champions of failure

Throughout this book there has been a nagging tension. I have argued
in favour of sport, always stressing the positive, uplifting effects and
its quality as a provider of achievement orientations. On the other
hand, I am forced to concede that many of the hopes stoked up by
sports involvement are destined to remain unfulfilled. When all is said
and done, sport is not a viable career for the majority of aspirants. But,
crucially, it will continue to attract black youth and, for that reason,
this work contains a warning.

For all its benefits, sport profits from failure: the failure of black
kids to integrate more satisfactorily, gain qualifications more readily,
find careers more easily. Social conditions militate against black youth
finding in school and work areas in which to develop potentialities.
With the psychologist Carl Rogers, I view all human beings as striving
productively for fulfilment and development: what he calls 'actualization' (1942; 1961). In Rogers' perspective, we are set at birth to grow:

we are active and forward moving and, if the conditions are permissive, we attempt to develop our potentialities to the maximum. The specifics of human growth vary from person to person. One individual may choose to become intensely involved in family life and the rearing of children, heightening his experiences in that context, whereas another may immerse himself in his occupation, improving his competence without pursuing domestic bliss. Yet, for Rogers, they may both share the same primary motive: the actualizing tendency.

Although the form of actualization differs from one individual to another, and from one population to another, there are some common features to the tendency: flexibility rather than rigidity is sought; openness rather than restrictedness; freedom from external control rather than submission to control. But the conditions must be conducive to such developments and, in sport and education, there are contradictions. Rigidity in learning may be a condition of flexibility in expression. Applying such ideas to black youth in modern Britain, it could be said that conditions are not conducive to their actualization in the spheres of education and work, so they turn to sport as the vehicle for actualization. Certainly, the fulfilment many derive from sport in terms of expression and identity is suggestive of this.

What can be done to make other areas with more tangible possibilities facilitate actualization? I have already acknowledged that many of the forces rendering vital areas bankrupt are beyond the sphere of influence. Raise employment levels, obliterate racist thought, eliminate racialist behaviour sound as naive and as futile as imperatives to change totally the capitalist system in one thrust; yet many would argue that the latter is a precondition of the former. I assume that, for the moment at least, the basic structure of society will remain intact and therefore the problems germane to this study will have to be confronted at another level – the immediate one.

There is, I feel, a growing understanding amongst Caribbean parents about the roles they must play in providing stimulating home environments for their children. I am mindful that the practical circumstances of many families often make the provision of such difficult or impossible and it may be a taxing request to make of parents who were rather poorly educated themselves in the West Indies, particularly those from Jamaica. As Christopher Bagley writes: 'One of the reasons for the underachievement of Jamaican children in English schools seems to be the relatively low level of educational achievement of their parents' (1979, p.69). Boxer Cecil

Williams, who was brought up by his illiterate grandparents, thought this problem would 'iron itself out with time'. As he says,

> There's no solution to it, now; you can't go about trying to re-educate all the parents. But, eventually, the next generation will understand the problems and pressures of school and give their kids help and assurance and the motivation to do well.

I endorse this view and add only the wish that some latitude be introduced into the often cruelly disciplinarian system of control in the Caribbean family. The investigations of Bagley, Bart and Wong revealed, amongst other things, that high-achieving black school children had parents 'who tended to be "non-authoritarian" ' (1978). Generalizing this tendency may bring higher achievements all round.

Discipline is also an issue at school. Most of the sportsmen feel that there is not enough of the right kind of discipline, the type that yields respect rather than fear or retaliation. Stories of hitting teachers back after provocation abound, a fairly typical one coming from Rupert Christie who recalled that, when 15:

> A teacher hit me across the face, so I punched him back. I could have stood him giving me the cane or something like that; I wouldn't have done anything. But hitting me in the face – I wasn't going to stand for that. He punched me back and we started fighting.

Whilst in his third year at school, javelin thrower Andrew Jarrett recounted similar episodes, one culminating thus: 'The teacher broke down and started crying in front of us. They're scared of some kids who'll stand up to them. But, if they insult you, you've got to have a go back at them.'

It seems such incidents are commonplace in the inner city schools and black kids accept them as part of the fabric of their school lives. Interestingly, however, the sportsmen generally find them unnecessary and undesirable. There is a dislike of indiscipline. Chris Egege, for example, moved from Birmingham to Bradford, where his educational performance benefited from more discipline and he reckoned: 'You can get on and learn something up here; the teachers were too soft in Birmingham.' He echoed the views of many.

An obvious factor behind this is that the sportsmen are more disposed to accept discipline either because they realize its possible rewards, having experienced the effect of rigidly supervised training in their performances, or because they may have been predisposed to accept discipline in the first instance before approaching sport at all – though I doubt it.

The expressed wish of the majority of black sportsmen, those at school and at work, is that teachers blend authority with imagination, that they set tasks the meaning and purpose of which are clear to all and reinforce the methods of achieving them, always straining to make obvious why certain methods are adopted rather than others. Sportsmen, of course, appreciate discipline and understand how coaches will subject them to almost sadistic treatments in order to produce results. 'He pulls it out of me', said Phil Brown of his coach. 'He knows I hate some aspects of my training, but he keeps making me do it. And I respond 'cause I know we've both got the same aim at the end of the day – even if it doesn't seem like it sometimes.'

Well, perhaps there are things to be learned from the relationships developed between coaches and sportsmen. Coaches 'pull it out' of their charges not because they impose their wills forcibly; sportsmen surrender themselves and obey instructions because they have trust in their mentors, a trust based on 'the same aim'. The goal is improving performance and it is shared by both. Might the attainment of skills, knowledge and the development of ability be goals shared in the classroom? Coaches do not encourage such affective goals as self-expression, fulfilment or self-analysis; they do not have to, they come through anyway. The sportsmen themselves create self-expression; they are merely provided with the fundamental equipment – fitness, strength, stamina, basic skills, etc. – by the coaches and given the avenues along which to develop them by competitive sport.

My conclusions tie in with those of Maureen Stone: 'Whilst not decrying all attempts at curriculum innovation and creativity, the need for schools to retain a commitment to the mastery of basic intellectual skills and competencies by all children has been expressed' (1981, p.254). The view is backed by the research findings of Michael Rutter and his colleagues who found that: 'children tended to make better progress both behaviourally and academically in schools which placed an appropriate emphasis on academic matters' (1979, p.114). Such an emphasis was found to fulfil pupils' expectations also.

Sport is an immensely fruitful area for creativity and expression, though these are not necessarily prime targets. Coaches and trainers establish the exact nature of the objective, whether it be a particular time to be broken or trophy to be won, and set about trying to reach it by pushing the sportsmen through routines which will give them the basic physical competence and mental alertness. These enable the sportsmen to be creative and express themselves. In sport, the conditions exist which are conducive to creativity: they aid growth in capability. To the uninitiated, the gym, track or training pitch may seem dominated by inflexibility, control and repression, but these are exactly the features which enable the sportsman eventually to be innovative, fluid, creative. Without undergoing the developmental rigours, he is impotent, lacking the capacity to create.

Accordingly, I am sceptical about many of the programmes of multi-racial education which stress the more expressive components of education for black youth: dialect classes, black drama, dance and music groups. These represent therapeutic devices for improving the supposedly problematic self-concept or self-esteem of black youth. Yet there is no satisfactory evidence to suggest that black kids do have inadequate self-concepts (see Kardiner and Oversey, 1951; Rosenberg and Simmons, 1971, for American studies). Because teaching personnel may have low expectations of black youth does not necessarily mean it translates into the youths themselves having devalued senses of self. As I have tried to indicate, there are many sources of identity; other people provide the all-important mirrors. Black kids do not rely on negative images from teachers, for they can seek alternative reflections, such as those they derive from other sportsmen.

If there are instructive statements to be drawn out of the study of one group of highly motivated, industrious, receptive, achieving black people, sportsmen, they are that learning and actualization are best promoted when certain conditions can be satisfied: when tangible objectives are specified and determined and when the methods for their attainment are established firmly; when such methods are directed towards the development of basic proficiency, skills and competence; when the methods are held together by discipline backed by a degree of authority; when periodic achievements are reinforced by rewards in order that the achiever feels his efforts are recognized and has palpable evidence of this; when individuals can feed off each other, sustaining each other's endeavours and helping each other improve – as sportsmen train collectively.

It follows that the more therapeutic elements of educational programmes aimed exclusively at black kids should be de-emphasized, that alleged problems of black self-esteem be forgotten, that teachers gear up their expectations of blacks in intellectual spheres and gear down those in relation to natural sports ability, orienting towards them as they would children of any colour while at the same time, recognizing what Winston McLeod called 'the special problems' experienced by black youth in home life. Black kids do drift away from others near school-leaving time or just after and perhaps some initiatives at school might be aimed at curtailing this, though it must be accepted that the critical factors behind this trend lie beyond the pale of the school. In a very pressing way, those critical factors outside the school are the ones which matter.

The study of black sportsmen is a study of success and a study of failure. A theme of this work has been that sport benefits from social adversity. My ambition has been to learn from sport in an effort to see how that adversity may be lessened. But, countering my lessons, there are seemingly immovable obstacles. How do we persuade a youth that the qualifications for which he is working have meaning in the context of proliferating unemployment? How do we convince him that the skilled or unskilled manual work for which he may be destined is not intrinsically dull and monotonous? How do we explain to him the contradiction of an educational system where the majority are fated to fall way short of the ideals set before them? How do we tell him that he will grow up in a world where the colour of a man's skin may well be the crucial feature of his entire life and determine his future? These are the questions of relevance which will inevitably undermine my conclusions.

Sport has and will continue to prosper from the massive contributions of young blacks. All black sportsmen give a great deal to sport in terms of skill, commitment, industry; all will take something, some much, much more than others. But this cannot disguise the more disquieting situations which effectively function to produce the phenomenon of the black sportsman. He is both a champion and a symbol of failure. They are time-honoured roles. From the 1770s and Bill Richmond to the 1980s and Garth Crooks, sport has been a route to fame and material comfort for thousands of blacks and will continue to be exactly that in future. For tens of thousands of others it will be illusory, only a route to nowhere. Sport conceals deep, structured inequalities and, for all the positive benefits it yields, it remains a source of hope and ambition for blacks only as long as those inequalities remain.

BIBLIOGRAPHY

Armstrong, Henry (1957), *Gloves, Glory and God*, London, Peter Davies.
Ashe, Arthur (1977), 'An open letter to all black parents', *New York Times*,
    6 February, p. 2.
Axthelm, Pete (1971), *The City Game*, New York, Simon & Schuster.
Bagley, Christopher (1979), 'A comparative perspective on the education of
    black children in Britain', *Comparative Education*, vol. 15, no. 1 (March),
    pp. 63-81.
Bagley, Christopher, Bart, M. and Wong, Siu-Ying J. (1978), 'Cognition and
    scholastic success in West Indian 10-year-olds in London', *Educational
    Studies*, vol. 4, pp. 7–17.
Banton, Michael (1977), *The Idea of Race*, London, Tavistock.
Baxter, Paul and Sansom, Basil (eds) (1972), *Race and Social Difference*,
    Harmondsworth, Penguin.
Bend, Emile (1968), *The Impact of Athletic Participation on Academic and
    Career Aspiration and Achievement*, New Brunswick, N.J., National
    Football Foundation and Hall of Fame.
Berger, Peter (1967), *Invitation to Sociology*, Harmondsworth, Penguin.
Bernstein, Basil (1971), *Class, Codes and Control*, vol. I, London, Routledge
    & Kegan Paul.
Bernstein, Basil (1975), *Class, Codes and Control*, vol. III, London, Routledge
    & Kegan Paul.
Birrell, Susan (1978), 'An analysis of the inter-relationships among
    achievement motivation, athletic participation, academic achievement,
    and educational aspirations', *International Journal of Sport Psychology*, vol.
    8.
Birtley, Jack (1976), *The Tragedy of Randolph Turpin*, London, New English
    Library.
Boyle, Robert (1963), *Sport: mirror of American life*, Boston, Little Brown.
Brake, Mike (1980), *The Sociology of Youth Culture and Youth Subcultures*,
    London, Routledge & Kegan Paul.
Brittain, E. M. (1976), 'Multiracial education 2', *Educational Research*, vol.
    18, no. 3, pp. 182–91.
Brower, Jonathan N. (1976), Whitey's sport', in Andrew Yiannakis *et al.*,
    Sport Sociology, Dubuque, Iowa, Kendall/Hunt.

Buhrmann, H. G. (1972), 'Scholarship and athletics in junior high school', *International Review of Sport Sociology*, vol. 7, pp. 119–28.

Butt, Dorcas Susan (1976), *Psychology of Sport*, New York, Van Nostrand Reinhold.

Cashmore, Ernest (1979), *Rastaman: the Rastafarian movement in England*, London, Allen & Unwin.

Cashmore, Ernest (1981a), 'The black British sporting life', *New Society*, vol. 57, no. 9.

Cashmore, Ernest (1981b), 'After the Rastas', *New Community*, vol. 5, no. 1.

Cashmore, Ernest and Troyna, Barry (1982), *Black Youth in Crisis*, London, Allen & Unwin.

Castine, Sandra C. and Roberts, Glyn C. (1974), 'Modeling in the socialization process of the black athlete', *International Review of Sport Sociology*, vol. 3, no. 4, pp. 59–73.

Chasey, W. C. and Wyrick, W. (1970), 'Effects of gross motor development program on form perception skills of educable mentally retarded children', *Research Quarterly*, vol. 41, no. 3, pp. 345–52.

Coakley, Jay J. (1978), *Sport and Society: issues and controversies*, St Louis, Missouri, C. V. Mosby.

Coard, Bernard (1972), *How the West Indian child is made ESN in the British school system*, London, New Beacon Books.

Cohen, Stanley and Taylor, Laurie (1976), *Escape Attempts*, London, Allen Lane.

Coleman, James S. (1960), 'Adolescent subculture and academic achievement', *American Journal of Sociology*, vol. 65 (January), pp. 337–47.

Coleman, James S. (1961), *The Adolescent Society*, New York, Free Press.

Commission for Racial Equality (1980), *Ethnic Minority Youth Unemployment*, London, Commission for Racial Equality.

Cooley, Charles Horton (1964), *Human Nature and the Social Order*, New York, Schocken.

Corris, Peter (1980), *Lords of the Ring*, Melbourne, Cassell.

Danford, Howard G. and Shirley, Max (1970), *Creative Leadership in Recreation*, Boston, Allyn & Bacon.

Daniel, W. W. (1968), *Racial Discrimination in England*, Harmondsworth, Penguin.

Davis, E. and Cooper, J. (1934), 'Athletic ability and scholarship', *Research Quarterly*, vol. 5 (December), pp. 68–78.

Davison, R. B. (1966), *Black British: immigrants to England*, London, Oxford University Press.

Delattre, E. J. (1975), 'Some reflections on success and failure in competitive athletics', *Journal of the Philosophy of Sport*, vol. 2.

Dougherty, Joseph (1976), 'Race and Sport: a follow-up study', *Sport Sociology Bulletin*, vol. 5 (Spring), pp. 1–12.

Douglas, J. W. B. (1964), *The Home and the School*, London, MacGibbon & Kee.

Douglas, J. W. B., Ross, J. M., and Simpson, H. R. (1968), *All Our Future*, London, Peter Davies.

Draper, Mary (1963), *Sport and Race in South Africa*, Johannesburg, South African Institute of Race Relations.

Dunn, J. and Lupfer, M. (1974), 'A comparison of black and white boys' performance in self-paced and reactive sports activities', *Journal of Applied Psychology*, vol. 4, pp. 24–35.

Dunning, Eric (ed.) (1976), *The Sociology of Sport*, London, Frank Cass.

Edwards, Harry (1970), *The Revolt of the Black Athlete*, New York, Free Press.

Edwards, Harry (1972), 'The myth of the racially superior athlete', *Intellectual Digest* (March), pp. 58–60.

Edwards, Harry (1973), *Sociology of Sport*, Homewood, Illinois, Dorsey Press.

Edwards, Harry (1976), 'The black athletes', in Andrew Yiannakis *et al.*, *Sport Sociology*, Dubuque, Iowa, Kendall/Hunt.

Egan, Pierce (1812–29), *Boxiana*, 5 vols, London, Smeeton.

Eitzen, D. Stanley (1976), 'Athletics in the status system', in Andrew Yiannakis *et al.*, *Sport Sociology*, Dubuque, Iowa, Kendall/Hunt.

Eitzen, D. Stanley and Sanford, David C. (1975), 'The segregation of blacks by playing position in football: accident or design?', *Social Science Quarterly*, vol. 5, no. 4 (March), pp. 948–59.

Eitzen, D. Stanley and Yetman, Norman R. (1977), 'Immune from racism?', *Civil Rights Digest*, vol. 9, no. 2 (Winter), pp. 3–13.

Eitzen, D. Stanley and Sage, George H. (1978), *Sociology of American Sport*, Dubuque, Iowa, W. C. Brown.

Essien-Udom, E. U. (1962), *Black Nationalism*, University of Chicago Press.

Farr, Finis (1964), *Black Champion: the life and times of Jack Johnson*, London, Macmillan.

Fleischer, Nat (1938), *Black Dynamite – the story of the Negro in the prize ring from 1782–1938*, New York, O'Brien.

Foner, Nancy (1979), *Jamaica Farewell*, London, Routledge & Kegan Paul.

Gainer, Bernard (1972), *The Alien Invasion*, London, Heinemann.

Gains, Larry (no date), *The Impossible Dream: an autobiography*, London, Leisure Publications.

Garvey, Marcus (1967), *Philosophy and Opinions*, 2 vols, London, Frank Cass.

Gillmore, Al-Tony (1975), *Bad Nigger! The national impact of Jack Johnson*, Port Washington, NY, National University Publications.

Glasgow, Douglas G. (1980), *The Black Underclass*, San Francisco, Jossey-Bass.

Guttmann, Allen (1978), *From Ritual to Record: the nature of modern sports*, New York, Columbia University Press.

Haerle, Rudolph K. Jr (1974), 'The athlete as "moral" leader', *Journal of Popular Culture*, vol. 8 (Fall), pp. 393ff.

Hare, Nathan (1973), 'The occupational culture of the black fighter', in J. T. Talamini and C. H. Page (eds), *Sport and Society: an anthology*, Boston, Mass., Little, Brown.

Hebdige, Dick (1979), *Subculture*, London, Methuen.
Henderson, Edwin Bancroft (1949), *The Negro in Sports*, Washington DC, Associated Publishers.
Henderson, Edwin Bancroft (1970), *The Black Athlete: emergence and arrival*, New York, Publishers' Co.
Hoch, Paul (1972), *Rip Off The Big Game*, New York, Anchor/Doubleday.
Jellinek, M. M. and Brittan, E. M. (1975), 'Multiracial education 2', *Educational Research*, vol. 18, no. 1, pp. 44–53.
Jones, J. and Hochner, A. (1973), 'Racial differences in sports activities', *Journal of Personality and Social Psychology*, vol. 27, pp. 86–95.
Jones, Peter J. T. (1977), 'An evaluation of the effect of sport on the integration of West Indian schoolchildren', unpublished PhD thesis, University of Surrey.
Kane, Martin (1971), 'An assessment of black is best', *Sports Illustrated*, vol. 34, no. 3 (18 January), pp. 78–83.
Kardiner, Abram and Oversey, Lionel (1951), *The Mark of Oppression*, New York, World Publishing.
Karn, Valerie (1977), 'The financing of owner-occupation and its impact on ethnic minorities', *New Community*, vol. 6, nos 1 &2, pp. 49–64.
Kenyon, Gerald S. and McPherson, Barry D. (1973), 'Becoming involved in physical activity and sport', in G. L. Rarick (ed.), *Physical Activity*, New York, Academic Press.
Knebworth, Viscount (no date), *Boxing: a guide to modern methods*, London, Seeley, Service & Co.
Kniker, Charles R. (1974), 'The values of athletics in schools', *Phi Delta Kappan*, vol. 56, pp. 116–20.
Landers, Daniel M. (ed.) (1976), *Social Problems in Athletics*, Urbana, University of Illinois Press.
Lasch, Christopher (1976), 'The narcissist society', *New York Review of Books*, 30 September, pp. 5–13.
Lasch, Christopher (1980), *The Culture of Narcissim*, London, Abacus.
Lashley, Horace (1980), 'The new black magic', *British Journal of Physical Education*, vol. 11, no. 1 (January), pp. 6–8.
Lawrence, Daniel (1974), *Black Migrants – White Natives*, London, Cambridge University Press.
Lee, Gloria and Wrench, John (1981), *In Search of a Skill*, London, Commission for Racial Equality.
Leonard, Wilbert Marcellus III (1980), *A Sociological Perspective of Sport*, Minneapolis, Minnesota, Burgess.
Leonard, Wilbert Marcellus III and Schmidt, Susan (1975), 'Observations on the changing social organization of collegiate and professional basketball', *Sport Sociology Bulletin*, vol. 4 (Fall), pp. 13–35.
Levine, Lawrence W. (1977), *Black Culture and Black Consciousness*, New York, Oxford University Press.
Lincoln, C. Eric (1961), *The Black Muslims in America*, Boston, Mass., Beacon Press.
Lomax, Louis E. (1963), *The Negro Revolt*, London, Hamish Hamilton.
Lombardo, Ben (1978), 'The Harlem Globetrotters and the perpetuation of

the black stereotype', *The Physical Educator*, vol. 35, no. 2 (May), pp. 60–3.

Loy, John W. Jr and Kenyon, Gerald (eds) (1969), *Sport, Culture and Society*, London, Macmillan.

Loy, John W. and McElvogue, Joseph F. (1970), 'Racial segregation in American sport', *International Review of Sport Sociology*, vol. 5, pp. 5–23.

Loy, John W. and Ingham, Alan G. (1973), 'Play, games and sport in the psychosocial development of children and youth', in G. L. Rarick (ed.), *Physical Activity*, New York, Academic Press.

Loy, John W., McPherson, Barry D. and Kenyon, Gerald (1978), *Sport and Social Systems*, Reading, Mass., Addison-Wesley.

Lueptow, Lloyd B. and Kayser, Brian D. (1973), 'Athletic involvement, academic achievement and aspiration', *Sociological Focus*, vol. 7, pp. 24–36.

McIntosh, N. and Smith, D. (1974), *The Extent of Racial Discrimination*, London, Political and Economic Planning.

McIntosh, Peter (1966), 'Mental ability and success in school sport', *Research and Physical Education*, vol. 1, p. 1.

McIntosh, Peter (1979), *Fair Play: ethics in sport and education*, London, Heinemann.

McKee, J. McClendon and Eitzen, D. Stanley (1975), 'Interracial contact on collegiate basketball teams', *Social Science Quarterly*, vol. 55, no. 4 (March), pp. 926–38.

McPherson, Barry D. (1975), 'The segregation by playing position in sport hypothesis', *Social Science Quarterly*, vol. 5, no. 4 (March), pp. 960–6.

McPherson, Barry D. (1976a), 'The black athlete', in Daniel M. Landers (ed.), *Social Problems in Athletics*, Urbana, University of Illinois Press.

McPherson, Barry D. (1976b), 'Minority group involvement in sport', in Andrew Yiannakis *et al.*, *Sport Sociology*, Dubuque, Iowa, Kendall/Hunt.

Maher, Charles (1968), 'The negro athlete in America', *Los Angeles Times*, sports section, 24 March, pp. 24–9.

Malina, Robert M. (1973), 'Ethnic and cultural factors in the development of motor abilities and strengths in American children', in G. L. Rarick (ed.), *Physical Activity*, New York, Academic Press.

Mandell, Richard D. (1971), *The Nazi Olympics*, New York, Macmillan.

Michener, James A. (1976), *Sports in America*, New York, Random House.

O'Connor, Ulick (1981), 'How running revealed man's best high', *Sunday Times*, 12 April, p. 29.

Odd, Gilbert (1978), 'Jeptha was the first', *Boxing News*, vol. 34, no. 36 (8 September), pp. 18–19.

Ogilvie, Bruce and Tutko, Thomas A. (1966), *Problem Athletes and How to Handle Them*, London, Pelham Books.

Olsen, Jack (1968), *The Black Athlete: a shameful story*, New York, Time Life.

Otto, L. B. and Alwin, D. (1977), 'Athletics, aspirations, and attainments', *Sociology of Education*, vol. 42 (April), pp. 102–13.

Pascal, Anthony H. and Rapping, Leonard A. (1970), *Racial Discrimination in Organized Baseball*, Santa Monica, The Rand Corporation.

Patterson, Sheila (1963), *Dark Strangers*, London, Tavistock.
Patterson, Sheila (1969), *Immigration and Race Relations in England, 1960–1968*, London, Oxford University Press.
Peach, Ceri (1968), *West Indian Migration to Britain*, London, Oxford University Press.
Pelé and Fish, Robert L. (1977), *Pelé: my life and the beautiful game*, London, New English Library.
Peterson, Robert (1970), *Only the Ball was White*, Englewood Cliffs, NJ, Prentice-Hall.
Phillips, John C. (1976), 'Towards an explanation of racial variations in top-level sports participation', *International Review of Sport Sociology*, vol. 13, no. 11, pp. 39–55.
Phillips, John C. and Schafer, Walter E. (1976), 'Consequence of participation in interscholastic sports', in Andrew Yiannakis *et al.*, *Sport Sociology*, Dubuque, Iowa, Kendall/Hunt.
Picou, Steven and Curry, E. W. (1974), 'Residence and the athletic participation-aspiration hypothesis', *Social Science Quarterly*, vol. 55 (December), pp. 768–76.
Pratt, Michael (1980), *Mugging as a Social Problem*, London, Routledge & Kegan Paul.
Quarles, B. (1964), *The Negro in the Making of America*, New York, Collier Macmillan.
Rarick, G. Lawrence (ed.) (1973), *Physical Activity: human growth and development*, New York, Academic Press.
Rehberg, R. A. (1969), 'Behavioural and attitudinal consequences of high school interscholastic sports', *Adolescence*, vol. 4 (April), pp. 59–68.
Rhodes, Lodis and Butler, Johnny S. (1975), 'Sport and racism', *Sociological Quarterly*, vol. 55, no. 4 (March), pp. 19–25.
Roberts, Randy (1974), 'Jack Dempsey: an American hero in the 1920s', *Journal of Popular Culture*, vol. 8 (Fall), pp. 411–26.
Roberts, Ron E. and Kloss, Robert Marsh (1979), *Social Movements: between the balcony and the barricade*, St Louis, Missouri, C. V. Mosby.
Rogers, Carl (1942), *Counselling and Psychotherapy*, Boston, Mass., Houghton Mifflin.
Rogers, Carl (1961), *On Becoming a Person*, Boston, Mass., Houghton Mifflin.
Rosenberg, Morris and Simmons, Roberta G. (1971), *Black and White Self*, Washington DC, American Sociological Association.
Rousseau, Jean Jacques (1974), *Emile*, London, Everyman.
Runnymede Trust and the Radical Statistics Race Group (1980), *Britain's Black Population*, London, Heinemann.
Rutter, Michael, Maughan, Barbara, Mortimore, Peter and Ouston, Janet (1979), *Fifteen Thousand Hours*, Shepton Mallet, Open Books.
Schafer, Walter E. and Armer, J. Michael (1968), 'Athletes are not inferior students', *Trans-action*, vol. 5 (November), pp. 21–6 & 61–2.
Schafer, Walter E. and Armer, J. Michael (1970), 'On scholarships and interscholastic athletics', in Eric Dunning (ed.), *The Sociology of Sport*, London, Frank Cass.

Schafer, Walter E. and Rehberg, R. (1970), 'Athletic participation, college aspirations and college encouragement', *Pacific Sociological Review*, vol 13 (summer), pp. 182–6.

Schur, Terry and Brookover, Wilbur (1970), 'Athletes, academic self-concept and achievement', *Medicine and Science in Sports*, vol. 2, no. 2 (Summer), pp. 96–9.

Scully, Gerald W. (1973), 'Economic discrimination in professional sports', *Law and Contemporary Problems*, vol. 38 (Winter/Spring).

Shattuck, Roger (1980), *The Forbidden Experiment*, London, Secker & Warburg.

Shneidman, N. Norman (1979), *The Soviet Road to Olympus*, London, Routledge & Kegan Paul.

Snyder, Eldon E. and Spreitzer, Elmer (1978), *Social Aspects of Sport*, Englewood Cliffs, NJ, Prentice-Hall.

Spady, William G. (1970), 'Lament for the letterman', *American Journal of Sociology*, vol. 75 (January), pp. 680–702.

Spivey, Donald and Jones, Thomas A. (1975), 'Intercollegiate servitude', *Social Science Quarterly*, vol. 5, no. 4 (March), pp. 939–47.

Spreitzer, Elmer and Pugh, Meredith (1976), 'Interscholastic athletics and educational expectations', in Andrew Yiannakis *et al.*, *Sport Sociology*, Dubuque, Iowa, Kendall/Hunt.

Spreitzer, Elmer and Snyder, Eldon E. (1976), 'Socialization into sport', *Research Quarterly*, vol. 47, no. 2 (May), pp. 238–45.

Start, K. B. (1967), 'Sporting and intellectual success among English secondary school children', *International Review of Sport Sociology*, vol. 2, pp. 47–53.

Stone, Gregory P. (ed.) (1972), *Games, Sport and Power*, New Brunswick NJ, Transaction Books.

Stone, Maureen (1981), *The Education of the Black Child in Britain*, London, Fontana.

Talamini, John T. and Page, Charles H. (1973), *Sport and Society: an anthology*, Boston, Mass., Little, Brown.

Thomas, J. R. and Chissom, B. S. (1974), 'Prediction of first grade academic performance from kindergarten perceptual motor data', *Research Quarterly*, vol. 45, no. 2, pp. 148–53.

Thomas, W. I. (1966), *On Social Organization and Social Personality*, Chicago, University of Chicago Press.

Thompson, Richard (1964), *Race and Sport*, London, Oxford University Press.

Tomlinson, Sally (1980), 'The educational performance of ethnic minority children', *New Community*, vol. 8, no. 3 (Winter), pp. 213–34.

Torres, Jose (1971), *Sting Like a Bee*, New York, Abelard-Schuman.

Troyna, Barry (1978), 'Race and streaming: a case study', *Educational Review*, vol. 30, no. 1, pp. 59–65.

Walvin, James (1971), *The Black Presence*, London, Orbach & Chambers.

Walvin, James (1975), *The People's Game: the social history of British football*, London, Allen Lane.

Watman, Mel (1968), *History of British Athletics*, London, Robert Hale.

Wells, Brian W. P. (1980), *Personality and Heredity*, London, Longman.

Willhelm, Sidney M. (1970), *Who Needs the Negro?*, Cambridge, Mass., Schenkman.

Willis, Paul (1977), *Learning to Labour*, Farnborough, Hants., Gower.

Worthy, M. and Markle, A. (1970), 'Racial differences in reactive versus self-paced activities', *Journal of Personality and Social Psychology*, vol. 16, pp. 439–43.

Yetman, Norman and Eitzen, D. Stanley (1972), 'Black Americans in sports: unequal opportunity for equal ability', *Civil Rights Digest*, vol. 5, pp. 20–34.

Yiannakis, Andrew, McIntyre, Thomas D., Merrill, J., Melnick and Hart, Dale P. (1976), *Sport Sociology: contemporary themes*, Dubuque, Iowa, Kendall/Hunt.

INDEX